CRITICAL ACCLAIM FOR
SHIPWRECK

"Smugglers, sinkings, survivors and sailors . . . Dave Horner has captured the spirit of exploration and adventure in treasures lost and found on the high seas. His research is astounding, with much new information welcomed by researchers and everybody else who's interested in the saga of Spain's great galleons."
—Ellsworth Boyd, *Sport Diver* magazine

"*Shipwreck* packs a wealth of data about Spain's treasure quest in the New World. Often speaking through the words of 17th century adventurer Padre Diego, Horner gives the reader a window into time, portraying the accumulation of stunning treasures, fierce naval battles at sea between the English and Spaniards, agony in death by drowning juxtaposed to victorious struggles to survive, and the inevitable trials in the courtroom."
—Richard T. Robol, General Counsel, Columbus-America Discovery Group

"*Shipwreck* is a true adventure and a history lesson . . . The book will appeal to everyone who is interested in ships and the sea, and the fulfillment of a dream. From the Spanish Main to the Armada of the South Sea, from Peru to Panama, from Cartagena to Cádiz, the story of the *Carrera de Indias* unfolds, defining mind-boggling treasures, disasters, and opportunities. It is a fantastic story."
—Herbert Humphreys, Jr., owner of the Marex Company that worked the remains of the *Maravillas*

RELACION DEL VIAGE,

Y SVCESSOS QVE TVVO DESDE QVE
salió de la Ciudad de Lima, hasta que llegó a estos Reynos
de España el Doctor Don Diego Portichuelo de Ribadeneyra, Racionero de la Santa Iglesia Metropolitana de aque-
lla Ciudad, y su Procurador general, Oficial, y Abogado
del Tribunal de la Inquisicion, natural de la Ciudad de Anduxar.

AL SEÑOR DON IVAN GONZALEZ DE VZQVETA
y Valdés, Cauallero de la Orden de Santiago, Señor de Boadilla, y sus
sierras, del Consejo de su Magestad en el Real de Castilla,
Indias, Iunta de Guerra, y Camara del las, y de la
Santa Cruzada, &c.

Año de   1657.

Con licencia. En Madrid. Por Domingo Garcia y Morras.

Title Page of Padre Diego's Original Diary

Photocopy of the title page of the vellum bound diary of Diego Portichuelo de
Ribadeneyra (Rivadeneira) showing his dedication to Don Juan Gonzalez de
Uzqueta y Valdes. Licensed publisher: Domingo Garcia y Morras, Madrid,
Spain, 1657. *Biblioteca Nacional, Madrid.*

SHIPWRECK

A
Saga of Sea Tragedy
and
Sunken Treasure

DAVE HORNER

ibooks
new york
www.ibooks.net

A Publication of ibooks, inc.

An ibooks, inc. Book

Distributed by Simon & Schuster, Inc.
1230 Avenue of the Americas, New York, NY 10020

ibooks, inc.
24 West 25th Street
New York, NY 10010

The ibooks World Wide Web Site Address is:
http://www.ibooks.net

ISBN 0-7434-4495-7
First ibooks, inc. printing June 2002
10 9 8 7 6 5 4 3 2

Cover design by Rob Johnson Design

Printed in the U.S.A.

For
Joey, Jimmy and Daniel

"The English turned on me next. I was sopping wet. My throat and nostrils burned from the salt water ingested. I trembled from an equal mixture of fear of my destiny and discomfort from my condition. My dripping clothes stuck tightly to my skin. In their search for jewelry or other valuables I might be carrying, they ripped my clothes completely. They stripped me with such fury I felt dismembered. Having them ravage my body was like being skinned alive. I was totally naked, left only with the flesh I had when I entered this world."

Padre Diego

ACKNOWLEDGMENTS

From thousands of hours of tedious research, and even more thousands of hours of difficult translation, to expert local knowledge and professional on-site recommendations, a number of people are responsible for bringing this book to fruition.

My thanks must go first to my wonderful wife, Jayne, who persevered in her translation assignments and tolerated my dog-headed stubbornness not to give in to almost impossible decipherings of ancient Spanish script. She also insured that, most of the time, my sentences were grammatically correct. Thanks, Jaynie!

Next, there are the researchers who deserve considerable accolades. Robert Sténuit, my good friend, author, diver and researcher *extraordinaire* in maritime history, handled the toughest assignments in his usual calm and professional manner. Because of his lifelong personal interest in the subject, Robert pursued difficult-to-find archive documents with an unfailing resolve. He deserves much credit for his competent efforts in the principal Spanish repositories and in bringing to light numerous heretofore undiscovered and unpublished details about lost galleons. Nice going, Robert!

David Nirenberg, Professor of History at Rice University, dedicated himself to my early research needs in Spain while he delicately balanced his Ph.D. thesis requirements. It was through David I had the pleasure of also working with Merce Gras Casanovas and Cristina Borau of Barcelona. Both women made several research trips to Seville in my behalf, in between their graduate study timetables.

Also in Spain, my thanks go to Admiral José Ignacio Gonzalez-Aller Hierro, Director of the *Museo Naval* in Madrid, and his competent public relations assistant, Rosa Abella Luengo, for their interest and assistance.

To my Spanish legal team of José Maria Alcantara Gonzalez and Esther Zarza at AMYA in Madrid, and Captain José Luiz Rodriguez Carrion in Cádiz, I express my gratitude for all their counsel and advice.

My appreciation is also extended to Dr. Luis M. Coin Cuenca, Professor of Navigation, Faculty of Nautical Sciences, University of Cádiz at Puerto Real, for his recommendations about old Cádiz landmarks.

I would be remiss not to single out Cristóbal Perez del Pulgar y

Morenes, the seventeenth Marqués de Montealegre, for his friendship and personal family historical recollections.

To my long-time friend, Felipe Gonzalez-Gordon Gilbey of Jerez de la Frontera, my thanks for his usual good advice and fine wine recommendations. *Muchicimas Gracias!*

Susan T. Moore tracked down English Admiralty letters, logs and files in London. Although we tried, we were regrettably unsuccessful in our attempts to locate the lost portraits of the two Baides teenagers. The boys, captured in the battle off Cádiz, were taken to England by Admiral Mountagu (Montague) along with the Spanish treasure. (Their paintings probably were burned in 1666 in the great fire in London that destroyed all the palace buildings, except for the banqueting hall.)

George R. Ryskamp, Associate Professor of History at Brigham Young University, assisted with difficult genealogical research in Spain and in the Americas.

American shipwreck researcher and friend, Bob Fleming, offered advice on early Spanish titles relating to subjects of interest.

A number of people are responsible for my direct personal involvement in the 1654 *capitana* off Ecuador. Herman and Cristina Moro, principals in SubAmerica Discoveries, Inc., got the ball rolling through their lease with the Ecuadoran Government in an area off El Real. This section of Ecuador's coast was of strong interest to me as well, as I truly believed the great lost galleon lay in that designated region. Their infectious enthusiasm provided motivation for me to spend money on geophysical surveys off El Real. The resulting actual discovery and recovery episodes are unique stories in their own rights.

My partners in Maritime Explorations International, Inc., Lou Ullian and Ed O'Connor, provided working capital and competent, technical decision-making capabilities so we could professionally follow through and assist SubAmerica in Ecuador.

My extremely able friend and maritime attorney, Richard T. Robol, provided timely legal counsel and prompt documentation when called upon. Thanks, Rick!

I highly appreciate the sound archaeological recommendations and advice John de Bry offered.

Thanks also to Norm Scott and Jerry Lee of Global Explorations who conducted two magnetometer surveys of the seafloor off Punta La Tintina.

In Guayaquil, Captain Michael Gordon offered his master mariner's hands-on advice and local knowledge about the seacoast around the Chanduy region. My friend and lawyer, José Modesto Apolo, did his best to keep me out of trouble there.

Gloria de Vinueza, along with her family, has been involved in the search for this great galleon for almost two decades. She deserves much credit for her aggressive perseverance on this sunken legend. Thanks also to her son-in-law, Santiago Cuesta, and Guayaquil attorney, Javier Vivas Wagner.

Diver Rob McClung deserves recognition for actually finding the long lost *capitana* when his hand luckily rested on the neck of a submerged amphora while diving about a mile beyond his jurisdictional area in almost zero visibility. Other divers, Dan McArthur, Mike McClung, Vicente Parrales, Don Schaefer, Vicente Arcos and Heniber "John" Egas (Agent 86) also played key roles in the 1654 *capitana* discovery. Joel Ruth did his usual good job of rare coin cleaning.

I also want to acknowledge and thank Contralmirante Fernando Donoso Moran, former Director General de la Marina Mercante y del Litoral, and his competent staff in Guayaquil. Also the brothers Rodriguez, Hector and Manuel, who are good attorneys and friends in Quito.

Captain Alberto Dillon, his wife Yolanda and son Douglas, always provided excellent sea food, sea stories, and a hospitable safe haven among the hills of Ballenita, Ecuador.

To Don MacKay, Bob Logan, Mike and Nancy Cundiff, Mick Murray, Captain Everrett Pastor, David Trader, Manny Casares and all the others who have offered advice, shared information and worked on this fantastic shipwreck, I extend sincere thanks. The entire episode has been an unbelievably dramatic chapter in my life.

My appreciation list on the *Maravillas* galleon wreck would almost constitute a book in itself, but there are a few who provided considerable assistance and deserve special recognition. Captain Herbert Humphreys, Hank and Beth Hudson, Jerry Cox and Tim Hudson of the MAREX Organization generously provided reference material, photographs and inside information on the Little Bahama Bank lost treasure hoard as a result of their seven-year search and hard work on this mysterious piece of Bahamian ocean real estate known in the early days as *Los Mimbres*. Certainly, "Herbo" Humphreys has been the most successful modern salvor on this famous lost galleon wreck and I sincerely thank him and his entire MAREX team for their friendship and assistance.

John and Betsy McSherry offered first hand experience from their gold sled and T-bar reef adventures, as did magging expert, Gene Evans.

Bob Colombo provided good back up archaeological support and meaningful information from his worldwide source of contacts, as well as being a good friend.

Captain Billy Gill, of the research vessel *Southland*, shared his views and thoughts on the *Maravillas* mother lode. Maureen C. Wilson, of the Bahamas Ministry of Public Safety and Transport (which supervises search and salvage leases), allowed me to review that agency's files. I am highly appreciative.

To the many divers and treasure hunters, including author and film maker, Sylvio Heufelder, who have passed along their thoughts and secrets relating to this and other lost galleon wrecks over the years, I say, "Thank You!"

Very real appreciation goes to Father Paul F. Reynolds of Saint Mary's Church, West Warwick, Rhode Island. Special thanks to Captain Father Louis V. Iasiello, Director for U.S. Navy Operational Ministry, CINCLANTFLT. I extend my sincere appreciation for the personal review of several chapters and for their Catholic ecclesiastical advice.

To Ken and Nell Haughton of New Smyrna Beach, Florida, who did considerable manuscript typing, I offer my thanks and appreciation for their secretarial services. To Maria Covey for translation assistance, as well as to my daughters, Julie and Vicki, who also helped with the manuscript.

And last, certainly not least, I want to acknowledge and thank Christina DiMartino for her meticulous and unrelenting editing and Dr. Neil G. McCluskey for his professorial advice and counsel. Dr. Eugene Lyon took time to review my manuscript and offer helpful technical advice which was much appreciated. I am particularly proud to recognize my friend, Eric Applegarth, whose superb sketches greatly enhance the overall quality of this book.

I extend to these special people my special thanks for a job well done!

CONTENTS

FOREWORD

The conquest of the Americas by the sword of the Spaniards has been correctly described as an "uninterrupted series of prodigies." The *Carrera de Indias* (Route of the Indies) from Seville and Cádiz to all parts of the New World was the passage used for the exploitation and administration of the outstretched American Spanish empire. It represents an uninterrupted historical chapter covering three centuries of prodigiously heroic and tragic feats.

Many of the men involved in the *Carrera* were heroes who thought themselves ordinary, dispensable soldiers or seamen. The sea voyages they engaged in were routinely made under conditions of hardship, no doubt considered unbearable by today's standards. Sea fights resulting in maiming or death were bluntly accepted. Honor left no alternative. Immense treasures were lost and stolen, accompanied by gripping stories, enough to make Hollywood productions pale in comparison.

People may never know the true story of the great galleons of Spain other than through an occasional, poorly researched television documentary or fiction feature. Fictional accounts of buccaneers, pirates and swashbucklers were produced on screen to enthrall audiences.

Yet there are millions of original documents at the *Archivo General de Indias* (General Archives of the Indies). They are complex, written in old Castilian script and fit together like an enormous, unmatched jigsaw puzzle. And few had ever undertaken the day-to-day digging through the dusty, centuries old, original Spanish papers.

But this is no longer the case. Now, thanks to this fine and well-documented book, relying on contemporary original manuscripts from Seville, the true story is finally told. A great writer, diver and researcher, Dave Horner creditably and unselfishly shares his source documentation.

Today, just as archaeologists are making incredible discoveries on land, and scientists are finding cures beyond comprehension, Dave turns his energy, efforts and his soul to what is buried beneath the power of the waves and currents. He then exposes it for all of us to learn from.

Dave Horner is the first in modern times to write and publish detailed accounts on the loss of the 1654 *capitana* off Chanduy,

Ecuador, as well as the sinking of the *Maravillas* in 1656. Both are chronicled in his 1971 book, *The Treasure Galleons*. Little did he know then how his passion would continue to grow, driving him steadily toward greater and more enigmatic sunken ship explorations. The countless millions left on ocean floors and the resulting astronomical economic damage to the Crown of Spain especially intrigued him.

"There is something about a sunken galleon that lures men on," Dave said in *The Treasure Galleons*. "After some twenty-five years of additional research, diving and traveling the world for new information, to say I'm lured on is an understatement."

Dave located Padre Diego Portichuelo de Rivadeneira's memoirs, originally printed in 1657, in the *Archivo General de Indias* in Seville. Dave's wife, Jayne, tediously translated the ancient writing. Captivated by the stupefying story, Dave absorbed himself in the unprecedented account, studying it relentlessly. "I became totally committed to learning every detail of each major circumstance of the amazing mid-17th century turn-of-events involving the padre," he admitted.

The combination of extraordinary catastrophe, millions in treasure, shipwrecks and sea fights, boggled his imagination. They led to nearly unbelievable human tragedy and spectacular losses of silver, gold and other valuable cargo. In its midst, Padre de Rivadeneira was miraculously rescued from the unrelenting sea claiming the galleons he was sailing.

Were it not for Dave Horner's undying efforts and passion for discovery, the world may have waited well into the future for the bounty of information he unearths and now shares. Worse, it may never have been uncovered. The world owes him a debt of gratitude for the treasure he found and the gifts he shares with each one of us today and for generations to come.

ROBERT STÉNUIT
Researcher in Maritime History
Brussels

AUTHOR'S NOTE

In 1971, while reviewing final proofs for publication of *The Treasure Galleons*, I received some late research from Spain. Hidden in the midst of the voluminous package of documents was an old Spanish publication with a lengthy and obscure title. The most interesting element of this material is that it was written by a witness of the sinking of the 1654 *capitana* off the desolate coast of Ecuador. The author's name was Padre Diego Portichuelo de Rivadeneira. Ironically, the padre finds himself experiencing a similar terrible ordeal as he continues his voyage to Spain later in the year, aboard the doomed *Nuestra Señora de las Maravillas*.

Being one of the few *Maravillas* survivors is not drama enough in the life of this modest clergyman. His adventure intensifies as he encounters enemy fire and feels the blood of battle within sight of his long sought destination of Cádiz. Culminating with the explosion of still another galleon, the events lead to his capture and temporary imprisonment. My excitement over this ancient document was second only to what I felt when the translation was completed.

This is the story of Padre Diego, based on his personal memoirs.

The diary reflects a remarkable endurance of numerous personal agonies, but does not relate how the consequences of these events combine to have historical effects. No doubt the padre had little idea of the magnitude of history he was participating in at the time. Nor did he consider the aftermath of those events lingering on in the lives of some of us today.

There are lapses in the good padre's diary. An attempt to fill these voids through research shows through in this book. Some of his casual or brief references justified more extensive detail. Ominous weather conditions, uncharted navigational hazards, unexpected predicaments of ocean salvage, a treasure ship's inventory register and the multi-faceted personalities of many people contributed to his story. In an attempt to add a measure of balance to the diary's references to the English, their side of the story is also told.

The dramatic sagas of the early salvors, as well as the exciting episodes of modern adventurers on the sunken wrecks, are all of historic consequence. Although Padre Diego was not a part of the early salvage diving on these lost galleons, the events directly involved him, causing grief and consternation.

Authenticity of this research is verifiable by letters, archive reports, court testimony and quotes from the men involved. It is now possible to relay in clear and understandable terms what it was like to have lived and experienced these events.

In cases of uncertainty involving a particular event, a meticulous review of hundreds of repetitious records was perused. The evidence was weighed to verify what probably was truth and how the actual events occurred. In every situation a sincere attempt is made to portray the facts. In doing so an amazing truth has been discovered, one much more astonishing than any element of fiction might have been.

I purposely took some liberty in interpreting characters and judging situations. In order to fully develop this remarkable story, to achieve a strong and interesting narrative, reinforced accurately and thoroughly with credible detail, I traveled many roads, air miles, and sea lanes. These journeys led to meetings with people from all backgrounds and occupations. Most of them graciously offered advice, assistance and information on the subjects herein. Numerous acquaintances were the result of this quest for new detail and unpublished information. Many of them have become close and lifelong friends. There are, unfortunately, a few enemies as well.

It has been a tremendous pleasure to work with some of the finest researchers in the world. The benefit from some of the most expert genealogical sleuthing not only provided good family background data, but also turned up living descendants of some of the book's key figures. For the modern salvors of these great shipwrecks, dedicated and expert diving efforts and undying loyalty and determination have earned them a rightful place in this chronology of history.

In looking back over the past two decades, and in reviewing the final galleys for this book, I'm convinced the effort has proven worthwhile. I found the challenge was inspiration in disguise while researching from South America to Spain, diving on Little Bahama Bank and off Cádiz, recovering treasure buried deeply in the sea hundreds of years ago. So long as there are ships lying buried beneath the sea, the drive and determination to discover them will continue.

DAVE HORNER

SHIPWRECK

INTRODUCTION

Within a hundred years after Columbus discovered the New World, Spain had become a great power. For more than three hundred years the flow of treasure to the mother country from the Indies, at first only a trickle, ultimately became a torrent. Streams of gold and silver continually gushed from the mines of Mexico, Colombia, Ecuador, Chile and Peru.

Goods badly needed in the new colonies were heavily loaded onto galleon after galleon sailing from the Spanish ports of Seville and Cádiz. Cargoes consisted of wine, cheese, hardware, nails, construction equipment, paper, glassware, pewter plates and buckles. Religious objects, medallions, books, cloth and clothes and other goods needed or desired in the colonies were included.

The Pacific colonial ports, a long distance from Spain, were important trading centers. Valparaiso and Arica in Chile, as well as Callao and Lima in Peru, were separated by many miles and a long journey from Panama. Maintaining an adequate transportation and communication link was an essential, though difficult requirement. Consistency in the flow of treasure was the highest priority.

Sailing from the southern reaches of long strung-out ports in Chile and Peru, the early Spaniards rode what is now known as the powerful northward-flowing Humboldt Current. The flow carried them to the latitude of present day Ecuador. There, this body of water takes a hard left turn, curving ninety degrees westerly to the Galápagos. Then turning southerly, it flows deeply into the South Pacific Ocean.

After losing the benefit of this current, Spanish navigators preferred to continue their northward voyage by piloting along the coast. This enabled them to visually sight landmarks and reference points to measure their daily progress en route to Panama.

In traversing the South American coastline, the armada of the "South Sea" (as the Spaniards referred to the Pacific Ocean during colonial days) confronted considerable natural and geographic obstacles. Seasonal navigational challenges, including adverse weather patterns, added to the difficulties facing many of the king's ships. Tidal ranges of between six and fifteen feet embracing the entire South American shoreline compounded navigational hazards. This combined to create added dangers for careless or inexperienced seafarers.

As an example, in today's Ecuador, a particularly significant peninsula protrudes westward into the sea for approximately eight miles. Known as Punta Santa Elena, the village of the same name is located just inside its protective hook. Northward from Santa Elena the land falls back to the east. It forms a gentle curve in the coast toward modern Colombia. The seacoast then curves again, in a westerly contour, before reaching Panama.

Spain, along with several of her European trading neighbors, depended on successful round-trip voyages to the Americas. One grounding, one sinking, one captured vessel were all considered devastating news. Each heavily-loaded treasure ship that did not return meant bankruptcy for many. It became a story too often told.

In exchange for arriving cargoes, vast treasure shipments from the fabulously rich mines of the New World received priority space aboard the homeward-bound vessels. Along with tons of silver and gold, the ships were filled with goods considered rare and desirable throughout Europe. Pearls from Margarita Island, diamonds from Venezuela, sisal and hides, Caribbean fruits and nuts, tobacco, cocoa and coffee were packed tightly, often filling the vessel's holds to over capacity. Honduras rosewood, Mexican jewelry of opals, amethysts and turquoise, pottery and glaze, cochineal (a scarlet red dye), indigo and numerous other items were registered on return manifests. Safe arrival of the exotic products was second only to the silver and gold eagerly anticipated by not only the Spanish hierarchy, but also most of Europe.

Each year witnessed increases in treasure production. The numbers and sizes of vessels necessary to transport it expanded proportionally. Larger ships carried more treasure, but when they failed to return, as a result of shipwreck, storms or enemy corsairs, they turned into more significant sea disasters and represented greater economic losses.

The galleons sailing to *Tierra Firme,* later known as New Granada and often referred to as the "mainland" (today the area of Colombia, Venezuela, parts of Central America including Panama) represented the greatest number of ships and cargoes from Spain. About forty percent of these vessels sailed into Cartagena, discharged cargo, then continued to the isthmus ports of Nombre de Dios and Portobelo. The convoy then returned to Cartagena to await word on the arrival of the *Armada del Mar del Sur,* the Pacific fleet from Peru, sailing along the South American Pacific coast to Panama. Often the wait lasted months.

Another thirty-three percent of incoming Spanish-European shipments and outgoing treasure cargoes cleared through the port at Vera Cruz. This group of ships was known as the New Spain fleet, or *plata flota*. The viceroyalty of New Spain included all of Mexico and Honduras.

The remaining approximate twenty-seven percent of treasure and general cargo shipping volume originated through the specific ports of the captain generalcy of Cuba, Santo Domingo and the immense viceroyalty of Peru, geographically designated today as encompassing Peru, Chile, Bolivia and Ecuador.

Philip IV ran this far-flung empire from Madrid, but his job was not easy. The vast kingdom was long, wide and paper-thin. Spain was at war with the detested English. Lord Protector Oliver Cromwell possessed all *de facto* powers in England and ordered a blockade of the major Spanish Atlantic ports, primarily Cádiz and Seville.

Spain was at war with Portugal. The Duke of Braganza, King of Portugal, was a close ally of England. This enabled English ships to re-furbish and revictual in Portuguese harbors. Having waged wars in Italy against neighbors of its peninsula possessions, King Philip also was at war with France, governed by Cardinal Mazarin. (Mazarin continued the politics of Richelieu, until Louis XIV took power in 1662.) This lasted several years, until the *Traité des Pyrénées*. At least Spain was at peace with the northern Netherlands. The two countries conducted brisk business.

However, the primary focus of the Royal Treasury was in the mines and mints of the New World. Increasing production of treasure and shipments back to the mother country was the principal goal.

Mining, refining, weighing, minting, stamping and transporting this treasure entailed every element of big business. Therefore, Spanish citizens were welcome to travel to the New World and operate a mine, so long as they took the oath to work on behalf of the King of Spain. Though most of the mines were operated privately, they were considered royal property.

Strict procedures and controls were designed to insure the king's allotment of the treasure. The royal *quinto*, or one-fifth, was the allotment claimed by His Majesty. As early as 1505 the royal share amounted to about fifty-thousand pesos. Twelve years later it grew to one hundred thousand pesos. The *quinto* later varied between one-fifth and one-tenth. Even so, royalties paid to the Royal Treasury continued to soar for more than one hundred years. Between 1556-1640, royalties paid to the king reached eighty-four million pieces-of-eight from the rich mountain of silver at Potosí alone.[1]

As silver production increased, the amount of contraband trade flowing between Old and New Worlds increased proportionately, in order to avoid the king's tariffs. This illegal commerce included treasure and commodities of every imaginable description. It was perpetrated by ship captains, merchants and "trusted" representatives of the Crown who constantly showed their palms and looked the other way. It reached epidemic proportions. King Philip was no longer sure he could trust captains of sea and war, lawyers, controllers, or local magistrates.

The Council of the Indies, managing the affairs of the *Carrera* for His Majesty, tried everything conceivable to contain, control, and otherwise thwart contraband cargoes. Spies were placed on board the king's ships. Vows of allegiance from sea captains and officers were demanded. Salaries were withheld until a vessel safely returned to Spain. Taxes and fines were levied when unregistered goods were discovered. Yet it was all to no avail. Illegal shipments constituted a greater portion of the trade than did the registered commerce.

In late October of 1654, the immense *capitana*, the "Queen of the South Sea," was sunk off the coast of Ecuador. The royal court in Madrid did not learn of the loss until the beginning of May the following year. The *capitana* carried an actual ten million pesos in treasure, but only three million was registered on the ship. Even at the lesser amount, the tragedy was not only a monumental loss to Spain, but also created havoc within the Viceroyalty of Peru.

In 1655, the citizens of Lima witnessed their homes, cathedrals and the palace of the viceroy destroyed by an earthquake. To pour more salt on Spain's open wound, it was also in the same inauspicious year that the English snatched Jamaica from Spanish control.

The devastating domino effect continued. In 1656 the king received news of the sinking of the 900-ton *Maravillas* on the wild and uncharted shoals of *Los Mimbres*. Six hundred people lost their lives and more than five million pesos in gold and silver were buried at sea with the galleon. History records this loss as one of the single worst shipwrecks in the *Carrera de las Indias*. This tragedy was yet followed by a disastrous battle with the English in September. Within sight of the Spanish shore, hundreds of lives and many more millions of pesos were also lost off Cádiz.

Spain's period of misfortune was not yet ended. The following April it was magnified by the complete destruction of the entire 1657 treasure fleet as it returned to Spain. While anchored in the highly-touted safest harbor in the Atlantic, Santa Cruz de Tenerife in the Canary Islands, it met its demise at the hands of the brilliantly daring English force. The consequences of this series of disasters were far reaching. Their combined effect greatly contributed to the decline of Spain as a major power.

Let's now go back in time to the middle of the 17th century for the complete story. This narrative of the trials, tribulations, life and death struggles of Padre Diego Portichuelo is based on his personal memoirs. The story is much more than just the diary of a man of the cloth. It is a moving account of historic maritime events following the Spanish conquest of the New World. From the small fleets of the South Sea to the huge armadas of the North (Caribbean and Atlantic), Spain endeavored to sustain its economic well-being with the resources of its newly established colonies. Many of the successes and failures of the *Carrera de las Indias* are revealed within the pages of this book.

While this book is based, at least in part, on the miraculous account of our good padre, it is much more. Indeed, it is an epic of sea tragedy and lost treasure.

Editor's note: For a better understanding of the material covered in the book and the Spanish terminology, the reader should consult Appendices A through D.

OLD WORLD

Madrid

King:	Philip IV, of the Spanish branch of the Hapsburgs (House of Austria) 1605–1665
Council of the Indies:	Grand Chancellor, Don Luis Mendez de Haro y Guzmán, Marqués del Carpio, and Count Duke de Olivarez, 1648–1661
President:	Don Gaspar de Bracamonte, Count de Peñaranda, 1653–1659
Public Prosecutor:	Don Antonio Pedro Galvez, 1654–October 1657
Succeeded by:	Don Antonio Feloaga, 1657–April 1658
Secretary:	Don Gregorio de Legina, 1650–1659
Chief Accountant:	Antonio Sanchez, 1632–to his death January, 1656
Succeeded by:	Don Pedro de Salinas y Sustaite, March 1656–1684
Treasurer:	Juan Bautista Everardo, 1652–1658
Court Reporter:	Don Fernando Jiménez Paniagua, 1640–1665

Seville

Casa de la Contratación (Bureau of Trade):

President:	Don Bernardo de Silva, Marqués de la Eliseda, 1649–November 1654
Succeeded by:	Don Pedro Nuñez Guzmán, Count de Villaumbrosa, November 1654–1662 (the younger brother of the Marqués de Montealegre)
Treasurer:	Andrés de Munibe, 1640–1659
Chief Accountant:	Don Fernando de Villegas, 1644–1675
Merchant Agents:	Don José Campero de Sorrevilla, 1650–1654
(Factors):	Don Jeronimo Ladrón de Legama, 1655–1656
Judge:	Don Martin de Oria, 1649–1654
Succeeded by:	Don Antonio de Leon Piñelo, 1655–1660
Public Prosecutor:	Don Antonio Abello de Valdez, 1657–1658

Cádiz

Casa de la Contratación (Bureau of Trade):

Chief Judge:	Lorenzo Andres Garcia
Captain General of the Ocean Sea:	Duke of Medinaceli

NEW WORLD

Viceroyalty of Peru

Viceroy:	Don Garcia Sarmiento de Sotomayor, Count de Salvatierra, 1648–1654
Succeeded by:	Don Luis Henriquez de Guzmán, Count de Alva de Aliste y Villaflor, 1655–1661

Lima

Bishop:	Don Pedro de Villagomez y Vivanco, 1640–1671
President of the Audiencia:	the Viceroy
Judges:	Don Pedro Vásquez de Velasco, 1651–1654
	Don Antonio Fernandez de Heredia, 1653–1660
	Don Julio de Vásquez y Llano, May 1654, to his death
	Don Andres de Villela, 1656
Regional Prosecutors:	Don Juan de Padilla, 1640-1660
	Don Bartolomé de Salazar, 1645–1659
	Dr. Don Bernardino de Figueroa y de la Cerda, 1651–1659
	Don Antonio de Quijano y Heredia, 1653–1659
Public Prosecutors:	Dr. Don Juan Cornejo, December 1654–1661
	Dr. Don Juan de Valdez y Llano, June 1651–May 1654.

Audiencia de Panama

President:	Don Pedro Carrillo de Guzmán, 1652–1657
Public Prosecutor:	Don Iñigo Perez de Lara, 1650–1660
Judge:	Don Diego de Valverde Orozco, 1650–1657

Audiencia de Quito

President:	Don Pedro Vásquez de Velasco, June 1654–July 1660
Public Prosecutor:	Don Diego de la Rocha, 1653–1660
Judge:	Don Tomas Berjón de Cairedes, 1653–March 1656
Succeeded by:	Don Fernando de Velasco y Gamboa, 1648–1660
	Don Antonio Diez de San Miguel, 1653–1660
Court Reporter:	Don Andrés de Augulo (later reporter in Lima)

Guayaquil

Governor:	Don Jorge de Rivera

Viceroyalty of New Spain (Mexico)

Viceroy:	Don Luis Henriquez de Guzmán, Count de Alva de Aliste, 1650–1653
	Don Francisco Fernandez de la Cueva, Duke de Alburquerque, 1653–1660

Going Down to Panama

For some unexplained reason, I experienced a nagging feeling of uneasiness, persisting for more than twenty-four hours.

IT IS A GLORIOUS DAY on Little Bahama Bank. Thirty-three feet under water, I'm digging in the soft sand of what the Spanish called *Los Mimbres*. Five Atlantic spotted dolphin are playing by my side. I would not want to be anywhere else in the world at this particular time but right here.

There is a trail of iron spikes and broken amphora, encrusted blobs of unidentified objects, a cannon ball, a corroded coin—make that several corroded coins, probably pieces-of-four *reales*, but heavily oxidized.

The hidden trail of treasure stretches beyond the edge of my underwater visibility. God, it's magnificent down here! The dolphin nearby are gesturing, "Dig here!" A barracuda hangs like a silent sentinel fifty feet away. It barely moves. Is it pointing the way? Breathtaking vistas of finger sponge and sea whips are swaying to the right as if to say, "The gold is over here." A colorful school of iridescent mackerel, darting back and forth, seem to communicate, "Follow us, it's this way." In this amazing undersea oasis, overlooking the brilliant reflection of clean, sand-bottom endlessness, with all this beauty among enormous currents—anyone who dares to understand and become a part of such an intriguing underwater environment can only dream big dreams.

I have lived, and relived, the story of the *Maravillas* for more than twenty-five years through endless hours of study and thousands of dollars spent on research. I am intimately familiar with the names and family histories of the major officers of the 900-ton royal galleon. I know the great ship's layout, armament, and treasure register. In my dreams I have met some of the 650 people who were on board, getting to know more about some of them than I care to admit.

I have become familiar with their individual strengths and weaknesses, habits and customs, their loyalty to the Crown of Spain, and to the Lord Almighty. It is interesting what one learns about a person after studying weeks of testimony and voluminous depositions, and after investigating years of genealogical trails.

I am speaking of the sacred vow of honor upheld by a Knight of Santiago. I am referring to the personal dedication and allegiance to the king by a humble but totally trusted silvermaster. I am discussing the "cover-one's-own-behind" maneuvers by the politically connected high-rankers. Does anything ever change over the centuries? I am relating to the crafty, cunning, scheming ways of opportunistic entrepreneurs who might retire after one successful round-trip voyage to the New World. I am referring to the timely courage of a single seaman versus the unmistakable faintheartedness of a high official, who paid handsome amounts for his privileged position. I am recalling the magnificent navigational skills and seamanship abilities of some of these long lost ancient mariners whose bones, tools, artillery, astrolabes, eating utensils and personal possessions lie buried beneath this fine white sand. I am remembering the steadfast kindness and unfaltering devotion to those who needed mercy and tenderness by one man of God, who served as chaplain aboard the galleon. All these diverse and remarkable deeds are revealed directly and between-the-lines through the diaries, letters, naval reports and testimony of those deposed, and the treasure and artifacts found on this stretch of ocean bottom.

Written in Castilian by scribes over the span of three centuries, their words reach out as if to show the way to the *Maravillas* mother lode—the unsalvaged, never-found chests of gold coins, the numerous boxes of rare emeralds, the luggage of the wealthy, with bags of jewel-studded crosses and exquisite medallions destined for the nobility of Spain and Europe, and the crates of once neatly stacked gold bars, along with row after heavy row of seventy-pound silver ingots in the lower holds. How much still remains, I wonder?

The mystic spell of the clear Bahamian water and the submerged history I'm dealing with have a mesmerizing effect. I am a transformed person, someone else, but I am not sure who. Having drifted back over the centuries to the mid 1600's, I've adjusted well. Still the question remains: Who am I? A ship's carpenter? A caulker? A cooper? A boatswain? A pilot? Yes, perhaps with my naval training in navigation and astronomy I was, and am, a pilot. Maybe even the master pilot of the *capitana San Josef*, whose errors in judgment caused the collision with the *almiranta*, and have led me to the small pieces of wreckage I am now sorting. Could I even possibly be the competent assistant pilot of the *Maravillas*, Gaspar de los Reyes, who returned to salvage much of the once great ship? It would be wonderful to be related to such a famous Spanish navigator and treasure salvor.

Wait a minute! What about the priest? Could I possibly be the reincarnation of Padre Diego?

Seville, Spain,
June 3, 1641

My name is Diego Portichuelo de Rivadeneira, Padre Diego to those who know me.[2] I was born in 1614 in beautiful Andújar, Andalusia. My parents entered me into the Seminary of El Escurial at age sixteen. This was my initial preparation for a life of service to Our Lord. I graduated from the University of Salamanca in 1638 with a bachelor's degree in canon law. From there I proceeded to Osuna to study for my doctorate, awarded in 1641. During my studies, I was appointed chaplain of the Metropolitan Cathedral of Lima in Peru by His Majesty on August 17, 1640. My position being non-salaried, the generosity of my sponsorship was granted by a noble patron, Don Juan Gonzalez de Uzqueta y Valdes, Knight of Santiago, Lord of Boadilla and its lands. I purposely note my sincere gratitude. Were it not for this support my Catholic purpose of bringing blessing to the infidels of the vast New World would not have been possible. I owe His Lordship a multitude of thanks for his benevolence, compassion and glorious spirit. It has provided daily motivation for my life and service to our Holy Father.

Presenting my royal order to the accounting department of the *Casa de la Contratación* (Bureau of Trade) in Seville, I requested they arrange passage to the New World for two servants and myself. Travel arrangements were expedited due to my royal decree. Soon after, I was on the high seas aboard the *San Estevan y los Angeles*, under the command of Juan Miguel de Ocuerri.

An arduous journey from Spain to the Viceroyalty of Peru consumed the last half of 1641. Thereafter, I assumed my post as a royal chaplain of the choir at the Holy Metropolitan Cathedral of Lima. My duty was to sing private masses paid for by individuals. I was also required to sing 240 masses annually for His Majesty, as well as for preceding kings. Mine was one of six such positions at the Lima Cathedral.

On February 8, 1642, the recently appointed archbishop, Don Pedro de Villagomez, entrusted me with teaching duties as vice-rector and regent of the Seminary of Santo Toribio. My work pleased the archbishop, resulting in my formal ordination as a priest the following year.

After ten years of dedicated service in every aspect of the cathedral's daily life, a *media ración*, a position paying half salary, became vacant. I purposely sought this nomination for years. It was a long hoped-for goal. It conveyed status as well as an income of 1,000 pesos annually. I was informed that my name was considered at the top of the list and was very excited. I had last been recommended for this position six years earlier. I again felt deep disappointment and resentment upon learning I was not chosen. Instead, the recipient of the prebend was Don Melchior Danalos Arvendaño.

Little did I realize how this occurrence would initiate an amazing chain of events in my life.

Soon after receiving the disappointing news, I was reprimanded by the Chapter of the Cathedral for not properly doing my duty as attendant of the choir. This brought the outlook for my somber life and career to a new low.

After much agonizing thought and prayer, I requested a special permit from the viceroy to travel to Spain and plead my case for a reasonable prebend before the Council of the Indies. The viceroy promptly approved my request. It was he who recommended me a year earlier for the prebend of a half salary.

"Don Diego has been chaplain of the choir and vice rector of the Seminary of Santo Toribio. He has devoted his best efforts for ten years in total satisfaction of the clergy of the church. I recommend him for an immediate half salary, not only on his merit, but because it will eliminate the necessity for his travel to Spain to appear at court and present his case for a prebend." (A.G.I., Lima 56 No. 8-10.)

The Cathedral Chapter named me attorney general of the court. Numerous dispatches, orders and requests were entrusted to me for safe delivery to designated church officials, convents and cathedrals within the Kingdom of Spain. I was also entrusted with a sizable amount of church funds for distribution. The unhappiness which had previously overwhelmed me quickly dissipated. In my excitement I wrote letters to my sponsor in Madrid and to my sisters in Andújar. A visit was planned with tender anticipation.

The request for a special visa was not a basic or simple one. Once he assumed his role as Viceroy of Peru in 1648, the Count of Salvatierra received numerous instructions from his friend, King Philip IV. These specifically recommended procedures for conducting the business of the Crown. Due to the steadily rising costs being borne by the Royal Treasury, the king included comments regarding the traveling habits of clergy members. He felt there was far too much unofficial and unnecessary travel to and from Spain under the pretense of "church business." As a result, a written authorization from the viceroy was now required, or a travel permit obtained from the authorities, and written approval by the bishop. No exceptions to these rules were permitted.

The clergy assigned to churches in Lima did not travel excessively. Life was pleasant there, especially compared to distant outposts in the cold and wild mountain ridges of Chile, or the heat- and disease-plagued stations in the jungle near Cartagena. Once settled in the beautiful "City of the Kings," few clerics desired to leave the area, or to serve elsewhere.

The viceroy did not hesitate to recommend Padre Diego for a prebend of *media ración*. It avoided the expense of his costly trip to Spain.

October 1, 1654

My official instructions included the responsibility of seeking authority and funds to complete the construction of the towers and porticos of the Lima Cathedral. After taking a century to build, the cathedral was finally dedicated to service in 1625. There remained significant work before it would be considered finished.

I was also instructed to inform His Majesty of the clergymen most deserving and in line for promotion. My intention was to include myself among this noble list.

One other important ecclesiastic mission assigned me was to seek permission for the prayers of the *Santisimo Sacramento* to be sung every Thursday, and the *Purisima Concepción* every Saturday.

I am sailing on the *almiranta* (the Admiral's ship) *San Francisco Solano* but I am not the officially designated chaplain. Still, at the request of Admiral Francisco de Solis, I agreed to assist the senior chaplain in any way possible. I also agreed to tend to soldiers and seamen becoming ill during the voyage, as there is not an official physician on board. In cases of extreme emergency, a surgeon who is assigned to the *capitana* (flagship of the captain general), in whose company we are sailing, will be called. The admiral entrusted me with the key to this vessel's medicine chest.

The chief chaplain agreed we will alternate in saying mass every other day, singing the *Salve Regina* in the afternoons and the *Ave Maria* each night.

I would not dare to put in your hands the following story were it not truth. However, I feel it is my Catholic duty to describe the prodigious miracles God repeatedly bequeathed upon this ordinary priest. I have been saved from the most torturous elements of weather as well as from the enemies of Spain. Because Divine Providence communicated His mercies upon me, and I am bestowed with the apostolate of priesthood, my hope is that this narrative of miracles will accrue to the great benefit of my Church. For me there can be no greater release from the gratitude owed to God than dedicating this narrative in His Honor.

Route of the Armada del Mar del Sur

Pacific colonial ports of Spain's New World centers were separated by many miles. Maintaining an adequate transportation and communication link was an essential though difficult requirement.

Word was received from Don Pedro Carillo de Guzmán, President of the High Court of Panama. The Marqués de Montealegre and his fleet have been waiting in Cartagena since August 22 to transport treasure brought from the great silver mines of Potosí to Spain. Every effort now must be made to expedite the departure of the South Sea armada. Each year this small fleet carries the silver from Peru, northward along the rugged South American Pacific coast to Perico[3], the port of Panama. The king's personal deputy in Peru, the viceroy, was under pressure to dispatch the vessels to Panama by previous orders. This should have been accomplished in May in order to meet the sailing schedule without unduly delaying the ships of the Atlantic Fleet.

Other than my long desired return to Spain, I am not eagerly anticipating my journey. I recall the long and tiring voyage bringing me here years ago. The Atlantic crossing from my mother country proved a trying experience. We also had to fend off outlaws on the jungle trail across the Isthmus of Panama. Enduring a 1,350-mile journey, we beat our way against the current to Callao, the port of Lima.

I am a simple man with basic needs. In my service to the Lord I can and have endured hardships. It is the endless days and nights of seagoing monotony and lack of activity that I complain about. I try to exercise, but the decks of this galleon are in such a jumble they are not conducive for walking. My muscles ache constantly, more from the cramped conditions than from physical over-exertion. In a few weeks I will probably be stoop-shouldered since the headroom in my cabin is barely five feet. Chests and boxes of cargo occupy much of the precious little space left. At forty years of age, I am still young enough to handle the discomforts of the cabin and of being at sea for months. Still, I long for the joy of a four-poster with feather pillows.[4]

I originally requested a room in the after-section of the ship. So many people are on board, my sleeping quarters must be shared with four others. Officers and gentlemen travelers have small cabins or larger bunk space than others, depending upon rank or their ability to pay. Still, they have little privacy, as the rooms are no more than ten to twelve square feet of space. I now prepare myself for the close camaraderie I will be subject to, and wonder if my roommates realize how long a voyage to Panama this will be. I was originally assigned to the *capitana* of Don Francisco de Sosa. However, it is even more crammed with people and cargo than our *almiranta*, so I was transferred, along with three dozen others.

We do not lack for provisions as we have on board many goats and hens. There is also ample wine (we are transporting thousands of jugs), biscuits and vegetables. We will pick up fresh fruit at each stop along our journey. Other than constant bleating, the goats do not seem to smell as bad as a herd of sheep or pigs. The weather was cool while provisions were loaded these past few days, so I may be speaking too soon. Nevertheless, those quartered on the gun deck or lower will certainly encounter some memorable aromas during the voyage. Though we must carry basic numbers of livestock for fresh meat, the noises and smells emitted by the animals can only be imagined. This, coupled with foul water from the bilges, no ventilation and the tropical heat, combine for unforgettable stenches and extremely uncomfortable living conditions. The small amount of privacy, worsening when difficult sea conditions occur, can cause shipwide seasickness.

While there is cause for concern over the many uncertainties lying ahead, it is crucial that I not openly display anxiety. So many look to me, their priest, for strength during this long passage. In our prayers we have already placed ourselves in the hands of Our Lord.

In the process of settling on board, I enjoyed several interesting conversations with agents of Don Francisco de Nestares Marin, a priest and former official of the Inquisition. A royal inspector, he was ordered to this viceroyalty by the king in 1648 to investigate reported problems at the *Villa Imperial de Potosí*. He was especially concerned about the problems involving the quality and purity of the coinage originating from the Potosí mint. Two of Nestares' most trusted aides are now returning to Spain to make a special report to the Council of the Indies. Hopefully, the Potosí coins, previously fraudulently debased, are under control, thanks to officially authorized counter stamps certifying true weights and values.

Initially beginning as petty pilfering and skimming on the part of the assayers and silversmiths at the Potosí mountain of silver, this grew into a monumental scandal when other nations trading with Spain began refusing to accept their coins at face value.

Many pieces-of-eight *reales* were found not to represent the full value in silver of one peso. It seemed a number of royal officials entrusted to all aspects of smelting, refining and minting were, for years, reducing the weight (especially) of eight *real* pieces, keeping the difference for themselves.

Consequently, in 1649, upon his arrival and investigation of the Potosí minting practices, Francisco de Nestares arrested dozens of Potosí officials. He also ordered the hanging of the mint assayer, Don Felipe Ramirez de Arellano, and the chief silversmith, Don Francisco Gomez de la Rocha. It was rumored both men buried some seven million of the debased coins before their execution.

A melting down order was issued on all Potosí small coinage recalled (two, one and one-half *reales*). Coins minted in 1650, 1651 and the first half of 1652, believed to consist of sufficient weight in silver to be considered "nearly full value," were counter struck. Various counter stamps were authorized for the sole purpose of restoring confidence in the Spanish colonial monetary system. This renewed credibility for the Royal Treasury. These particular coins were valued accordingly at 7½ and 3¾ *reales*.

The pride of the newly reorganized and revitalized Potosí Mint management is evidenced by the shiny new coins from the design personally decreed by King Philip IV, and first minted in late 1652. Thousands of eight and four *reales* bearing either newly designated counter marks or the new Potosí design are brought aboard for transport to Spain. This is proof to the administration that the monstrous minting scandal is now contained. I sincerely hope so. Still, the world appears to be filled with evildoers and thieves.

Our scheduled departure from Callao passed several months ago, but politics within the merchant guild prevailed creating the delay. Now we are hurrying to leave. The merchants know that plans for the fair are underway in Portobelo. Anticipating our arrival in Panama, they must be represented, if for nothing else but their pursuit of the almighty peso. Our decks are piled high with goods and products. It seems they have sufficiently delayed us in order for them to drive their prices much higher for those products in the greatest demand.

As our fleet was being readied to sail, an incident created much excitement. A short while before our departure, the viceroy made an unannounced inspection of the huge flagship. An enormous amount of silver ingots and silver wedges were discovered stored in the private cabin and luggage of Captain General Don Baltasar Pardo de Figueroa.

The general was immediately arrested. Four armed soldiers were ordered to escort him to jail. "Let go of me! Let me explain! Villains!" he shouted as they hauled him away.

His senior admiral, Andres de Aguilar, was in line as successor. However, he was earlier ordered to sail to Acapulco on the galleon *Santiago* to fetch the former Viceroy of Mexico, Count Alva de Aliste, Don Luis Henriquez de Guzmán, who was recently promoted to new duties in the much larger viceroyalty of Peru.

Under the circumstances, Francisco de Sosa was named captain general of this year's 1654 *Real Armada del Mar del Sur*. He previously served as admiral of the 1652 armada, and has made ten previous voyages to and from Panama. This command is the highest level he has reached in a career spanning nearly four decades.

Second in command of the *capitana* is Captain of Sea and War Bernardo de Campos. Captain Campos is also the designated silvermaster. He is extremely busy inventorying the many thousands of bars of silver brought aboard the *capitana*.

When the viceroy's aides were finally satisfied that there were no more smuggled goods, the fleet generals announced their readiness. The Viceroy of Peru, Garcia Sarmiento de Sotomayor, Count of Salvatierra, issued the sailing orders, bidding us a good journey.

Port of Callao, Peru,
October 18, 1654

Following a prayer service, and amidst the ringing of bells from our Holy Cathedral of the City, the 1,150 ton galleon of forty-four guns (cannon of bronze) *Jesus Maria de la Limpia Concepción*, Royal Flagship of the South Sea Armada with its new general in command, was the first to weigh anchor. However, fate intervened: The anchor cable parted, sending several tons of heavy iron to the bottom of the Callao sea floor.

Divers were ordered to retrofit the cable and recover the anchor. This took all day. While it was being attended to, sailors gossiped and rumors began. "Is this an evil omen? A portent of the uncertain voyage ahead? An ill wind blowing no good?"

It was nightfall before the *capitana* was ready to sail. Our *almiranta*, the *San Francisco Solano*, is also a large galleon of 1,000 tons. Loaded with people and treasure, it was the next to weigh anchor.

Among others of nobility aboard the admiral's galleon was Don Francisco Lopez de Zúñiga, fifth Marqués of Baides, Knight of the Military Order of Santiago and former Governor and Captain General of Chile from 1639 to 1646. He was returning home to Spain with his wife, Maria de Salazar, daughter of the judge of Charcas, and their five children; the oldest daughter, 19, the oldest son, Don Francisco Lopez, 16, Doña Josepha, 18, Don José Zúñiga, 12, and Doña Catalina, 9. They carried with them all the goods they accumulated while living in Chile and later, Peru.

The marqués is the son of the Count of Pedroso, fourth Marqués de Baides. He has distinguished himself in service of many years to the king. He contained the revolt of the Araucanian Indians, negotiating a peace treaty during his tenure in Chile. He is also responsible for repulsing a Dutch attack under Cornelius Brouwer, who attempted to take an area at the mouth of the Rio Valdivia in Chile.

Besides the two principal royal galleons of this small armada, there are two *chinchorros*, or *pataches* (small, fast vessels intended as tenders to the large, slow galleons, for reconnaissance and rushing dispatches). These avisos are under the command of Luis Vaez Camiña.

Around midnight on October 18, 1654, our fleet managed to sail into a shoal area known locally as "Pins and Needles." After several moments of shouting to and fro, the pilots agreed on a quick course change to port. This enabled the vessels to safely maneuver around the shallow undersea hazard.

The westward change of direction continued for most of the remaining hours of darkness. Captain Miguel Benitez de Alfara, the head pilot, decided to continue tacking seaward on a west-northwesterly course in order to gain sea room. The following day we were overtaken by a fast *patache* sent by the viceroy. He directed the captain general to send our avisos ahead to Panama to alert them of our forthcoming arrival, and of the large amounts of silver being carried by both the *almiranta* and *capitana*. This news would be sent to Cartagena so *Tierra Firme* galleons could be readied. By the end of the day the sails of the avisos were no longer visible on the horizon.

Soon we left the Islas de Lobos downwind. The following day Cabo Blanco was sighted off the starboard bow. It was anticipated that our northwesterly course would enable us to safely pass well clear of Punta Santa Elena.[5] This notorious headland projected some eight miles westward into the South Sea from the normal coastline of the Quito province.

This was a deviation from the usual procedure of piloting northward with the coast in sight, taking advantage of the great northward flowing current.[6] It was the first of several faulty decisions.

The voyage of the South Sea galleons was usually made by sailing along the coast to the port of Paita, some 515 nautical miles north of Callao. The fleet then would sail seaward from Paita for at least three days, in order to pass the dangerous promontory of Santa Elena. Otherwise, if a stop was contemplated at Guayaquil, they would sail to an anchorage at Puna Island, at the entrance of the Guayas River.

After sailing northwestward for an uneventful six days and nights, the pilots joined for a meeting. At noon a sun sight was taken. It placed the vessels at three degrees south latitude. Believing they had gained enough sea room to safely pass Punta Santa Elena (latitude 2° 11' South), they decided to change course toward Isla de Plata,[7] located about 54 nautical miles northward of Punta Santa Elena (latitude 1° 17' South). Their hope was to reconnoiter the port of Manta soon afterward.

The *capitana* and our *almiranta* were sailing along nicely, taking advantage of the current and a favorable southerly wind. For some unexplained reason, I experienced a nagging feeling of uneasiness which persisted for more than twenty-four hours. Peering over the dark, uncertain horizon that night, we saw the eerie glow of the *capitana*'s big stern lanterns. My anxiety would have been lessened if at least one of the avisos had remained with the two royal galleons.[8]

On what proved the fateful night of October 26, the lookout of the *capitana*, half asleep and rubbing his eyes, suddenly viewed a sight all seamen dread: breakers ahead!

The *capitana* immediately fired several guns to alert our *almiranta*, following nearby astern.

Captain Francisco de Solis lost no time bringing his *almiranta* into the wind. Taking soundings he found himself in four and one-half fathoms. He hastily dropped anchor. Everyone rushed on deck, still wearing their nightgowns.

Captain General de Sosa later recalled in his testimony, "About eleven o'clock, the silhouette of land and breaking seas was seen by the watch. It was very near and dead-ahead. Orders were given to fire a gun as the pilot yelled, 'Fall off! Fall off! Head into the wind to stop the vessel'. In turning we found ourselves in the midst of reefs. After hitting three times, our rudder fell off. The pumps were started because the shock of each impact was splitting our seams. Water was pouring through the caulking. In addition to the three pumps being manned, everyone on board was bailing with jars and bowls. We worked all night. At daylight we had eight feet of water in the ship. Everyone was exhausted."

The *capitana* lit as many lanterns as possible to aid passengers and crew aboard the stricken vessel. Guns and muskets fired throughout the long night, signaling the *almiranta*. Those of us on the *almiranta* kept diligent watch through the night. We prayed and sang hymns until dawn. All eyes strained to penetrate the darkness and view the fate of our sister ship.

Pilot Alfara later explained. When they saw the breakers and began bumping bottom, the night was clear. It was approximately eleven o'clock, almost everyone on board was asleep. He tried to drop the sails and anchor simultaneously, but all the windage from the sails and rigging caused the ship to be dragged over the bottom. Suddenly they experienced three severe blows. "The last one being so hard, the ship striking with such force, no one aboard remained standing. The rudder broke off like a mere splinter of wood. We had difficulty getting the anchors down because there were mountains of unregistered goods stored on the foredeck and on top of the anchor cables," the pilot admitted during his trial.

Two anchors were finally dropped. The hooks took hold in twelve *brazas* (fathoms), but the mariners soon found seawater gushing into the lower hold of the vessel.[9]

The captain general was beside himself. He realized he was in the worst possible predicament. The rudder was already lost on a lee shore, and now his flagship was taking on vast amounts of water. Frantic officers were shouting orders to even more frantic seamen. People were pushing, shoving and climbing up and down ladders in an attempt to collect personal valuables from their quarters. The main deck was filled with frenzied passengers who crowded the waist of the ship, preventing the sailors from doing their tasks. The entire ship was turning into a madhouse.

In an attempt to establish some semblance of calm out of chaos, the general directed all passengers to form a bailing line. They passed buckets and containers of water from the depths of the bilged hull. A beleaguered Francisco de Sosa then retired to his cabin.

A ship's officer later testified he witnessed General de Sosa naked in his cabin during the evening and in the midst of the events of the fateful night. He was eating the hallucinatory and addictive *paraguas* plant, a narcotic mushroom. The captain obviously decided if he was about to die, he may as well do it in a euphoric state.

Early the next morning the general returned to his ship's charge. He ordered the launch put over the side where it moored until daybreak. It was then to sail to the *almiranta*, now anchored approximately a half-league away, to seek assistance.

In charge of the launch was Don Francisco Tello de Guzmán y Medina. His boatswain, longtime soldier and seaman, Francisco Barragan, recently received a disciplinary downgrade in rank from captain. Still, he was known to be adept at handling smaller vessels. At daylight the launch approached the *almiranta*, requesting help.

No one slept during the night on either vessel. I watched as the longboat drew near our ship in the early mist of dawn.

As the launch pulled alongside our galleon, I witnessed a loud verbal exchange between our admiral and those in the small boat. "The captain general is demanding your assistance," they shouted. Our hull was sound, the *capitana*'s was full of water. With the tide now ebbing, our own ship was bumping bottom. Admiral de Solis's primary concern was saving his own *almiranta* by any means possible. In his predicament, and with a firm belief in the survival of the fittest, he felt there was no time to assist the *capitana*.

Lowering his longboat, he cut the *almiranta's* anchor loose and tied the cable to the longboat. It took eight strong oarsmen much straining and pulling, but eventually our galleon was towed to deeper water—and to safety.

The *capitana's* launch returned empty-handed to the lee side of the stranded vessel. A piercing sound of wailing and cursing streamed across the salty air, ultimately fading, as though the cries were traveling to the heavens themselves.

"I trusted Don Francisco Tello with the launch to the *almiranta*, half a league away. We asked for their help in unloading and saving His Majesty's silver. They refused to assist in any way. Soon after, they merely sailed away," declared General de Sosa in a letter written to the viceroy on October 29, 1654. "By abandoning the *capitana* and refusing to answer my signals, they did much insult to His Royal and Catholic Majesty."

His Majesty was not to be the only one insulted. General de Sosa ordered the launch to stand by the beleaguered *capitana*. Its assistance was needed to transport people and treasure ashore. He then called a council of the ship's officers to decide the best course of action. The consensus was to try to beach the vessel. The fear, otherwise, was that the great ship would sink in deep water, where nothing could be recovered.

There was considerable panic in the midst of this meeting. Passengers screamed, alarming crew members even more as their pitch intensified. Some grabbed planks and jumped over the side. Others plunged into the chilly seas holding on to chicken crates, in an attempt to reach shore. Most totally abandoned their valuables—in exchange for saving their lives. Some attempted swimming, weighted with money belts. Twenty people drowned trying to reach the beach.

Persuaded by the panicking people, Boatswain Barragan released the longboat's painter tied to the mothership. Accompanied by Captain Guzmán y Medina, and the few others comprising the crew, he sailed the small boat directly to the beach. Desperate passengers clung to both sides of the gunwales of the small craft, holding on for dear life.

General de Sosa later testified: "Upon reaching the rock strewn beach, the boat was broken apart and rendered useless. This left the *capitana* and its remaining passengers and crew a considerable distance from shore with no means to reach land."

Don Francisco Tello de Guzmán y Medina was fined 30,000 ducats, payable to the Royal Chamber of the *Hacienda*, for his cowardly action in abandoning the *capitana*. He and four of his crew were sentenced to ten years of hard labor. En route to Spain to serve his sentence, he lost his life when the *Nuestra Señora de las Maravillas* met its destiny on the Little Bahama Bank. Francisco Barragan voluntarily turned himself in to the jail in Guayaquil. After being interrogated, he confessed to his uncourageous deed. He was sentenced to ten years of service in the wars in Chile, on half pay. He was so affected by the charges that he ultimately lost his mind. He was admitted to the madhouse wing of the hospital of San Andrés where he grew more furious each day.[10]

October 27, 1654

As daybreak turned into morning, the tide began to flood. The *almiranta* sailed for Punta Santa Elena to report the disaster and to seek assistance for the *capitana*.

October 31, 1654

Our pilots determined our distance from the *Punta* to be only about six leagues. However, the set of northwesterly currents flowing against us was so severe, it took four long days tacking back and forth to cover the six leagues.[11]

Finally anchoring in sight of the *Pueblo* (also known as Santa Elena) within the protective peninsula of the *Punta*, we gave thanks to God's gracious Providence for our safe arrival.

I was fascinated with the glorious mountain ranges and foothills of this part of the Presidency of Quito. This place reminded me of pleasant boyhood memories of the Sierra Morena in the province of Jaén, not far from the upper reaches of the Guadalquivir River, where I grew up.

Word was sent overland to President Velasco, advising him of the *capitana*'s great peril. The *almiranta* was then ordered to continue its voyage to Panama to inform the president of the disaster, and to request divers and necessary salvage equipment to save the treasure.

November 20, 1654

We safely reached the port of Perico today. It is the eve of the day of Our Lady of the Presentation. I was overjoyed to disembark and walk on dry land. Immediately following a prayer service giving thanks to our Almighty Father for our safe deliverance, I made arrangements for transport to Portobelo and Cartagena. It is my hope to book passage to Spain on one of the vessels of the Marqués de Montealegre.

Upon hearing the disturbing details, the President of Panama, Don Pedro Carillo, responded diligently. Within six days, two *chinchorros* with dozens of divers and salvage personnel and equipment were en route from Panama to the wreck site at Chanduy. News was already sent to Lima, via Guayaquil, presenting a full account of the accident to the viceroy and requesting assistance.

The courier reached Lima on Sunday, November 15, and told the story of the sunken *capitana*.

"News has just arrived: the *capitana*, sailing to *Tierra Firme* with His Majesty's treasure valued at 13,060,000 *patacones*[12], was lost between Punta de Carnero and Chanduy, fourteen leagues downstream from Guayaquil.[13]

Viceroy Sotomayor immediately responded. He ordered Don Pedro Vásquez de Velasco, the President of Quito, to hasten to the wreckage site and take charge. The District Attorney of the Audience, Don Diego Andrés de la Rocha, was ordered to maintain careful records of the treasure being retrieved, along with an account of any actions deemed harmful to the interests of the viceroy or the king. Accompanying Don Diego Andrés was an appointed tax attorney, Don Bartolomé de Solorzano, who was ordered to take with him "all the registers of this year . . . and the records of the royal fifth" in order to make positive identification of the recovered treasure officially registered and sent aboard the *capitana*.

Records of the Lima Royal Treasury chronicled that the *capitana* carried 865 silver bars for the Crown (valued at 867,778 pesos), and 1,219 ingots for private accounts. Also included in the ship's register were 151 boxes of eight and four *reales* from the Potosí mint, as well as twenty-five chests of worked silver. This was the official register of the *Jesus Maria de la Limpia Concepción*.

The official register of the 1654 *capitana*[14] was "reconstructed" in 1655 following the disaster at Chanduy, Ecuador, and the subsequent scandal exposed as a result of the shipwreck. This 1655 register reflects a total of 2,212 silver bars with an average weight of 68.5 pounds each, instead of the 2,084 reported on the original register. There were also 216 chests of coins (with 2,500 coins per chest), instead of the 151 chests initially reported. The difference may be the result of those persons stepping forward and reporting their previously unregistered treasure after the shipwreck in order to prevent their valuables from being confiscated for the king.

Descriptions of Registered Treasure
Aboard the 1654 *Capitana*
A.G.I., Contratación 2425

Silver Bars (for the account of the king)

From Potosí	697
From Lima	137

Silver Bars (for private accounts)

With assay, weight and identifying marks	810
With no markings or weight	568
(average weight per bar was 68.5 lbs.)	

Total Registered Silver Bars   2212

Chests of Silver Coins

2,500 coins per chest (mostly eight and four *reales*)   216

Boxes of Worked Silver

Candelabra, water and wine goblets, pitchers, trays, etc.   22

2

Salvaging the Queen of the South Sea

Nowhere has one ever seen so much silver piled in mountains as though it were wheat.

BACK AT THE SITE of the *capitana*'s troubles, the general ordered all masts severed in order to lighten the water-logged vessel. In later testimony, he provided an account of his strategy to rescue the treasure.

"We waited for high tide to cut our cables and drift from the spot we were moored the night before, some three leagues out. By using the spritsail to our advantage, we negotiated a narrow channel. We luckily succeeded in avoiding a reef dangerous enough to demolish our vessel if we had collided. The *capitana* came permanently to rest near a rock pile in four and one-half fathoms, less than a league from shore. The wind veered westerly, causing the galleon to roll to starboard.

"With the ship listing so, it was impossible to refloat her, but fortunately she stranded cleanly. The bottom is neither muddy nor sandy, rather it is hard and firm. We were hard aground, about a quarter of a mile from El Negro[15], in front of a small bay with a curving shoreline like a horseshoe. Punta Chanduy is to the east-southeast. The water is four fathoms deep at low tide and six fathoms at high tide."

Lima, November 26, 1654

The viceroy primarily focused on immediate salvage. "Divers are needed, but there are none available in the area. Organize all available divers in Callao and nearby areas. Exclude no one. Send them to the wrecked *capitana* without delay. The most seaworthy ship in Callao must be expediently prepared to sail to the site. It is to transport the divers, equipment and necessary supplies. In charge of this important mission will be Admiral Martin de Camudio. He will be assisted by Captain Diego Dias."

Don Pedro Carillo, the President of Panama, also responded diligently. Within six days two *chinchorros* with dozens of divers, salvage personnel and equipment were en route from Panama to the *capitana*.

December 2, 1654

By the end of November, Vásquez de Velasco completed setting up camp at Chanduy. He took his responsibilities seriously, as evidenced in one of his first reports.

"Concerning the loss of the *capitana, Jesus Maria de la Limpia Concepción de Nuestra Señora*: In view of the frauds occurring in past years, as well as this year, and regardless of His Excellency's reasons for not registering the silver, gold and goods embarked on the *capitana*, the following will be effected immediately: All items recovered from the wreck, and regardless of the rightful owner, will be fully counted and manifested. All rights and dues will be paid to His Majesty. Anyone who has embarked silver, gold and other goods must declare so within twenty-four hours to officials of the viceroyalty. In doing so those persons will be granted immunity from prosecution for undisclosed goods or seizing of same. The taxes due will be assessed. Goods not declared will be forfeited to the Crown."

A further warning is issued: "Persons acting under the pretext of aiding the owners in saving their treasure, or those who have embarked and now escaped with large stolen amounts will be denounced. They will be punished with the utmost severity. This official notification is to be publicly announced and exhibited in writing in the usual meeting places.

"This order applies also to white silver not carrying markings, such as unrefined silver or silver cones and bars. It is known that much treasure of this description has been stolen by persons entrusted by the original owners for safekeeping following salvage."

Immediately after the shipwreck, Captain General Francisco de Sosa organized a volunteer diving effort, admirably performed by a handful of his sailors. Results of the initial salvage effort were extremely good, considering the circumstances. Francisco de Sosa was stranded in an inaccessible section of the coast where there were only a few inhabitants scattered among several poor Indian villages. They had minimal drinking water, available from only a few deep wells.

"The place is a desert," stated an early report. Until help arrived, de Sosa had no real divers, very few tools, and most of the work could be performed only at low tide. The seas were then calmer, and more grounded superstructure was reachable. With as much as thirteen-foot tides in the area, it was nearly impossible to continue salvage operations at any other time. Fortunately for those stranded on the beach near Chanduy, a large quantity of assorted provisions and wine was saved.

The silver recovered was from sections of the galleon not completely flooded. "I took a quantity of silver from the cabins, berths and poop. Using the jolly boat I transported it to the beach. It was then stored nearby and guarded," de Sosa reported.

Although his was a desperate effort to save face, the amount recovered was a wonderful accomplishment under such adverse conditions. Admittedly, the amateur divers sought out the most accessible boxes and chests in the upper deck areas. What they found and brought to the surface was mostly personal and unregistered cargo. Nevertheless, the inventory of treasure rafted ashore at low tide and stashed in lime kilns under guard was impressive.

To accomplish this salvage, General de Sosa enlisted the services of local Indians who provided their personal canoes and rafts to ferry the heavy silver ingots from the wrecked ship, sometimes through heavy surf, in order to safely reach the beach. More than once a *cayuco* was overturned in the breakers.

De Sosa also opened the hatches above the *pañoles* (storage rooms) not totally immersed. He requested volunteers to enter to see if anything visible was salvageable.

The general later reported, "Three or four men dared to enter the dark and fouled bowels of the ship. Much silver belonging to Your Majesty and private persons was saved. When Vásquez de Velasco arrived, the following was already recovered from the upper section:

291 bars belonging to Your Majesty
373 bars belonging to private owners
109 boxes of *reales*
12 boxes of ornamental silver trays, pitchers, candelabras and various other items
31,000 pesos in bags
1,009 small bars
4 cones (the *quinto* was paid on 3)

11 flat sheets of silver
22 guns and some cables"

Vásquez de Velasco brought six divers with him and hired fourteen other volunteers from Guayaquil.

Getting into the lower hold was not an easy task. Stacked on top of the silver were 11,000 jugs of Chilean wine, 4,000 large blocks of salt, 2,000 bags of flour, each weighing fifty pounds, many hundreds of flagstones, an assortment of copper pots, baskets of raisins, crockery and boxes of *plata labrada* (silver ornaments and utensils such as plates and candlesticks). Not only did this bulk combine to hinder the diving and salvage efforts, but strewn on top of all of this were stacks upon stacks of burdensome bales of vicuña wool, 12,000 bales in all. This unbelievable quantity of merchandise was expressly forbidden to be carried aboard the king's royal galleons!

Another major problem the divers faced was the vessel's serious list toward starboard. Several intermittent westerly squalls caused even further instability of the hull. Each storm tide surging over the wreck increased the angle of starboard roll. As a result, there was considerable sanding-in on the right side of the submerged hull. These storms not only halted salvage efforts, but further destroyed what remained of the *capitana*.

The first *chinchorro* arrived at the Chanduy wreck site with fourteen divers from Panama in early December. Under the charge of Sergeant Baltasar de Salvatierra, they received a loud cheer and round of applause from the exhausted crew of the shipwrecked *capitana*. Many of the seamen-turned-volunteer-divers had been working from sunrise to sunset since the accident. Those not diving were assigned other necessary chores, including making repairs, building floats, fishing, clamming, cooking, seeking fresh water and gathering firewood. The general made certain everyone was busy, even those guarding the silver.

In the meantime, Juan Vincincio Justiniano, General Commissioner of the Artillery of Panama, was ordered by the president, Don Pedro Carillo, to hire several dozen of the best pearl divers he could find and proceed directly to Chanduy with appropriate salvage equipment. Justiniano was a highly regarded, loyal and energetic, middle-management official who related well to the soldiers and pearl fishery divers, with whom he previously worked. In only a few days he was ready to depart Panama with thirty-two divers.

The President of Panama stated, "It would be difficult to find in the Indies another man more competent. Therefore it is important that you offer him every assistance and give him good accommodations.

"I have instructed him to allow the divers to work underwater in turns throughout the day, but under no circumstances are the divers to do any other type work. They should be well treated because they are held in high esteem in this country. Furthermore, the amount of their value has been insured to the benefit of their owners, in the name of the king, should they die."

Since the divers were slaves, albeit well cared for, if any died the king was under obligation to purchase replacements for the private owners. The divers were considered so valuable to the success of the recovery operation that the President of Panama sent six of his soldiers to guard and protect them, both afloat and ashore. He also sent a cook to see to their needs, along with provisions and water for thirty-five days. They were paid four pesos for each silver bar recovered, eight pesos for each box of *reales* recovered, and twelve pesos for each chest of worked silver.

Justiniano also signed on a man from Spain, a great diving expert whom he brought with the thirty-two native divers, and "all the necessary tools to do the job, including iron hooks, hatchets, crowbars and claws. All have been forged between last night and this morning in the foundries of this city."

When Justiniano and his skilled divers arrived on the scene with fresh reserves, they too were warmly greeted by the other professionals, most of whom were nursing bruises and cuts. Some of the Panamanian divers were strong enough to individually wrestle a single bar weighing seventy pounds to the surface. Consequently, an amazing amount of treasure was recovered during November, December and January.

When Don Pedro Vásquez de Velasco arrived to take charge, he gave credit to the captain general for his recovery and inventory of the huge pile of treasure. General de Sosa's words to Velasco were:

"I have recovered all the silver stored on or near the upper decks. With the divers now here from Panama, let us hope, with the help of God we can get it all. However, I must ask you to close your eyes on the smuggling of the merchants who have suffered considerable losses. Otherwise you will ruin what little remains of their investments and make even more desperate their plight, as well as that of the entire trading profession.

"As of this writing there are remaining only a few crew and eight of the passengers. I have on shore two hundred bars from the second deck of the infantry. Since it is unregistered silver, I have confiscated it for His Majesty. I am sure there is a great quantity more of the same still aboard. I hope to quickly recover it and expedite it to Panama."

The first shipment of recovered treasure was sent to Panama on the *Nuestra Señora de Los Angeles*, skippered by Captain Francisco Benites on December 28, 1654. The total value of this first salvage operation was 1,870,525 pesos. The *Los Angeles* was nicknamed the *Ship of Gold* because none of the crew had ever seen so much treasure.

"Nowhere has one ever seen so much silver piled in mountains as though it were wheat. For this reason the fleet—leaving from Cartagena—will be delayed until the end of July or mid-August. Despite the accident resulting in a great shortfall of funds, it will be judgment day for all of Spain if the treasure does not arrive at all."[16]

Many of the *capitana*'s sailors, including a number of officers and petty officers disappeared. "More than sixty crew members departed with sleds and packs carrying one million pesos," one report stated.

Witnesses reported some leaving camp late at night with bags and boxes of stolen plunder. Others ran off in broad daylight, burdened with bundles of assorted goods. It was said they were living in style in nearby towns.

Deputy Silvermaster Juan Cortes, and the *capitana*'s chief scribe, Bartolomé de Chavarria, were accused of hiding many chests of silver on shore during the night. Artillerymen Francisco Fuentes, Francisco Davilla, Juan Buenano, the guardian of the galleon, Francisco Gil and a passenger, Geronimo Gabrera, were all charged with carrying private treasure ashore, amounting to some 24,000 pesos in gold. They refused to turn the treasure over to the rightful owners. They were ultimately captured and sentenced to death.

Four others refused to declare silver discovered in their personal lockers when uncovered by divers. The men included Francisco Medero, boatswain, Geronimo Lozano, a demoted sergeant, Lieutenant Pedro Farfan, and Bernardo Ortiz de Meneses. Each was fined 2,000 pesos and sentenced to four years in Callao garrison on half pay.

The thievery was so massive, it was said; "Those who left Callao

Salvaged Silver Shipped Aboard the *Los Angeles*

Treasure Description	His Majesty's	Private Registered	Private Unregistered	Unidentified	Value in Pesos
Silver Bars Standard Size	386	711	267	4	1,355,688
Boxes of "White Silver" (small bars and sheets)	3 (546 *marcos* wt.)	159			43,097
Boxes of *Reales*		151	8		397,500
Reales (separate)	440	3,800			4,240
Boxes of Silverware		25	3		70,000
Total Treasure Recovered up to December 28, 1654					1,870,525

poor were now rich, and those who left rich and powerful were now poor and disgraced."

Señor Velasco issued another memorandum on December 28, this one directly to the viceroy. It indicated he recognized what had happened at Chanduy beach in only a few weeks.

"Since it has been impossible to prevent all fraud, it will have to be dealt with upon arrival of the galleons in Panama or Spain. It is presumed there was more treasure unregistered than registered. I wrote to Your Majesty regarding this problem three years earlier. You may recall my suggested remedies: Smaller ships. No wool on ships due to the amount of space it occupies versus the small profit and tax revenues. No more boxes of worked silver on which the *quinto* has not been paid: this is simply an excuse for sending silver without paying the tax. It also occupies too much space. Finally, all ships from Callao to Panama should be required to clear at Paita. Such clearance would have prevented the accident of the *capitana*."

New Year's Day, 1655

Captain and Silvermaster Bernardo de Campos was a busy man from the moment the galleon was grounded. The largest portion of His Majesty's treasure was stored on the starboard side of the ship, now inaccessible. De Campos was particularly concerned. He convinced de Sosa to cut open the galleon and burn part of the superstructure in order to gain access to some of the starboard *pañoles*. His responsibility as silvermaster was being tested. It was imperative he do everything possible to save the treasure.[17]

Using axes, holes were cut into the side of the vessel. Hatch openings were enlarged in order for divers to enter the submerged portion. Divers previously reporting zero visibility were now aided with a small beam of sunlight filtering through the dark and dangerous hold. The prow portion remaining above water was burned to the surface in order to provide easier access. The work, nonetheless, was slow and arduous. Tons of rope, tackle, shipboard gear and assorted merchandise were strewn about, hampering salvage efforts even further. One diver, while probing the waters beneath the dark forecastle, became entangled in submerged lines of hemp. Fellow divers were unable to reach him in time. He became one more victim of the *capitana*'s plight. His limp body was retrieved by his own brother, himself barely making it back to the water's surface.

Only days later a diver from Panama was working the wreck during morning hours. He suddenly shot to the surface, screaming in spastic agony. His shipmates quickly dragged him into the *chinchorro* in an attempt to aid him. His convulsions increased, his eyelids drooped and his jaw muscles were so tightly locked he was unable to speak or swallow. After a few moments of incoherent mumbling, he lapsed into unconsciousness. A few minutes later he was dead. An inspection of his body revealed several neat pairs of small circular red dots on one leg, about one-half inch apart. The leg was already swollen. The only explanation was the dreaded *culebra de mar*, a deadly venomous sea snake located in tropical Pacific waters.[18] The snake was never found.

In a letter to the viceroy in Lima, Vásquez de Velasco wrote, "Two divers are dead from salvage-related accidents. The others are now fearful. All assorted cargo has settled above the silver loaded on the starboard side. It cannot be reached. It is not possible for divers to recover the extremely large amounts in the lower holds and between the ballast. Nor is it possible to recover the registered silver not stored in the upper strong rooms, due to the wreck heeling greatly to starboard."

To the Peruvian administrators, at first glance, it would appear that the salvage recoveries of the *capitana* were tremendously successful. In little more than three months almost 3,000,000 pesos had been recovered. This was the approximate amount of the ship's register.

On February 14, 1655, 1,061,455 pesos were transported from the salvage camp near Chanduy to Panama on the reserve galleon *Santiago* of Captain Juan de Vidaurre.

By March 1655, a series of weather patterns brought the treasure diving to a halt. The viceroy ordered the shipwreck site "be watched until underwater operations can resume next summer."

When he arrived in Lima in February 1655, one of the first orders of business for the new viceroy, Count of Alva of Aliste, was to arrest General de Sosa, as well as the pilots of the *capitana*. The viceroy also ordered Andres de Villela to reopen the case originally handled by Pedro Vásquez de Velasco in Chanduy and Guayaquil. New inquiries were made, more depositions were taken and new accusations came forth.

The captain general knew that all kinds of memorandums and reports, official and unofficial, would soon begin circulating. He also knew of his tremendous potential personal liability for the treasure, lives and merchandise lost. He was fully aware that his responsibility for wrecking the largest galleon built to date for the Crown would not be taken lightly. He was correct. Evidence against him was accumulating, and pressures were mounting. He later reported:

"Your Majesty, I tell you in all good faith, and in hope of a fair distribution of justice, if I should be charged, I should be punished. Yet I hope you will remember I have served Your Majesty for thirty-seven years, and I am now getting old, and have sons . . ."

The most serious charge against him was that he had sent the *chinchorros* ahead, probably to some clandestine rendezvous with smugglers from Guayaquil. The scout ships were not available to reconnoiter the coast and survey the best possible course for the *capitana* and *almiranta*.

"Had even one of the *chinchorros* been available, to sail ahead of the *capitana*, it would have seen the land, realized the impending

Salvaged Treasure Shipped Aboard the *Santiago*

Treasure Description	His Majesty's	Private Registered	Private Unregistered	Unidentified	Value in Pesos
Silver Bars Standard Size	340	513	22	26	952,351
Silver *Barretones*			93 (579 *marcos* wt.)		4,967
Boxes of "White Silver" (small bars and sheets)	217 (1,378 *marcos* wt.)				11,823
Boxes of *Reales*		5			12,500
Reales (separate)	65,814*				65,814
Boxes of Silverware			2	1,049 (*marcos*)	12,919
Taken as Taxes	126 (*marcos*)				1,081
Total Treasure Recovered from December 28, 1654 to February 14, 1655					1,061,455

* In reconciling the early salvage reports there is a question whether this number is in *reales* or pesos. It is being carried forward as pesos.

dangers, and could have warned the armada. The *capitana* would not have been lost."

General de Sosa responded to the charge by producing an original written order from the former viceroy, Count of Salvatierra, concerning the mission and uses of the *chinchorro*.

"You have no right to blame me for the absence of the *chinchorros*," he testified. "The (former) viceroy ordered I send them ahead, even before we departed Callao."

Even so, several witnesses testified that Captain Luis Baez Camiña, skipper of the *chinchorro*, *San Pedro*, put into Isla de la Plata and Paita for personal reasons. When he finally returned to look for the squadron, he found the *capitana* aground a mile off the beach. Captain Camiña admitted being concerned for his own safety and was not able to get close to the stranded galleon. For his unresponsive action he was sentenced to ten years of war service in Chile, on half pay.

As to the responsibility for the shipwreck of the *capitana*, the captain general stated it rested entirely in the hands of the pilots. These included Captain Miguel Benitez de Alfara, First Pilot, and Julio Caballero, Second Pilot, whose poor judgment caused the misfortune.

"The responsibility cannot be placed on the general," proffered his lawyer, citing article six of de Sosa's sailing orders. "The general had no obligation to be an expert in navigation, and his instructions were not to interfere with the decisions of the pilots. They are paid to be knowledgeable about the set of tides, currents and behavior patterns of the sea.

"As to having taken on board large quantities of wine and flour, he confesses. He was required to feed an extremely large number of important people on this voyage. These provisions had to last for not only the trip to Panama, but also while he remained in that harbor. These rations also were necessary for the long return voyage to Callao, as sufficient quantities of such supplies are not available there.

"The wine and provisions brought aboard by the general were quite reasonable quantities when considering the length of the passage and the number of merchants and passengers needing to be fed. These people eat at the expense of the general and other officials with whom they negotiated the price of their passage," stated de Sosa's defense attorney.

The captain general was given credit for maneuvering the heavily ladened ship into a shallow, hard-sand bottom where it grounded in a small channel between two rocks. He was also credited with the recovery of much of the sunken silver.

"He was not afraid to go into the water himself, and did so in depths reaching beyond his chest, to move some large rocks hindering the landing of the dinghies. He worked constantly, like any humble seaman, to save the silver and artillery. When Pedro Vásquez de Velasco arrived, much of the first silver to be shipped to Panama and most of the artillery was out of the water," stated a friendly witness.

While it was determined that extremely strong westerly winds and currents were the factors causing the *capitana* to run aground, there were many witnesses who confirmed that the pilots did not follow the normal, previously established route from past years. And somebody had to be blamed for the great loss of the "Queen of the South Sea."

Francisco de Sosa, with ten previous voyages to and from Panama to his credit, was one of the most experienced mariners in the *Armada del Mar del Sur*. His flimsy answers and excuses for the wrecking of the *capitana* were not taken lightly by the investigating officials of the Crown.

Why was the ship so extremely overloaded with cargo, as well as people? Why did de Sosa sail with only half the required crew to handle a galleon this size, many of them untrained Indians or mulattos with little knowledge of their jobs? Why did they not follow normal sailing directions with their course having been set along the seacoast? How could such a staggering amount of contraband silver have found its way into the *capitana*'s lower holds without the captain general's knowledge? (One witness testified the amount of contraband cargo was so immense, it would have filled the entire Square of Lima.)

Consequently, Francisco de Sosa and the two pilots were sentenced to death by the Viceroy of Peru, and a date for their execution was arranged.

They were transported from Guayaquil to Callao to meet their fate. As it turned out, the skipper of the small coastal vessel carrying them was a distant relative of one of the pilots, and was sympathetic to their cause. He had heard many stories of the fantastically successful salvage work.

"Surely you did not turn in *all* of the recovered silver?" he questioned.

The convicted men smiled. Their two guards smiled. A deal was made.

The trio was put ashore at Punta Jambeli. They cautiously made their way across the Santa Rosa estuary to the village of Huayala (today Puerto Bolivar). From there they traveled to Machala. Taking refuge in a small cathedral, they requested asylum from the resident priest where they remained in the sanctuary for some time and were well succored. The priest noted their seemingly endless supply of Potosí pieces-of-eight *reales*.

However, their luck was short lived. The fugitives were betrayed by a member of the church. When the viceroy learned of their hiding place he immediately ordered an armed patrol to the location.

Although their number of treasure coins was dwindling, they were able to acquire the services and sympathy of an ecclesiastic attorney and judge, who was quickly persuaded to come to their rescue.

The judge notified the viceroy that his death penalty was out of order. He demanded the execution be suspended until His Majesty could intervene and determine the proper punishment.

Don Francisco de Sosa was summoned to Spain to be tried by the Council of the Indies. He was jailed and finally released after two years.

While the hundreds of documents relating to the Chanduy tragedy indicate that the new viceroy was attempting to make every effort to punish those who might be guilty for the disaster, the voluminous files also strongly point to flagrantly loose controls at every level of the colonial system. The merchant community boldly shipped treasure and goods without declaring them. Men like Juan de Navarrete, the principal guard responsible for the loading of the silver aboard the *capitana* at Callao, received only a slap on the wrist after the discovery of such huge amounts of contraband came to light, since "blame could not be placed upon just one person."

There were numerous recorded admissions of clandestine attempts to smuggle treasure ashore from the shipwreck site in "bundles of linen, personal luggage, and even in the barrel of a cannon." Testimony after testimony and document after document provided unmistakable signs of a system out of control.

3

Everyone Is a Smuggler

Although the capitana's registered amount was 3,000,000 pesos, there were, in fact, very close to 10,000,000 pesos on board. There also was 7,000,000 pesos unregistered. I have manifested all saved and recorded it.
Juan de Valdés y Llano

IT WAS GENERALLY UNDERSTOOD in Lima that 13,060,000 pesos had been shipped aboard the fleet bound for Panama on the 1654 *capitana* and *almiranta*. Official records, however, indicate that registered pesos of only 3,000,000 for the king and private accounts were aboard the *capitana*. Later, 1,883,193 pesos were acknowledged by merchants who stepped forward and paid the *avería* tax to avoid confiscation after shipwreck, even though some of their declared goods were not recovered.

Public Prosecutor Juan de Valdés y Llano stated in a letter to the king dated December 31, 1654, "Although the *capitana*'s registered amount was 3,000,000 pesos, there were actually on the *capitana* very close to 10,000,000 pesos, 7,000,000 of which were unregistered. I have manifested all that was saved and recorded it."

Confirming this, another interesting comment was made the following day, in a letter sent to the king on January 1, 1655, by Coamana de Figueiroa: "The *capitana* was carrying more than nine million."

In a letter to the Marqués de Montealegre asking him to wait in Cartagena until some of the salvaged silver reached Panama, the President of Panama wrote:

"While there are various opinions as to how much treasure was on board the *capitana*, I can affirm it was nothing less than eight million. The loss is not only the greatest in the memory of these seas, but probably the waters of the north as well . . ."

The monstrous scandal of contraband and unregistered silver, revealed as a result of the shipwreck of the 1654 *capitana* near Chanduy, highlighted the problem identified with the *Carrera de Indias* for years. Because ships of the *Armada del Mar del Sur* were considerably fewer in number than those plying the Atlantic and Caribbean waters, one can visualize how the percentage of illicit cargo might increase in proportion. Still, *three times more* than the registered amount is difficult to comprehend. Surely, the captain general, the silvermaster and everyone involved in loading cargo and keeping the books had to have been entangled in the scheme. Everyone truly was a smuggler, and the causes were inbred from previous generations. By the mid-1600's the problem reached epidemic and uncontrollable proportions within the Spanish Empire.

Document after Spanish document reflects the reluctance of merchant traders to send anything duly registered, fearing the merchandise would be confiscated by representatives of the king upon port arrival, under the pretext of a *voluntary loan*. Such actions happened repeatedly and caused disastrous effects. Certainly, if the king was under financial stress, many merchant shippers relying on the galleons to bring goods to and from the colonies for their own livelihood also claimed empty pockets if the ships were delayed, or did not arrive at all.

As a result, the Bureau of Trade (*Casa de la Contratación*), exercising the system of audit and control over the *Carrera de Indias*, adopted a new attitude in dealing with smuggled goods. Knowing it could neither monitor nor control smuggling, much less stop it, the Bureau allowed certain private goods labeled "to be registered." In reality this meant it was agreed by both shipper and receiver that the owners would step forward and declare the goods if an unusual circumstance, such as shipwreck, occurred whereupon they were caught red-handed with unregistered goods. Then, and only then, would they be required to pay the duly declared fees, assessments and taxes. The system was so well organized that few smugglers ever were caught. This was, indirectly, part of the king's problem. He was not receiving a fair tariff for the goods of every description occupying space on his vessels. Yet he bore the expense of transport.

The official observers turned a blind eye and were rewarded for doing so. Disembarkments at night, or just prior to arrival while still out at sea, were well organized and common occurrences. There was always a bevy of small boats loitering around a recently returned galleon. Traders made their deals and considerable cargo went over the side of the hull into waiting auxiliary boats. The goods were shuttled ashore—cash and carry.

With the king's treasure receiving most of the attention, personal luggage generally was not checked. Smuggling was a game played at all levels. If someone was caught, clemency usually was recommended by the controllers of the Bureau. They knew there were not a lot of men walking the streets of Spain or Peru who would ordinarily risk their necks at sea for galleon wages. Harsh punishment, as the law requested, would mean the ruin of both the men and the trade. Except in cases where it was unavoidable (such as shipwreck or blatant act of theft), few actions were brought against smugglers. Everyone knew everyone was a smuggler. From the captain general to the youngest sailor, everyone going to the Indies or sailing in the South Sea Armada planned to make as much money as possible on the side.

Sailors and other crew members of a treasure galleon had their own particular code of conduct and standards of ethics. Few gave a second thought to their smuggling activities being punishable by fines, jail or possibly death. Few dared to report the contraband activities of their shipmates. Absolutely none of them ever admitted that bringing unregistered goods into any port governed by the Crown of Spain was a purposeful act of fraud against the king. Silence and loyalty among the seafaring brethren reigned supreme throughout the *flotas*. These men certainly did not sign on for a long and hard voyage for paltry seamen's wages. They were on their particular ship for the same reason as the captain general, sergeant major, boatswain, and even the royal scribe,—for a piece of the action and an opportunity to participate in the immense profits to be made from almost every imaginable aspect of the New World trade.

Even after the Crown positioned official observers or constables on board the galleons to watch for illicit trade, the practice of smuggling continued to proliferate. These same officials soon began receiving bribes greater than their salaries, encouraging them to look the other way, or lose count of the numbers of boxes, chests, crates and bars of bullion brought on board unregistered.

The contraband scene ran rampant for years as officials of the Crown continued to allow illegal shipments and contraband imports. Key magistrates of the king, whose responsibility was investigating and collecting the tax, often met with military and administrative officers of an incoming fleet for customs clearance (if such was not already arranged). If goods were declared, percentages often were levied to compensate merchants (smugglers) for their costs, plus a general bonus to the captain of the galleon, usually representing five percent of the total value. Spanish records are replete with cases involving rank and file officials who were indicted for everything from improper conduct to bribery at every level. Traders and adventurers from every direction flocked to Cádiz, Cartagena de Indias, and Peruvian ports to participate.

Various methods were utilized and rules imposed to attempt controlling excessive fraud and smuggling. Captains' salaries were not paid until the vessels returned to Spain or the colonial home port. This provided a source of offset should deceitful merchandise be exposed.

Surety bonds often were required, particularly of captains who were named to those positions for the first time. This extra insurance fee, in most cases paid by the skipper of a galleon, in itself promulgated smuggling as a means of recapturing the *unnecessary* and *unwarranted* funding of such bond.

Amounts of surety bonds levied against key officers sailing to the Indies in 1647[19]:

Position	Ducats
General of Armada	8,000
Admiral of Armada	4,000
General of Flota	4,000
Admiral of Flota	3,000
Captain	2,000
Veedor (Overseer)	2,000
Accountant	2,000
Governor of the Infantry Corps	2,000
Sergeant Major	1,500
Warrant Officer	1,000
Navigator/First Mate	1,000
Royal Scribe	1,000
Royal Constable-Bailiff	1,000
Governor of Water	1,000

Second Lieutenant	500
Silvermasters	500
Pilots	500
Scribes of Rations	500
Storekeepers	500
Custodians - Watchmen	300
Chiefs of Infantry	300
Medics and Surgeons	300

Every fleet commander and ship captain swore oaths of homage and allegiance to the king and promised never to transport treasure or merchandise outside of registry. This was a prerequisite of being named to the position. They swore before God and All Saints to defend the king's treasure until their death. They pledged never to surrender their galleon even after it sank to the ocean bottom. They agreed to fight the enemies of Spain until no life remained. However, no one ever acknowledged being overpaid, nor affirmed there were no dangers or hardships in going to sea. What was good for their ancestors Francisco Pizzaro or Hernando Cortez certainly was good enough for them. If the captain, who paid homage with his oath of allegiance and his surety bond, did a bit of informal importing and exporting, it surely was equally appropriate for the second lieutenant or sergeant of infantry or cabin page. Smuggling of treasure and contraband cargo could only be tolerated—never stopped. It was impossible to regulate illicit commerce. Admiral Pedro de Ursua stated in 1640[20] that even if he inspected the luggage of every merchant and passenger for contraband he could never guard the several dozen ports and hatches through which baggage and chests might be passed.

It was extremely difficult for the authorities to enforce the rules relating to unregistered goods. Many of the high ranking officials who conspired with the galleon captains lobbied simultaneously against enforcement. They stated the *avería* was not so much affected by what little might be brought in concealed by the seamen. It was the large unregistered merchant shipments causing the loss of taxes and fees to the king.

The *avería* was a forced duty, a contribution expected to be paid to the king as a partial offset of the cost of protecting the fleet. This duty was assessed and levied on the value of the goods being transported under the protection of the king's galleons or the regular

Armada de la Guardia de la Carrera de las Indias, as well as the *Armada del Mar del Sur*. The *avería* would reimburse the Royal Treasury for the depreciation and maintenance of ships and artillery, and cover the wages of those soldiers who were on board the royal galleons.

During times of relative peace the *avería* charge was a modest two to five percent. However, after the Dutch and English began sending marauding war fleets in search of the Spanish *flotas*, and piracy was a way of life for many, the *avería* fee averaged as high as twenty to twenty-five percent for protection during a particular year. The fiscal administrators of this transport duty constantly faced the problem of catching up with the shortfall of the previous year and staying current. If there were major losses at sea, or major shipments undeclared, the king seldom recovered his justly levied duty.

Sometimes extreme decrees were ordered. Following the loss of the 1654 *capitana*, the *avería* went to thirty percent.[21]

For the official controllers the situation almost always was one of catch-up due to shipwreck, fraud and undeclared cargoes. Honest merchants paid heavily for those who refused to declare and pay their fair share. With so many freeloaders in the business there was constant turmoil and protesting about the modus operandi of the Council of the Indies and of those in responsible positions of enforcing the armada taxes.

If the Council of the Indies showed leniency by permitting a grace period of ten days or two weeks to allow time for illicit cargo to be correctly manifested and the *avería* tax and other required assessments paid, the Council of the Treasury, on the other hand, flatly refused any pardon period. This administrative agency stated that those who took the oath agreeing to serve His Majesty must recognize His Royal Rights. No exemptions should be permitted anytime, anywhere, to anyone. Most importers and exporters laughed at such stern posture.

If caught and pressured to pay the tax, many merchants and sea captains with unregistered cargo threatened to sell their treasure or merchandise outside the Kingdom of Spain with expediency. Consequently, the custom of granting certificates of amnesty became a time honored tradition. The habit cost the Crown millions in lost revenue.

Crown officials constantly complained about the excesses of smuggling and swore to increase vigilance in order to contain the fraud. However functionaries and judges were involved virtually everywhere. Therefore quantities of contraband goods seized and punishments levied were never significant.

Cádiz, El Puerto de Santa Maria, Sanlúcar, Huelva, Ayamonte, and other ports along the Atlantic Andalusian coast were naturally situated to take advantage of the galleons going to and coming from the Indies. Coastal boat builders were barely able to meet the demand for a particular type of longboat known locally as a *lancha*. The utility vessel was designed specifically to shuttle goods out of register between shore warehouses and ships anchored at pre-designated positions in the Bahía de Cádiz. Apparently, there were so many *lanchas* operating at all hours that the *avería* tax collectors petitioned for the sinking or de-rigging of every longboat in the vicinity. Of course, nothing ever came of this. In 1647[22] the Council of the Indies recognized that, if the day ever came when longboats would be prohibited, the smugglers would simply develop some other means of moving their cargoes.

To combat the importing of contraband cargoes the *Casa de la Contratación* commissioned special barges armed with musketeers to move throughout the bay looking for any suspicious activity on recently arrived ships. After a short while the embarrassed *Casa* admitted that the barge guards were paid by the smugglers more not to look or shoot than they made in salary. All Spanish ports continued to remain open to fraud.

For the South Sea trade, clandestine activities involving smuggling of contraband cargoes took place near many Pacific coastal seaport towns. Arica was a customary stop-over point for ships bringing goods to and from Chile. Silver and copper also were shipped from this port, much of it having been brought down from the high elevations of Potosí, Oruro and other mining towns in the *Audiencia de Charcas*.

Callao, the port town of the Peruvian capital of Lima, provided continuous opportunities for loading and off-loading cargoes out of registry. For years there was insufficient security at the port. Only when vessels of the Crown were inbound or outbound were sufficient watches established, and many of these turned a blind eye when adequately enticed.

Before reaching the Gulf of Guayaquil, Paita was a routine replenishment stop. Afterwards, there was Santa Clara Island, and then the numerous anchorages off Puna Island. A favorite was near Punta

Mandinga on the east side, and in the Canal del Morros, off the cliffs at Punta Trinchera on the west side. These and other sites provided rendezvous spots a convenient distance down river from Guayaquil.

Farther up the coast, the bight of Santa Elena, Manta and Isla de Plata proved to be popular meeting sites for swapping, bartering and trading every conceivable cargo to escape brokers' margins and the *avería* tax. Other opportunities presented themselves at Esmeraldas, Isla del Gallo, where Pizarro drew a line in the sand to challenge his mutinous crew, and the Pearl Islands off Panama.

European merchants of many nationalities were establishing themselves in Spanish Old and New World ports. Those who married native women of Spain were considered native themselves, and approved for transacting business in Spain and its colonies. Still, many of their *business transactions* did not benefit the Spanish tax base or economy since the silver and merchandise they traded were illicit. Many of these goods never touched Spanish soil.

Inbound vessels from Caribbean ports often were met one or two days out at sea or at a nearby safe anchorage. Cargoes belonging to allied traders, such as Dutch, French or Italian merchants, were transferred. When the ship anchored at its destination port there was only the registered cargo to be off-loaded. The movement of unregistered goods was so easy to accomplish, much of it was blatantly done between various ships anchored directly off Cádiz, as well as numerous New World ports.

Council of the Indies officers complained continually about the massive presence of foreigners in not only Cádiz but also Cartagena and Lima that were monopolizing the silver trade and clandestinely eluding the register. The power of these merchants grew, ultimately becoming immense. In the colonies, especially at Lima, merchants generally determined the dates when the trade fairs were held, and consequently, the dates the galleons would sail. They warehoused their merchandise until the prices they wished to attain were committed, or the barter they desired to achieve was accomplished.

Other European countries took advantage of the power and influence of their agents at Cádiz and Lima making sure their consignment of treasure and merchandise came directly to them after being unloaded. We will never know how much treasure and merchandise never reached the tax assessment books of the *Casa de la Contratación* in Seville.

In 1645[23] a servant of Fleet Admiral Don Pedro de Ursua was detained by the authorities while delivering a letter to the wife of the admiral. The admiral wrote to his wife that his inbound fleet from the Indies was only thirty leagues from Cádiz. The servant, along with a number of merchant traders, had disembarked days earlier. They were hustled into Cádiz by means of one of the fast avisos to make arrangements for transferring their cargoes prior to the arrival of the fleet. Neither the *Casa de la Contratación* nor the Council of the Indies was notified of the armada's impending arrival. Similar delays took place when the Indies bound fleet departed Cádiz. This allowed time for illegal shipments of assorted goods to be brought aboard, intended for selling or swapping in the New World. Such galleon movements and illegal transfers had to be sanctioned in every instance by the galleon leaders, who were as heavily involved in the trade as were the merchants. Had they not been, the deals could never have been consummated. These clandestine actions were initiated and approved at all ports where Spanish vessels called.

After a thorough investigation of the registers of the *Carrera de las Indias*, Dr. Earl J. Hamilton[24] calculated that between the years 1503 and 1660, a total of 447,820,931 pesos of registered treasure was reported being brought into Spain. This figure was based on a tally of 117,386,086 pesos for His Majesty, and 330,434,845 for private accounts. If this large sum was the officially registered total, one can only speculate as to the real value of silver, gold, emeralds, diamonds, pearls and all the many other goods entering outside of registry.

The amount of treasure transported by the royal *capitana* of 1654 ranged from a minimum of 4,883,193 pesos, as established by archival documents, to a maximum of 10,000,000 pesos, as confirmed by officials of the government of Spain. In sheer weight, this means treasure, primarily silver, valued at the equivalent of 132 metric tons minimum to 270 metric tons maximum!

The amount of actual treasure left today in and around the wreckage of the *capitana* on the seafloor near Chanduy is impossible to determine accurately. Good research makes it possible to reasonably estimate how much *might* still remain. The problem is not knowing how much was stolen.

Successive salvage projects were sponsored almost annually for eight years under the direction of two viceroys: Don Garcia Sarmiento de Sotomayor, Count of Salvatierra, viceroy from September 20, 1648 to February 24, 1655, and his successor, Don Luis Henriques de Guzmán, Count of Alva of Aliste, Viceroy of Peru from February 24, 1655 to July 31, 1661. Viceroy Guzmán was succeeded by the Count of Santiesteban.

From these official expeditions we know 3,339,751 pesos were reported as having been salvaged during those eight years, with almost 3,000,000 having been recovered during the first year alone. What we will never know is how much was salvaged later but never registered officially.

Our estimates also should include an amount covering what was misappropriated during the confusion of shipwreck. This additional estimated amount was stolen by crew members who disappeared shortly after the first silver was brought ashore. These were the very men who were assigned the responsibility of guarding it. The galleon's silvermaster was the officer in charge of security and accuracy of the treasure inventory aboard. It was also his responsibility to collect all dues and taxes owed to the king, such as the *avería* charge. He was the king's trusted agent whose primary job was to safekeep the silver, as well as minimize the shipment of contraband goods.

However, it was this very officer, Bernardo de Campos (also master of the ship), who was accused of methodically ransacking passenger luggage, stealing whatever he could lay his hands on while everyone else was manning the pumps and bailing sea water for all they were worth, after the big galleon struck the reefs and began sinking. His later indictment brought forth accusations that considerable personal gold and jewelry were stolen by him, together with some of the king's own treasure, also in his entrustment. It is certainly likely he did misuse his position of authority during and after the shipwreck.

"Numerous accusations evolved around the silvermaster, Bernardo de Campos," claimed His Majesty's lawyers. "Because he knew certain silver and other private treasure had not been registered, he decided to keep much of it for himself. He hid it in various places. He threw some into the sea, marking it with buoys so it could later be fished up at night and re-hidden. Furthermore, both he and the captain general helped load the wine on board for which they received handsome payments from the wine merchants."

Concerning the smuggled silver, he later testified he brought none aboard for his own account because he had all he could do to keep track of the official silver registry for the king.

"If any silver found its way to my cabin, some merchant must have stored it there without my knowledge," he stated during the deposition. Bernardo de Campos went on to describe how he alone was responsible for confiscating most of the unregistered silver and bringing the bullion to shore where it was inventoried for Don Pedro Vásquez de Velasco.

Continuing his defense, "This effort of recovering the heavy bars, hauling them to shore as best we could, storing, counting and guarding the treasure, required so much of my time and effort, I could not possibly have been able to take any for myself. These people, whose unregistered treasure I confiscated, became my enemies. They have consequently made these very unjust declarations against me, whereupon I was just doing my job."

As to the large cargo of wine brought aboard (11,000 jugs certainly appeared to be a large measure), Bernardo de Campos stated,

"Really, Your Honor, the amount of wine was actually not a very large quantity when you consider the number of merchants and passengers whom I had to feed at my table."

One merchant testifying against Bernardo told how the places where smuggled silver had been stashed by the silvermaster were well known. After receiving their directions, the divers could go straight to the hidden treasure.

"Each time a diver broke the surface for air, his hands carried *piñas* of silver or smuggled bars. Every location a diver was told to search revealed various articles of unregistered treasure. There was unquestionably more unrecorderded silver on board than officially recorded, and this is the fault of the silvermaster, who must be held accountable."

While investigating officials gave much credit to Bernardo de Campos and Francisco de Sosa for the silver that was salvaged, the captain general and silvermaster had to be held accountable for the loss of the great *capitana*.

"In consideration of the silver that was saved, and the fact that his records totally agreed with the silver we inventoried on the beach of Chanduy, I sentenced him (Bernardo de Campos) to four years of service in the Presidency of Callao on half salary, plus a fine of 4,000 pesos to be paid to the Royal Chamber," reported Don Andres de

Villela in a letter to the King of Spain. The fine would be dealt with by the Council of the Indies.

On September 4, 1656, Villela also told the viceroy:

"While General de Sosa should be considered as the primary officer responsible for the shipwreck, evidence indicated the silvermaster was undoubtedly considered by many to be the biggest thief."

Villela, as the "oldest and most experienced judge" within the *Audiencia de Lima*, was appointed by the Crown to deal with any wrongdoings in connection with the shipwreck of the great *capitana*.

While some of the silver stolen from the beach of Chanduy was later recovered from the very thieves who "were helping to safekeep it," we have no idea how much may have been stashed, spent, lost or otherwise never reclaimed. An auditor of the king suggested that one million pesos probably were stolen during and after the shipwreck.

In a letter to the king on January 1, 1655, the viceroy stated, "The value of the Royal Fifth and the *avería* tax, plus freight levied on the smuggled goods, will more than repay the loss of the ship."

While this was definitely a personally protective comment, it meant one-twentieth of the value of the treasure fraudulently minted and smuggled aboard, but salvaged after the shipwreck, and the *avería*, plus the freight (none of which was paid because the goods were contraband and/or not registered), would actually bring more to the coffers of the king than His Majesty lost in the sinking of the *capitana*.

Here we have in one sentence a summary of three typical methods of defrauding the Royal Treasury. There were others, including innocently shipping *personal* silverware, also not taxable, and hiding jewelry, gold chain, and gold coin in the lining of coats, belts, shoe soles and other personal luggage. Treasure was also successfully hidden in boxes of commercial merchandise, including cocoa, barrels or sacks of food such as beans or flour.

Finally, there were several reports to the king stating essentially,

"Almost everything had been recovered."

This apparently was intended to convey the meaning that almost everything either directly belonging to the king or unregistered goods claimed by the king had been saved. Other than dealing with the unscrupulous people, the disaster had been repaired.

One must ask, if there were 5,000,000 to 7,000,000 pesos remaining in the sunken hull after more than 3,000,000 was salvaged, why would all this money be abandoned?

There are likely two answers. The Spanish were, just as we are, unsure exactly what remained since the ex-owners of the *hot property* would never step forward and acknowledge its existence. Many of these people were merchants and speculators who suddenly were filing for bankruptcy. The other reason was likely due to natural elements. Digging out submerged objects from under tons of sand on the ocean floor was no easy job, nor was blindly rummaging through tons of shipboard gear submerged in a lower hold.

The President of Panama confirmed that the large quantity of vicuña wool placed on top of the silver bullion was heavily soaked, making it extremely difficult for divers to get through it and reach the treasure.

"The mass of wet, stagnant wool not only smells terrible, but combined with the thousands of wine jugs and olive jars it provides an obstacle course considerably hindering and endangering the divers."

Even with these problems, the divers recovered thirty-three bronze cannon by the end of 1654. Most of these guns had been positioned on the main deck.

Because of severe tides and currents, the wreck could only be worked at low tide. Even then it was very dangerous. The diving season was dictated by the *vendavales*, a heavy weather system consisting of strong westerly winds. Even today they raise rough seas along this coast, generally from April through November, leaving only the months of December through March when fair weather prevails. Storms across the Pacific sent long rollers crashing into the wreck area, as waves concluded their endless journey, breaking upon the Chanduy beach.

With the proximity of the Equator, tropical borers and teredo worms soon left little of the wooden ship exposed. Almost everything man-made eroded, disintegrated, or was covered with sand. Only the anchors and cannon, tons of silver bullion and the heaviest timbers would stand up to the elements of time.

Of the 44 bronze guns on the *capitana*, 40 were recovered during primary salvage of 1654-1655. One more was reported having been retrieved in 1656. They were stated to be worth 5,000 pesos each, for a total of 205,000. The two primary anchors were dropped when the ship first stopped in 12 fathoms of water. Since their cables were cut at high tide the next day to allow the galleon to drift toward the shallow shore, the anchors would not be found on the ballast pile, but offshore of it.

The *Capitana's* Hull Was Like
a Floating Safe Deposit Vault

This athwartship cross-sectional drawing illustrates the manner treasure and cargo were stowed aboard the galleons. Heavy bullion bars of silver normally were packed in the lower hold to supplement rock ballast and lower the ship's center of gravity. Chests of coin, casks of small bars and wedges along with worked silver were placed one deck higher for easier handling. The most valuable smaller items, such as gold and jewelry, diamonds, emeralds and pearls, were stored in the sterncastle cabins of the principal officers and wealthy merchants and passengers where they could be carefully guarded. Generally registered treasure was stored in a large orlop located aft, abutting the transom.

Construction of the *capitana*, *Jesus Maria de la Limpia Concepción*, was initiated in 1640, under orders of the viceroy, the Marqués de Mancera, at the Puna Island shipyards, where the Guayas River meets the Bahia de Guayaquil. Vessels of all types needed in the coastal trade had been constructed in this region for a century, and it had become the primary shipbuilding and naval refurbishing site within the Peruvian viceroyalty.

Martin de Valenzequi, chief magistrate and yard supervisor, was provided with scme 200 pages of construction specifications and rigging instructions.[25] These building specs detailed everything from the recommended size of the ship, height of the masts, rigging and cordage designations, to the types of wood and other materials to be used including bolts, nails, spikes and cable. Most of the iron fittings came from Spain, as well as anchors and chain. Copper for kettles and lamps was available from Chile. Cordage, cotton canvas and caulking was brought from nearby Quito. Tar, pitch and oakum was available locally at Guayaquil.

Most masts and spars were produced from a wood known as *palos maria*. *Guachapelí* was the preferred wood for heavy timbers such as keels, keelsons and even ribs and planking. The *guachapelí* tree was abundant in the forests of Bulubulu, in the district of Yaguachi. "Aside from its firm resistance to water rot and shipworm, it has the special quality of being easy to handle with the axe, adze, chisel or auger."[26]

There were few naval architectural drawings. Once they agreed on approximate dimensions, shipyard managers and engineers sketched on any available piece of wood, and even in the river sand and dirt around the cradle to determine angles, shapes and ultimate lines and composition. The results of their enterprise and successful planning, as well as the soundness of the vessel, would not be known until the time of launching, when they would see if the ship actually floated and was reasonably balanced.

"The ships are so irregular that they appear distorted—their sides are as straight as walls."[27]

As chief magistrate, Valenzequi was paid an annual salary of 2,000 pesos. Working under his direction, Lorenzo de Bances León was responsible for selecting and cutting the timber and getting it to the construction site. Having been in ship construction for a number of years, León was in charge of the day-to-day supervision, and in directing the hundreds of skilled and unskilled workers. While he probably was more valuable to the total effort than Valenzequi, León received a salary of 1,000 pesos. Assisting him were a master metalsmith, a master ship's carpenter, a supply officer, a chaplain, and other key people.

Official decrees[28] during this period generally limited the size of the South Sea vessels to a maximum of 500 tons in order to facilitate sailing and maneuvering against prevailing strong tides and currents. However, the men who ran the Guayaquil area shipyards were their own bosses and built the galleons as they pleased. These independent entrepreneurs owned some of the vessels which they constructed and often were offered tips or percentages by the merchant shippers, all of whom favored larger ships capable of carrying more cargo, and therefore more economical for transporting large quantities of treasure and products. Consequently, the size of ships and carrying capacity were more likely to be determined by a consortium of yard foremen working hand in pocket with the merchant guild than by royal orders.

The keels of both the *Limpia Concepción* (intended for the designation of the *capitana*) and the *San Francisco Solano* (the *almiranta*) were laid on June 8, 1641. After three years of continuous work by hundreds of Indian and mulatto craftsmen, the two vessels were launched in July of 1644. The cost of building the two galleons exceeded 257,000 pesos, funded by the Lima treasury. (Another report stated the *capitana* alone cost môre than 300,000 pesos.)[29]

In the first half of the 17th-century, a vessel built in the Guayaquil-Puna region would likely have a length/beam ratio of 2.66 to 2.75.[30] As an example, a ship with a breadth of 20 *codos*[31] (about 38 feet) would have a resulting length of keel of 53 to 55 *codos* (about 96 to 105 feet).

Cargo carrying capacity would be measured in tons[32]:

Tons	Beam	Keel Length
297	13 *codos*	37 *codos*
755	18 *codos*	44 *codos*
1252	22 *codos*	53 *codos*

The *capitana* was 122 feet long, had a beam of 40 feet, and a draft of 19 feet below her main deck. This galleon of 1,150 tons was designed intentionally large to intimidate, and defend herself, against English, Dutch and French pirates. As the largest galleon yet built, she was pierced for 60 guns, and specifically reinforced in the lower hull and keel, which measured 95 feet.

The chronicler Bernardo de Torres in his *Crónica Augustina*, published in Lima in 1656 stated, "The royal *capitana* was the Queen of the South Sea. She also could be the Queen of the North Sea with her size and beauty."

4

Captain General of the Fleet
(The Marqués de Montealegre)

*The marqués was so determined to begin the journey through Ha-
vana, then on to Spain, he left only three days later. The weather
was turbulent and questionable.*

THE COUNCIL OF THE INDIES met regularly during the early
1650's to discuss its concerns about the large English ship
movements in the Caribbean. By mid-February 1654, more
alarming news was received in Spain. Oliver Cromwell, Lord
Protector of England, not only ordered more armed vessels to the
Caribbean, but was readying a fleet of warships to patrol from Portugal to Gibraltar.

Spain was officially at peace with England, but the large concen-
trations of men-of-war were ominous signals to the Spanish Crown,
not to be ignored. Consequently, in 1654, King Philip IV sent a military armada to the Indies to transport his treasure from the New
World, instead of the usual fleet of numerous merchantmen and
armed hulks.

The armada's mission was to carry requisitioned clothing, hardware, tools, paper, glassware, religious accessories and numerous
other European articles highly in demand in the colonies. They were
then to return safely to Spain with several hundred tons of bullion and
coin accumulated in the forts and castles of Lima, Cartagena, Portobelo, Vera Cruz and Havana.

King Philip was not the only one concerned. Many of the merchant shippers and money lenders were worried over the safety of
their cargoes and investments. The 1654 armada was in fact created
through numerous loans "extracted" from the wealthiest merchants
and individuals in Seville, Cádiz and Madrid. Due to the financial
woes of the Royal Treasury, the 1654 fleet was not to be a large one.

On October 10, 1652, the Council of War had proposed three

names to the king for general of the armada of *Tierra Firme* for the year 1653. They included Don Juan de Tchaverri, Don Antonio de Isasi and the Marqués de Montealegre. King Philip replied, "I name Don Juan de Tchaverri general of the galleons for the coming year. I name the Marqués de Montealegre general of the said armada for the voyage following this one."

This appointment was made after a consultation with the President of the Council of the Indies on August 13, 1653. It was confirmed by a royal decree in Madrid on November 28, 1653. The following week the Council of War in Madrid issued a memorandum questioning the appointment of the Marqués de Montealegre as general of the armada in full title. No doubt, this was due to his lack of naval experience.

The king did not change his mind.

Little is known of the "professional" career of the marqués prior to being named captain general. Certainly, he had never sailed to the Indies before. King Philip granted the title of *Marqués* to his father, Don Martin de Guzmán III, Señor of Montealegre, in 1625.

The name can be traced to 950, when Count Don Niño Munion y Muñoz built a castle in Roa, between Burgos and Valladolid, in a place called Guzmán. The nobility of the house was proven repeatedly in all the military orders of Spain.

Our Marqués of Montealegre, Luis Francisco de Guzmán, was the first son of the Señor of Montealegre and Isabel Niño de Silva y Ribera, from Toledo, Spain. Don Luis married Doña Juana de Borja, the daughter of Iñigo de Borja, Governor of Antwerp, and Doña Elena da Hanin, one of the old, prestigious Belgian families.

Despite objections from the Council of War, the commander-in-chief of the 1654 armada was destined to be Captain General Don Francisco Luis de Nuñez y Guzmán, the Marqués of Montealegre, Knight and Commander of Calatrava, personal ally of King Philip, and an influential business man in Spain.

Galleon commanders were chosen for their important posts by means of a time-honored tradition within the kingdom. Criteria included having a track record of long-term allegiance to His Majesty. Respected military service was also highly favored. The noble status of their names and heritage was an important consideration, as well as tenure of service. It went without saying that these commanders of royal ships were God-fearing men of strong character and reputation, willing to risk their lives for the king. The favored skippers were those demonstrating continuous examples of honesty, fairness and discretion in handling officers and crew.

One overriding fact was clear. When decision-making time came, as far as the king was concerned, it was beneficial for one or more of these *hidalgos* to own a galleon or two, or at least exhibit a willingness to front money to fund a good part of the expenses. Unfortunately, the amount of money advanced to the Royal Treasury often determined rank or position of authority within the fleet, rather than leadership or seamanship qualifications.

We know Don Matías de Orellana "loaned" the king 30,000 pesos for his position as admiral.[33] The Marqués de Montealegre, leader of the fleet and not a military person, may have paid as much as 100,000 pesos for the honor and privilege of serving as captain general. As a member of the powerful Mendoza family he really didn't *need* to purchase his position. In actuality he may have paid the king even more than this amount. This belief stems from the fact his title was not only for the 1654 sailing, but *propietario*, permanently for the rest of his life. He was paid 4,000 ducats a year for this position.

"He who is chosen by the king to be general of the galleons advances to him fourscore, or a hundred thousand crowns, repaid him in the Indies with great interest. The other captains also advance money to the king proportionate to the size of the vessel they command."[34]

Upon his appointment, the marqués asked, as a favor, that one-fifth of any prizes the armada might take be given to him as a share. On May 23, 1654, his request was transmitted by the Council of War. The king answered, "Affirmed." Preparations now underway, the small but heavily armed fleet readied to sail westward.

Seven weeks later, on July 10, the fleet sailed from Cádiz. This *Flota de Tierra Firme* reached Cartagena on August 22, relieved to have enjoyed a pleasant and uneventful Atlantic crossing with no tropical storms thwarting the passage.

The Viceroy of Peru, Count of Salvatierra, had already notified Don Pedro Zapata de Mendoza, the Governor of Cartagena, that His Majesty's silver was ready to be shipped from Callao, the port of Lima, to Panama. He awaited further orders.

Route of the Armada of the Marqués de Montealegre

The fleet sailed from Cádiz on July 10, 1654. They reached Cartagena on August 22. Their return voyage was delayed while they waited for the salvaged treasure from the Chanduy, Ecuador, shipwrecked *capitana*. Finally, the heavily loaded fleet departed Havana on January 1, 1656, bound for Spain.

The Marqués of Montealegre was delighted with the news. Word was immediately sent overland from Cartagena to the viceroy to ship the king's treasure as soon as possible. Montealegre promptly wrote the king saying, "If the silver arrives in Panama by the end of September, I should be prepared to depart for Spain by the end of October."

However, the travel arrangements and subsequent scheduling of the marqués did not evolve as smoothly as planned.

In the midst of these events, the *capitana* of the South Sea Fleet struck a reef off Chanduy. On October 27 it sank in four-and-one-half fathoms. The marqués was forced to wait for some of this treasure cargo to be salvaged. Not only was he delayed, it also meant a long winter for the entire fleet.

January 15, 1655

The marqués sailed from Cartagena to Portobelo in January. He was to procure some of the *capitana*'s salvaged silver and take on passengers who made their way across the isthmus after disembarking at Perico on the Pacific side of Panama. These included passengers, cargo and treasure shipped on the *San Francisco Solano*, the *almiranta* of the 1654 South Sea Fleet.

Unaware of the large amount of salvaged treasure from the *capitana*, the marqués arrived at Portobelo on January 28. He issued two small tenders to carry the silver to Cartagena. The lack of transport capacity and protection for the Royal Treasury sparked a major controversy in Panama.

Many ingots were buried in the houses of Portobelo that night. Some pack animals still en route were turned back on the trail. Montealegre was openly criticized for his lack of preparation and defense of the king's treasure.

Within a few weeks the incident was defused. The silver to be shipped began being inventoried on the Royal Register at Portobelo.

Easter Sunday, 1655

By April the Marqués de Montealegre had returned to Cartagena. He was ordered to remain there as more salvaged treasure was en route from the *capitana* shipwreck. Furthermore, the viceroy in Lima had another million pesos from Potosí, already shipped from Callao. He re-scheduled his departure plans once more. May appeared to be the new embarkation date for his armada.

Unbeknown to many officials in Peru as well as the galleon commanders waiting at Cartagena, a colossal scandal was in the process of being exposed as a result of the sinking and subsequent salvage of the 1654 *capitana*. By mid-February 1655, accountants of the king reported that 2,932,000 pesos were salvaged in the three-month period following the shipwreck. This was not only a tremendous accomplishment, but the disclosed sum amounted virtually to the registered total of 3,000,000 pesos. It was now recognized that this total represented only one-third of what was actually on board, but not reported. This revelation leveled a sledgehammer blow, stunning the Peruvian royal administrators. They now scurried to cover their hides and place blame on others.

Although the Marqués de Montealegre was not part of this bureaucratic bungle, he was forced to wait to receive the salvaged treasure, if and when it arrived. His correspondence home relayed his strong desire to leave for Spain in May, or, at the very least, soon after.

The news was bad. An extremely large fleet of some fifty English ships, spotted earlier in the Caribbean, was now attacking Santo Domingo. The marqués faced a longer wait, much to his dismay.

Cromwell ordered the English fleet to rendezvous at Barbados, then sail to capture Santo Domingo, the capital of Spanish Hispaniola. However, the Spaniards at Santo Domingo were not easily intimidated. Advance word of the impending attack rendered them well prepared. They fought their aggressors with furious determination, and the English were contained within the harbor.

Withdrawing, they sailed for Jamaica. It was, perhaps, a means of saving face. They knew Spanish defenses there were slight. They reached the island on May 10, 1655, and immediately ordered their marines ashore. Within two days every Spaniard found was captured or killed.

Jamaica's magnificent natural harbor soon became a buccaneering stronghold. In time, with massive fortification, it became a major English-Caribbean possession.

Among the soldiers and renegades left to defend the newly acquired English territory was a young Welshman, Henry Morgan. He soon became a bloody scourge to every Spanish port throughout the Caribbean.

July 1, 1655

The torrid summer melted the Caribbean in 1655. Repetitive delays
and oppressive heat began wearing down the Marqués de Montealegre, Numerous family and business affairs needed his attention at
home, causing him to be impatient to leave for Spain. After all, he had
waited in sultry Cartagena for almost a year.

At long last the king sent the awaited directive. It reached Cartagena on July 1. The marqués was instructed to immediately bring the
treasure to Spain. He summoned his captains and weighed anchor, totally ignoring the tropical wave of low pressure now sweeping through
the region.

"The marqués was so determined to begin the journey through
Havana, then on to Spain, he left only three days later. The weather
was turbulent and questionable," another captain reported.

The Marqués de Baides remained, justifiably, in Cartagena. His
travels previously took him and his family from Callao to Panama,
carrying their worldly goods. Then he traversed the isthmus to Portobelo, and finally arrived at Cartagena. His wife, seven months pregnant, suffered setbacks caused by the arduous journey. He had no
choice but to remain in Cartagena until the baby was born.

By July 17, the small fleet approached the southern Cuban coastline, giving a wide berth to the Jardine rocks. As they cautiously
probed their way toward the westerly tip of Cuba, they spotted a large
number of tall sails on the horizon. Unidentified, these soon disappeared behind the Cuban coastal mountains. Adverse winds forced
the fleet to tack for two days before reaching Cabo de San Antonio on
the southwest point of Cuba. They knew watches were posted on
their behalf.

Captain Don Mendo de Contreras put his launch overboard to
seek the latest news. His men soon returned, accompanied by two
Cuban lookouts. They reported the events of the preceding day in
great detail. Twenty-seven English ships of war passed by the Cape.
These were the sails spotted two days earlier. If only the English had
known the treasure fleet was so near!

The large English fleet caused serious consternation among the
Spanish captains. They knew Jamaica was taken earlier. They were
concerned over what the next English target might be. A council of
war lasted all day as they weighed the potential problems of proceed-

ing to Havana. Some Spanish skippers questioned whether the English had spotted their ships and were waiting behind the western shore of Cuba to attack as they rounded the Cape. Finally they ordered the small boat back to the Cuban coast with a sealed letter for the governor and the king of Spain. The letters reported their uncertain situation and their decision to head for safety at Vera Cruz.

After an uneventful voyage the treasure fleet anchored at the port of San Juan de Ulua in Vera Cruz on August 2. Several smaller merchant vessels of the fleet held back for a few days. They reached Havana safely after the English left the coast.

The Duke of Albuquerque, Viceroy of *Nueva España*, was notified of the arrival of the king's ships. The captain general gave an account of their voyage and requested money and provisions to prepare his fleet to depart before the season of the northerlies arrived.

Accordingly, the viceroy issued 40,000 pesos with an order that the armada be given hardtack, flour and dried vegetables, including chickpeas and kidney beans. He also commanded four companies of soldiers to reinforce the infantry on board the galleons, along with considerable gunpowder, shot and assorted additional armament.

Word was received from Havana on August 25. The coast was clear. Though the reason is not known, it was September 7 before the fleet departed.

October 10, 1655

Good weather and good fortune enabled the treasure fleet to anchor at Havana on October 10. Havana, a favorite liberty port, was not to be enjoyed by the entire crew. There was much work to be done prior to the Atlantic crossing.

All ships were checked over before beginning their long voyage. Worn rope and rigging was repaired or replaced. Hulls were scraped and cleaned and sheathing repaired. A great quantity of food and stores were purchased, firewood acquired and water casks filled.

The *capitana* was refitted with a new cutwater, bowsprit and rudder. The *almiranta* also received a new rudder, as well as additional futtock knee supports under the main deck to reinforce those cracked.

Cuban products including hides, sugar and tobacco were brought aboard, as well as money representing the annual royal taxes.

Besides local assessments, anyone dying intestate forfeited his assets.. These automatically became the property of the king. Royal collectors annually remitted distributions from the deceased who did not leave wills.

While the vessels were careened, caulked and marine growth was cleaned from their bottoms, officers and elite among the passengers were wined and dined by Havana's aristocracy. Crew members toiled at making the ships ready for sea while the fleet's noblemen enjoyed the fishing, beaches and frivolities of the city.

Just after Christmas, a council of ship's officers was called to determine the readiness of the armada. Most of the captains reported they were prepared to sail for Spain. The remainder were ordered to ready themselves and their vessels immediately.

A recommendation was made for them to wait for the fleet of Marcus del Puerto, whose ships would provide additional armament in case of enemy attack. Also the seasonal weather pattern would improve in several months, reducing seagoing risks.

The advice, however, was considered out of the question to the marqués. He was ready to sail.

5

The Sinking

The confusion of the moment held a death-hold on me. The uncertainty, the cold and dark, the ghoulish wind, the eerie dreadfulness of the night, the screams and wails, all combined to envelop me in pincer-like jaws.

PADRE DIEGO EMBARKED on the *Maravillas* at Cartagena. Eager to continue his journey, he was hoping for a peaceful and uneventful voyage. His memoirs reflect the anticipation felt by all on board. After the fateful sinking of the *capitana* off Ecuador, he prayed that God would now watch over and protect their continuation homeward to Spain.

Havana, New Year's Day, 1656

After welcoming the New Year in intriguing Havana, all were eager to put to sea. The warm January sun on our backs, the fresh clean whiff of salt air in our nostrils and the effervescent and dark-blue hues of the northward flowing current in our sights mingled to create an exhilarating sensation. We were finally homeward bound. At long last the treasure fleet sailed from Havana on January 1, 1656.

Aboard my ship, the *almiranta*, named *Nuestra Señora de las Maravillas*, were officers and crew of approximately 300. The official list of personnel aboard the *Maravillas*, when she sailed from Spain in July 1654, totaled 259 persons. It included fourteen officers, twenty-seven able seamen, seventeen seamen, thirteen pages, thirty-five gunners and 153 infantry, five being officers. Additional soldiers and arms were brought aboard at Vera Cruz and Havana. Several source accounts indicate 650 persons are on board. We are obviously crowded beyond comprehension, as well as totally overloaded with treasure and general cargo.

The additional passengers and royal officials boarding in Havana contributed even more to the extremely cramped quarters. Besides the large number of people, the 900-ton vessel carried treasure for the king and private accounts reported by numerous merchants at 5,000,000 pesos. I registered a large sum with the silvermaster, representing significant allocations for my church.[35]

Our admiral is Don Matías de Orellana. A forty-five year old Knight of Santiago, he is from Casas de Reinas, a village in the Province of Badajoz in Extremadura, between Portugal and New Castile.

We sailed from Havana in favorable weather conditions. Everyone foresaw a pleasant voyage. The *almiranta* was at full sail, her low prow and new sails making the ship very fast. Even flying less canvas, she passed the *capitana* and led the way. I suspected Don Matías, having served as fleet admiral for eight years, and very much aware the marqués was not an accomplished seafarer, was cleverly testing the mettle of the captain general. Under all circumstances, and according to the king's policy, the captain general was to lead the armada.

Unfortunately, I was confined to my cabin off the poop deck for several days, suffering from fever and aches. I took some stomach medicine after dinner, then attempted to sleep. Others played games or engaged in conversation. The guard on duty contemplated the evening.

Painful stomach cramps prevented me from sleeping peacefully. Only several days out of Havana, the maggot grubs in my mealtime biscuits and the thought of other hidden molds and fungi lurking in my food left me nauseous and queasy. Spoiled foodstuff was commonly the fare toward the end of a voyage, not at the beginning. I lay perspiring on my cot, considering what strange and alien biological germs might be breeding in my intestines. This, with the incessant rolling of the ship, combined to make me miserable.

My dinner consisted of the aforementioned ship's biscuit, a modest portion of stewed tortoise with onion and garlic, and several ounces of cheese and raisins. All was washed down with a clear, golden amontillado from Jerez de la Frontera. A number of Havana tortoises were stored on the galley deck to be readily butchered as needed. Hanging there also were salt pork, hams and great slabs of dried meat. Dozens of cages packed with live hens were aboard. Four wealthy merchants brought several pigs aboard. Tied together by their legs, they were secured in a dark corner with small ropes. The constant grunting and squealing of the hapless animals disturbed everyone, further detracting from the shipboard dining atmosphere. By the time we finished our meal, a seaman from Honduras had cut six-inch pieces of papaya wood and rammed the sticks well into the rectum of each swine. This maneuver immediately quieted the animals. The wooden sticks being hollow, the only noise the pigs emitted was an occasional whistle when wind was passed through the papaya twigs.

Daily Rations Served Aboard the *MARAVILLAS*

During the early weeks of a voyage the following rations were served daily to each man. Officers and wealthy passengers brought their own private stock of provisions, kept in their quarters. First Class passengers ate the captain's fare at his table. Of course, to do so, they paid handsomely.

Biscuit	1½ pounds (1 Castilian pound equals 460 grams)
Wine	about 1 liter
Meat (22 days a month)	6 ounces of bacon with 2 ounces of chickpeas or beans
If fresh beef not available	12 ounces of bacon.
Rice	2 ounces, served on the days of fish or meat
Salt Fish	6 ounces served 8 days a month with 1 pint of vinegar. This was allocated for every three men, along with 1 ounce of oil.

Heavy weather days   No cooking was permitted during
                                      rough seas. An allowance of 6 ounces
                                      of cheese and 2 ounces of peas with ½
                                      ounce of oil was substituted.

A special diet was provided for those who were sick. This included
raisins, almonds, sugar and white biscuit.

Pushed by a balmy and moderate breeze from the south-southwest,
aided by a three-knot current, the fleet was making excellent headway.
Just before sunset the following evening, the lookout reported from
the crow's nest that he could see much of the coast of Florida off the
port beam.

Shortly thereafter the wind freshened as its direction veered from
south-southwest to northwest. Air temperature dropped by ten degrees almost immediately. Sails were flapping and luffing as sailors
rushed to the tops (crow's nests) to handle running rigging to adjust
and trim the canvas.

With the wind now from the northerly quadrant, and the force-
ful current coming from the opposite direction, a strange and uncomfortable chop developed in the confused seas. Waves now slapped
against the sides of the vessels in place of the smoothly flowing fur-
rows and the long, deep swells experienced a short time earlier.

The distant blackness of the horizon ahead began to clutter and
haze. Still, there were a million stars flying by, as if part of a glittering
psychedelic scene. The sea astern was as black as the sky, except for the
lonely trail of phosphorescence undulating in the wake of each labor-
ing galleon.

Everyone aboard every ship in the fleet appeared active. Some
donned additional warm clothing. Others double-checked loose gear
and belongings now beginning to shift unrestrained, to and fro. Sails
were furled or trimmed. Hatches and ports were checked and double
battened. An extra guard was posted by the fire box located near the
base of the main mast in the "waist" of the ship, as some were not finished cooking dinner. The vessels soon began to pitch and roll nervously. An increasing concern about loose pieces of fire or sparks
being dangerously tossed out was obvious. The cook stove was finally
shut down, the fire completely extinguished.

Several hours passed and the *almiranta* continued to lead the
fleet as the ships plunged and rose against the increasing wind and

seas. The *capitana* was nearby astern. Lights from the other ships were clearly visible in the near distance.

Sailors handled the heavy, soaked lines of hemp with groans and curses. Given the motion of the ship, it was extremely dangerous handling lines from the upper tops. Still, there was no choice. The topsails needed to be trimmed and furled. Someone must brave the wind and salt spray to do the job. Whenever an opportunity permitted, men on deck took shelter in any leeward corner they found in a futile attempt to dodge the cold and wet northwester. Time and again they braced themselves as they watched the high and unsympathetic seas pound the ship's side. The cool salt water cascaded over the weather rail, flooding the forecastle and rolling over the main deck. Finally replaced by a change of watch, men retired to bunks and hammocks. Miserably wet and salty stiff, they were noticeably exhausted from the strain of battling adverse conditions.

Off to port of the *Maravillas* the horizon was becoming obscured and muddled. A few intermittent stars still glimmered on the starboard beam, dim and vague above a vast, wet wilderness of white caps and spray.

A conclave of officers huddled in conference at the binnacle. They knew they did not have adequate angle on the wind to make good their desired course. The chief pilot recommended they steer another couple of points[37] toward the east. In doing so, perhaps more northerly progress could be made. The assistant pilot argued it was too great a change in course.

Suddenly a plunge of the galleon into a wall of water sent a shock wave through the entire vessel, as if she struck something solid. A few moments of stillness passed as green water washed over the main deck. Salt spray flung hard upon the worried faces there to receive it.

Those on deck knew the weather was worsening. Those below deck felt the uneasiness of the ship. Their nervousness showed as they bit their nails. Everyone was aware the galleon was heavily laden. Accordingly, it rode low in the water. They wanted to assume this was the reason for the annoying pounding they began to experience.

For a flickering second the low hanging clouds were unveiled by a flash of lightning. Those on deck felt the sinister intent of the foaming crests of oncoming waves.

Earlier the fleet was close along Florida's coast. Now it wallowed dangerously in the depths of the dark and menacing Bahama Channel. Unknown at the time, the set of the uncompromising current, coupled with an unforgiving northwest wind, caused a serious north-easterly drift.

January 4, 1656

Shortly after the page on duty called out *"Second watch glass"* (2200 sailor's time) the boatswain's shouts from the prow reported a shallow depth. His shouts startled me awake. I later learned they noticed the waters were whitish and awashing, indications the bottom is near. Soundings revealed thirteen fathoms.

I jumped from by bed, dressed hurriedly and went on deck. Many others already gathered there, alarmed and confused.

The *capitana* sailed near us, but the other ships were some distance behind. We fired a cannon to alert the fleet of the danger. Most of the ships changed course toward Florida and deeper waters. The pilot of the galleon of Juan de Hoyos must have misinterpreted our cannon shot. Thinking it meant to signal our shift more to the east in order to improve our sailing ability, he maintained his course. His galleon struck a rock with such force the entire rudder was knocked away from its gudgeon, falling into the sea. The galleon bounced aground, then anchored in four fathoms of water.

The *capitana* now was frightfully close to the *almiranta*. The sounding lead was revealing dangerously shallow water depths. The pilots and cap-tains of both vessels knew they desperately needed to change direction. But what direction? Obviously the coast of Florida was somewhere distant off the port side, but it was the direction of the wind. Turning quickly into the wind might prove disastrous in such shoal water and adverse sea condi-tions.

Aboard the *Maravillas* the pilots were yelling over the noise of the breaking seas to the *capitana* to steer past the stern of the *almiranta*. Doing so would provide sea room enough for the galleon to tack away from the reefs. The wind also screamed through the rigging, while waves broke with strange high-pitched hissing sounds against the side of the ship.

After we fired our guns in warning to the others, the admiral ordered the helmsman to turn the ship away from the shoals. His orders carried through, the helmsman repeated the orders and the course. The bow now headed south with the wind on its starboard quarter. The ship was gaining speed. Suddenly the *capitana* was bearing down on us.

Everyone ran to the starboard side, screaming for the *capitana* to luff. There was no response.[38] Our chief pilot ordered us to fall off to leeward. It was too late.

Suddenly, in an attempt to turn, the *almiranta* bumped bottom. In a heartbeat the *capitana* appeared directly in front of her. The extreme veloc-ity of the surging current made it impossible to maneuver. With a great crash the bowsprit of the *capitana* passed from the starboard through to the port side of the *almiranta*. Its anchor demolished and opened a huge gap in her stem. She was now turned sideways to the weather.

The spritsail spar, recently constructed of seven-inch-thick mahogany in Havana, now hung haphazardly, projecting from the bowsprit of the *Maravillas* and broken into three pieces. The ship's plankings from the waterline down were now mere splinters.

A sailor in the process of furling the spritsail on the *almiranta* was knocked off his perch above the forepeak from the collision. Instead of falling overboard to certain death, he landed miraculously on his feet on the foredeck of the parting *capitana*.

Amidst the confusion everyone came forward. Mattresses, sails, blankets and clothing were stuffed into the hold in the prow in an attempt to stop the sea water now gushing into the vessel.

The beakhead, anchor and cables were partially entangled at the time of collision. After what seemed an eternity of grinding and breaking timbers, the *capitana* broke clear, drifting astern the *Maravillas* and into safe water.

The northwest wind and currents quickly shoved the *Maravillas* into the white water shoals where the nine-hundred-ton vessel anchored as it awaited daylight.

All four pumps aboard her now operated continuously. Those aboard haphazardly organized into lines with jugs, bowls and buckets attempting to bail the rising water in the galleon. No matter how much scooping, pumping and bailing was done, the water soon reached the second deck.

In the predicament, after the ship's two anchors finally dug in, the wind and currents combined to position the galleon to broadside strikes from the onrushing northwest seas. Pounding waves began breaking the ship into pieces, filling the waist of the galleon.

I groped through the confusion to reach Admiral Don Matías de Orellana. "Admiral, what should we do?" I asked. His frankness was shocking. "We will be lost without remedy. Please confess all who wish to be absolved."

I struggled to the highest cabin of the sterncastle where hundreds crowded. I found the great lanterns of the galleon still lit, reflecting an unearthly glow against the pitch-darkness. Everyone was begging for God's mercy.

I was astonished at how many people packed themselves into the poop house. They retreated there because it was the highest deck on the ship. I tried to console them. With competition from the crying crowd and the howling northwest wind, I endeavored to minister.

Their determination was very real as everyone knew their time was limited. Even though their despair was great, I began confessing them of their sins. Shortening the penitential form as much as possible, I blessed them despite the circumstances.

I climbed atop a chest in order to be visible above the wailing crowd. I tried earnestly to calm them. Getting their attention was difficult because of the noise of wind and sea. But, speaking as loudly as possible in order to be heard, and trying not to tremble (for I, too, was upset and frightened), I finally, though momentarily, managed to compose them. For a short time, at least, their cries and sobs silenced.

"My children, I am your priest. Hear me out!" The strength of my own voice both amazed and helped to calm even me. I proceeded to read from the Bible.

"The Lord *is* my rock and my fortress, and my deliverer, my God, my strength in whom I will trust; my buckler, and the horn of my salvation, *and* my high tower.

"I will call upon the Lord, *who is worthy* to be praised: so shall I be saved from mine enemies.

"The sorrows of hell compassed me about: the snares of death prevented me.

"In my distress I called upon the Lord, and cried unto my God: he heard my voice out of His temple, and my cry came before him, *even* into his ears.

"He sent from above, He took me, He drew me out of many waters.

"He delivered me from my strong enemy, and from them which hated me: for they were too strong for me.

"They prevented me in the day of my calamity: but the Lord was my stay.

"He brought me forth also into a large place; He delivered me, because he delighted in me.

"The Lord rewarded me according to my righteousness; according to the cleanness of my hands hath he recompensed me.

"For I have kept the ways of the Lord, and have not wickedly departed from my God."[39]

As I lowered my Bible and looked at them, they began sobbing again. I raised my hand, the Bible clutched tightly in it, and began hearing individual confessions. I then offered a general absolution to all the others.

A large section of flooring from the poop deck was lifted. Securing it with rope and sleeping bags, it was lowered over the leeward side of the sinking ship.

A number of desperate people clambered over the side and jumped to the wooden platform saying, "Father, we are throwing ourselves on this board and in company with *Our Lady of Solitude* we will go comforted to where God will carry us."

A framed image of Our Lady of Solitude was removed from one of the priest's cabins along with a crucifix. One person preparing to abandon ship removed the image from its frame. Pressing it against his heart, he jumped upon the large plank tethered to the side of the ship by ropes. Don Diego de Castro handed me the crucifix. I placed it around my neck between my shirt and skin.

I soon found myself staggering around in a senseless condition, trying to come to grips with the situation. A frightful blackness and despair engulfed me. The gale appeared to be attacking me personally. I had confronted bad weather and discomforts at sea in the past, but never a shipwreck. My hand found a gallery rail. I wrapped both arms around it. Breath came only in asthmatic-like gasps. I sorely wanted to disbelieve the irrefutable reality of my plight. Perhaps a dream, a dreadful nightmare caused my mind not to work, my courage to flee. A cold water drenching from a gigantic wave helped me recover my senses, returning me to the bitter reality.

Voices called me, some in violent tones. Although I wanted to tell them I would remain with them on the ship, I could not. As I stared into the sea I saw a large desk float by, about ten yards away. Several sailors urged me to go to it. Not able to swim, I dared not jump into the water.

The confusion of the moment held a death-hold on me. The uncertainty, the cold and dark, the ghoulish wind, the eerie dreadfulness of the night, the screams and wails, all combined to envelop me in pincer-like jaws.

Surely there must be something I, or someone can do. There must be some way to save the ship, the passengers and crew. How can we allow these people to perish? For a fleeting moment I clasped my hands and bowed my head.

"Our Father who art in Heaven, hallowed be Thy name. Thy Kingdom come, Thy will be done, on Earth as it is in Heaven . . . Please help me, for I know not what to do."

When I began to focus on these multi-dimensional nightmares unfolding before my very eyes, my stomach became queasy and my knees began to shake. My tongue was so thick and swollen I was unable to move it. It felt full of cotton. I looked furtively for a place to hide.

Suddenly I snapped into reality. Despite my clenching fear, this was no time for personal emotions, especially self-pity or fear. I would not allow myself to be afraid. There was no choice but to stay strong for those who needed me. Though I wanted to be alone with God, to say my own vows, no one allowed me my solitude. Not even God Himself.

In the darkness I somehow found Admiral Orellana. He abandoned the pumps only moments before because the rising water within the hold could no longer be contained. Totally soaked with sea water and shriveled to the bone, he calmly reiterated there was nothing more to be done to save the ship. He placed his hand on my shoulder. "Our energies, Padre, must be used to assist and give solace to those who seek it," he offered. "If it is God's will, we must also endeavor to save ourselves."

He started away, then turned back, looking straight into my eyes. He added, "Do not fear death, Father Diego. I do not, for it will catch us both sooner or later."

Without further hesitation the admiral began to assist his sailors, now desperately trying to launch a longboat. Regrettably, with the wild ocean thrashing us, the boat was smashed into the side of the ship, swamped by the seas, then lost.

This was the last I saw of our gallant Don Matías de Orellana. But I shall never forget how his eyes shone through the nether gloom of the evening, when he attempted to assuage my fears.

The weakened vessel now shifted somewhat to starboard. I knew the galleon was definitely on the bottom and beginning to break. I began running to the mid section of the main deck. The seas were already entering over the gangway area and waves were breaking with great force over the side of the ship.

A man near the gangway stood over a chest. As I approached him, I realized it was Gaspar de los Reyes, the assistant pilot. Without speaking a word he hastily undressed. He motioned to me to follow suit. We both stripped to only our shirt and underpants.

Following him, I groped my way along the rigging of the mast on the port side. (The main mast and tackle, already broken and fallen into the sea, were now banging destructively against the side of the galleon.)

I watched the pilot dive into the water head first. I knew it was time for me to make a decision. The sound of the ship splitting apart indicated what little time remained.

I realized the hull of the ship, as well as the sterncastle, were in the process of collapsing. Because I could not swim, I looked for the portion of the main mast and rigging in the sea, still secured to the port side.

The cracking and splintering of the after-portion of the galleon increased with the intensity of the north wind, adding to the agonies of those still alive.

The cold was unbearable. The incessant noise created terror and fear. With sea water now covering my feet, I noticed a hatch floating alongside. The current literally brought it to me. I jumped quickly and clumsily in its direction.

My body weight sent me plummeting. I sank unfalteringly beneath the water, but was not submerged long. I soon found myself being squeezed between some brackets and planks. This is where I nearly drowned. Totally terrified because of my inability to swim, I managed somehow to maneuver, squirming and struggling with all my strength, to achieve an upright attitude on the miserable piece of wood, now my temporary salvation.

As I clung to the hatch cover trying not to be washed overboard, the entire sterncastle of the *Maravillas*, all three decks of it, crashed in a tumbling fall, astern to starboard. The tower of breaking wood sent horrified and screaming people sprawling into the sea in every direction.

The huge structure came down with such a thundering crash it seemed to eerily equalize the bashing of the high wind and eruption of the seas, mollifying the nightmare everyone now faced.

I desperately hung on, though frightened beyond belief and trembling with cold. Freezing and drenched to the bone because my shirt had ripped from my body as I struggled to climb upon the hatch cover, I cried a soft prayer, knowing death would soon come.

If God in His infinite mercy had not placed the board in the sea near where I was, the stern cabin would have broken me into pieces when it fell. No doubt but I would have perished.

In the darkness, two men suddenly came swimming toward the hatch where I perched. Coughing and gasping, they caught hold of an iron ring. With one arm around my waist for leverage, they climbed upon my platform.

Recognizing me, they both immediately began confessing. In the serious situation we found ourselves, the three of us consoled one another with words spoken from our hearts and through our tears.

Then I heard other voices in the sea. Some cried for help. Others begged for mercy, questioning what sins they committed to bring on this unbelievable tragedy.

Waves rocked the partially submerged hatch. Somehow, with the help of my mates, I managed to stand. One held me by the waistband of my underpants. The other steadied my legs while I held on to his hair, tied in a queue.

As I stood shivering in the cold air, the fear of death left my mind. The crucifix in my hand, I said with a strength of voice surprising even myself, "My children, I am with you. It is your padre. I am here to absolve you."

It is not possible for me to repeat exactly what happened this awful night. I may have even forgotten some of the details. But I will never forget the cries of so many through tears and grief as they beseeched God for the blessing of their souls.

Some bluntly shared their many sins. Others simply gave me their names and asked for absolution. The lamentations of some, the groans of others, the weeping and wailing, all combined with the noise of the wind and waves to sap my strength. I was unsure how long I could continue with the Blessed Sacrament of Forgiveness.

But our Lord God worked His miracle and I endured. The sea manifested its compassion upon those around me. Whether they floated in the water alone or held on to hatch covers or hen houses, the first light of day found us drifting together in a somewhat calmer sea.

In the distance we saw the silhouette of part of the bow and foremast of the *almiranta*, still protruding above the surface of the ocean. There were a few people hanging on to those sections of the ship, but the voices I heard near me in the water were now only a few, and they sounded very weak.

Just before sunrise, I fainted from exhaustion, falling over the hatch into the water. My companions dragged me back aboard our death plank, telling me to "Cheer up. Today is another day. Besides," they offered, "we do not intend to die without having a priest on hand."

As the day brightened we saw an unknown black thing coming toward us. Was it a vicious marine beast coming to do us further harm? As it drew nearer, we recognized it was a bedroll of palm matting. My friends quickly grabbed it and threw it over me, hoping it would help shield me from the cold. I felt I was wrapped in a blanket.

Now daylight, we spotted a barrel floating nearby. It was full of lemons. I grabbed for one and quickly ate it. It caused such retching, I vomited for an hour.

Our eyes burned from the salt water. Our eyelids encrusted with salt, we still managed to spot a galleon, apparently anchored about a league away. We watched as a small boat tried twice to head for us. Because of the heavy ground swell and strong currents, twice they turned back.

The small vessel finally reached several survivors in the water near us. I watched Gaspar de los Reyes, the assistant pilot of the sunken *almiranta*, climb in it, thinking surely they could pick up more than a few men. But for fear of capsizing, they returned to the anchored ship.

Hours passed. We had little hope of living. Hungry, weak and shivering uncontrollably, we were numbed by the cold. One of my hatch companions, a soldier, hadn't spoken for several hours. He lay slumped on the side of the hatch, partly leaning against me and partly in the water. I tried to roll him over into a better position, but was unable to support him. He slid off into the sea. We then realized he was dead. I said a short prayer for him.

I suppose there were about 150 of us in the water during the night. By morning we numbered only forty-five.

By midday the sun was out, but the seas remained high. Fortunately, they were considerably more settled than the previous evening.

Our problem of survival now centered around the degree of cold and wet we could endure.

I attempted to cheer those floating nearby in the water by telling them the story of Saint Paul's miraculous survival of a shipwreck.

"Stay calm and listen carefully," I instructed them. "As the Apostle Paul once said, 'There shall be no loss of any man's life among you, but of the ship. For there stood by me this night the angel of God, whom I am, and whom I serve.'"[40]

I told them how those who cast themselves into the sea would reach land, some on boards and some on broken pieces of the ship, just as Saint Paul did. Then we all prayed. I began singing *Te Deum Laudamus*, crying so hard my voice could barely whisper the verses.

As the sun began to fall in the afternoon, I was certain my own death was near and imminent. My face and chest were sunburned. I was so parched that my tongue was badly swollen. I was desperate for a drink of water. I came to rely on words of encouragement from my hatchmate, a knight of the Order of Christ and resident of Lima. Don Domingo de Vega proved to be a very heroic man. I still visualize the magnificent Cross of Malta he wore around his neck, enameled in blue with golden letters, I H S. He was quite proud of having been ordained in this small select habit. He explained it was created in 1615 by Pope Paul V. He repeated, "Hang on, Padre Diego. Hang on. They will send a boat and we both shall live." As I reflect back on this ordeal, I give Don Domingo much credit for helping me "hang on."

We were repeating Acts of Contrition when suddenly rejoiceful shouting began. I saw not one, but two small boats approaching us. One was skippered by Gaspar de los Reyes, who returned first to the sunken *almi-*

ranta to pick up survivors from the collapsed foremast. I also saw a chest in the bow of his boat.

"Over here," I shouted. "I am a priest. Pick me up!"

They finally came for my hatchmate and me. They dragged me over the side of the launch as the lower half of my body was paralyzed from the cold. Although my teeth chattered, I was barely able to move my jaws.

I noticed the chest in the boat was open. The reason for the delay in picking us up was to enable the sailors to take as much as they could possibly hide within their clothing. This was not easily done as the chest contained silver bars of various sizes, plus a number of silver cones.

We were picked up by the long boat about four o'clock, and arrived at the galleon shortly before prayers. It was the *Jesus, Maria y Josef* of Juan de Hoyos. They had lost their rudder, but the ship's hull was intact.

6

The Survivors

Let this lesson on the frailty of life give us the inspiration we need to live each new day to the best of our God-given abilities.

January 5, 1656

Rescuers wrapped me in a sheet and laid me on a cot. They provided hot wine and brandy, then dinner. I began to recover my strength. An invitation to sit at the captain's table was extended.

Captain Juan de Hoyos' words flowed with emotion as he related his version of the evening's events. "After the *almiranta* fired the warning shot, I realized we were probably on the edge of the *Mimbres*.

"We hit a rock and the rudder kicked off, breaking the whipstaff. It happened nearly simultaneously. The hard coral also stripped away some fourteen feet of keel sole. It was a miracle the galleon was not broken to pieces like the *almiranta*. We anchored in less than four and a half fathoms and spent the rest of the night firing guns in a call for help, and to warn the others.

"When daylight came, we saw part of the *almiranta*'s wooden foremast sticking out of the water, a little less than a gunshot away. We watched as it broke and sank. Naked people signaled for help, right before our eyes! I immediately ordered the launch and longboat lowered."

Shortly following my rescue I watched as the *patache de la Margarita* and the *capitana* of the Marqués de Montealegre appeared on the horizon. I knew it was the *capitana* as I recognized its flag. We fired several cannon hoping they would come alongside the stranded *Jesus, Maria y Josef*. Instead, they soon turned and sailed away. We never saw them again.

I slept very well that night. The next day I celebrated the Holy Sacrament, giving thanks for the incredible mercy bestowed on me. A monk of San Juan de Dios offered me one of his tunics. Although it was from a different habit, it was very respectable.

We anchored there for six days. Captain Juan de Hoyos offered 1,000 pesos to those of the crew who could construct and install a new rudder. The men worked diligently, and with much industry and creativity.

Throughout the night and day, the small group of carpenters and craftsmen worked on the new rudder. Assorted pieces of wood and nails were taken from other parts of the ship. From miscellaneous pieces of scrap iron found on board, a blacksmith forged large pinions to hang the rudder. It seemed impossible to me to have among us men with such talent and understanding of what needed to be done.

All the while Captain Hoyos continually encouraged the men to build the replacement rudder as strong as possible, so we might sail out of this dangerous place. I doubt he slept at all during the six days it took to perform this important work.

Finally the huge piece was finished. They requested I hold a special service. A large harness was rigged and, with the rudder hanging inside it, the entire sling was lowered over the side and into the sea. In only three hours the men were able to position it into the gudgeon sockets on the stern and secure the pins. I blessed the rudder and asked for the Lord's blessings.

Desperate men are often capable of ingenious improvisations during life and death scenarios. The creative construction and installation of an impromptu rudder was not only a major feat; given the conditions on the uncharted waters of *Los Mimbres*, it was more of a miracle.

The size of a typical rudder for a 900-ton galleon of this era measured between fifteen and twenty feet in length, and might weigh as much as a ton.

The rudder was moved to port and starboard by a long tiller located on the lower gun deck. The tiller was shifted to the left or right on a steadying sweep by a whipstaff, activated through an opening one or two decks above. Larger ships over 400 tons might require as many as six or eight men to move or hold a whipstaff in heavy weather. At times the whipstaff and tiller might be so uncontrollable, a large block and tackle rig would be utilized to brake the movement. Consequently, the helmsmen on duty were unable to see where they were headed. Orders were yelled down to them via the hole in the deck. For better or worse, the ship plowed ahead to its destiny. Those physically steering never saw where they were going, or what they were heading into.

January 15, 1656

Finally, our foresail was up. The launch led us, taking soundings as we picked our way carefully off the shoals. We passed through five fathoms, then six. We were soon in eight, then ten fathoms of water. Within a half hour we watched the bottom disappear from sight.

A course was set for the *Jesus, Maria y Josef*. It was an attempt to follow the intended route of the *capitana* northward to a latitude of 31 degrees, then eastward, passing south of Bermuda. Onward toward the Azores, and finally to Spain.

However, after sailing for only a short distance we approached the latitude of Punta Canaveral, where we encountered adverse weather. The galleon was considerably lightened while anchored at *Los Mimbres* of Little Bahama Bank. Now the ship rolled heavily in the large swells.

Hatches were battened down and artillery ports were closed. The *Jesus, Maria y Josef* was forced to sail in the direction dictated by the wind. Fortunately, we were able to proceed in an east-northeasterly direction. We maintained this heading for the next three days.

All 350 people on board spent much of their time in prayer. Soldiers and sailors, never before knowing the need, were now seen on their knees with heads bowed and hands folded against their hearts. They were all fully aware they were among the lucky few who survived.

Several masses were held as a memorial to those lost in the *Maravillas* tragedy. Survivors confessed their sins at all hours to the five priests on board the galleon. I say with certainty, there was no one who was not confessed, some citing sins committed thirty years before. Some of the sailors had spent almost their entire lives on these ships. They never practiced religion or received sacraments. Now the Lord worked wonders on their souls through the miracle of their conversion. Even as I was laying on my cot at night, I welcomed all with love and tenderness who wished to see me. What a glorious occasion it was for me to receive all those wishing to repent, and now place their trust in God.

Ours became a ship of love and thanksgiving. Not one curse or oath was heard aboard the galleon. All soldiers, sailors and passengers appeared to be in a divine state of peacefulness. Even those who pilfered silver bars and clusters of treasure from the chest of the *almiranta* in the *Mimbres* returned everything to me during their confessions. I surrendered it all to the captain and silvermaster. It was counted and placed in the storeroom for His Majesty's register. It seemed to me a great quantity of treasure.

January 30, 1656

We sailed eastward for the next nineteen days, always with contrary weather and winds. As we attempted to tack against the strong headwinds, we realized we were not making headway. Maintaining this course was futile[41] as the ship was unable to sail into the wind, now constantly on our nose. Provisions and water were critically low. Juan de Hoyos also was concerned about his makeshift rudder.

It was decided to change course for Puerto Rico. The bow of the *Jesus, Maria y Josef* soon headed in a southerly direction. The north-easterly wind now on the port quarter, our square-rigged sails filled nicely. The galleon plowed along making good headway with the seas following.

On the Day of San Blas, February 3, we spotted land on the horizon. To the dismay of all on board, however, it was not Puerto Rico. Instead it was the cays of the Isle of Mayaguana, some 400 nautical miles northwest of Puerto Rico.

Those on the ship were bitterly disappointed. After so much torture and misfortune already experienced, this only added to our overall discouragement. Perhaps the *almiranta*'s dead were truly the lucky ones. At least they were spared the additional suffering and continual ordeals we were now forced to endure.

I made a strong effort to console the distraught passengers. Standing at the quarter-deck rail I raised my voice to all. I told them we must appeal to God, our only salvation. I then offered a mass to the glorious San Blas, asking for his intervention in our behalf. Alms were offered by everyone, the amount distributed among the five priests who prayed fervently.

Favorable winds continued to propel the galleon under full sail. Juan de Hoyos navigated as carefully as he and his pilots were able, making sure they gave *Los Abrojos*[42] a wide berth near where the New Spain *almiranta* of 1641 was previously lost.

A few days later everyone awoke to hear the ship's officers conferring excitedly. Land was spotted off the starboard bow. One of the more experienced pilots recognized it as Isla Desecheo, positioned in the Mona Passage, about fourteen miles to the west of Puerto Rico.

The galleon's heading was brought around to the east. Moments later the mountains of Puerto Rico stood out prominently in the morning light. The headland of Punta Borinquen soon began to be recognizable.

Everyone on board was ecstatic. San Juan was only sixty miles away! Still, we needed to proceed cautiously. This is an area of the Caribbean favored by pirates. Isla Mona is a known popular hangout for scoundrels of the sea. Located at the center of Mona Passage, it provides a perfect lookout spot for shipping to the west of Puerto Rico, or on the easterly side of Hispaniola (Santo Domingo).

Passengers and crew assembled in the forecastle chapel of the *Jesus, Maria y Josef*, to give thanks for safely reaching Puerto Rico. The first pilot headed the galleon directly for the *Aguada de Puerto Rico*, the river emptying into a small bay on the western shore of the island. This location serves as a common anchorage and watering hole for the New Spain fleet.[43] Fresh water and provisions will be loaded while we are here. Even though sea currents are extremely strong in the Mona Passage, an onshore breeze brought us safely to the anchorage at daybreak the following morning.

February 24, 1656

Water casks and jugs were filled. Fruits, including bananas and oranges were acquired. Pigs and poultry were purchased from local inhabitants. Our people enjoyed bathing themselves on nearby beaches. Captain Juan de Hoyos sent a letter to the governor of Puerto Rico with a report to be forwarded to the king, informing His Majesty of the Hoyos' trials and tribulations. The vessel, its passengers and crew rested at the *Aguada* anchorage for three days.

Rescue Route of Juan de Hoyos

From Havana, to the disaster at Little Bahama Bank, finally reaching Puerto Rico, and then Cartagena—a period of sixty-nine days.

The captain, concerned about our westerly exposure, weighed anchor and continued to San Juan. The vessel struggled for sea room all day in an attempt to make the turn off the Puerto Rican coast around Punta Borinquen. Nightfall found us still within a league of our previous anchorage.

The nightmarish memory of the currents and reefs of *Los Mimbres* still fresh on his mind, and fearful of the equally dangerous current we fought all day, Juan de Hoyos did not want to be caught on a lee shore in a westerly blow. As night set in he made an expedient decision to go with the wind. Bringing the clumsy, rolling ship about, he pointed the beakhead southward and left Puerto Rico on his stern.

The wind and current swept us away. We literally flew past Isla Mona and headed for *Tierra Firme*. With the strong, favorable breeze and following seas, we raced toward Cartagena.

March 10, 1656

We arrived in wonderful Cartagena in six days, Ash Wednesday, March 10. Our battered galleon brought with it the alarming news of the lost *Maravillas*, the miseries of the survivors, and the tallies of the dead to the governor, Don Pedro Zapata. Hearts and pocketbooks of the people of this great city were generously opened to us.

For weeks Cartagenians catered to the needs of Juan de Hoyos and the crew. They were especially generous to those of us who survived the sinking of the *almiranta*. An enormous amount of food, money and clothing were offered to the survivors.

It pleased me greatly to be invited to hold a memorial service at the Santa Iglesia Cathedral. We celebrated Lent by blessing all who lost their lives in the shipwreck of the *Nuestra Señora de las Maravillas*. The entire city participated in the ceremony. We remained in the Holy House all day.

For this special service I offered a mass of Thanksgiving. Each of the forty-five survivors came forward to express before God and the congregation their personal thanks to Him for their rescue. Following this I said a short prayer: "Lord, our God and Savior, please allow those who have lost their friends and relatives on the *almiranta* to share in the benefits and blessings those survivors have received. Let us be reminded how fragile our lives truly are. Let this lesson on the frailty of life give us the inspiration we need to live each new day to the best of our God-given abilities. Help us to care for each other as our Savior has commanded."

The *Jesus, Maria y Josef* was being careened for bottom cleaning and caulking. A new rudder was also constructed. Don Pedro Zapata was busy equipping six frigates, the largest being 100 tons. Armed with soldiers and staffed with forty divers and necessary gear, they prepared for the search and salvage of the sunken *Maravillas*.

Juan de Somovilla Tejada was placed in command of the search and salvage fleet. He had previously served on the *Tierra Firme* galleons for many years. He also worked as an engineer under Cristóbal de Roda, the nephew of the famous architect Juan Bautista Antonelli, chief engineer in Cartagena from 1591 to 1609.

Somovilla helped build the fortifications at Cartagena, as well as the walls and forts of Havana, Portobelo and Puerto Rico. He took part in the battle for the island of San Martin and participated in the invasion of the Islas de San Andrés y Mosquitos, previously occupied by the English who were ousted.

During these years of service in the Indies, he had numerous occasions to use his technical skills in construction and in underwater salvage. His knowledge and energy were utilized in the successful salvage of the *capitana Concepción* and the galleon *Bom Sucesso* of the Portuguese armada of Don Rodrigo Lobo de Silva. Both vessels ran aground in the Bay of Cartagena on March 17, 1640 as they were entering Boca Grande, even though local pilots were aboard. Following a sudden breeze one night, the towering *capitana* rolled over on her side. Governor Melchior Aguilera ordered Somovilla Tejada to oversee the urgent salvage operation and put all the resources of Cartagena at his disposal. Somovilla managed to retrieve all eighty of the ship's cannon, and everything else of value in only twenty-two days, though the galleon was lost.

Second in charge of the salvage operation was none other than Captain Gaspar de los Reyes, the assistant pilot of the lost *almiranta*. It was he who carefully placed the marker buoys on the wreck site. He also measured the meridian altitude of the sun to determine the latitude of the location. It was now to be his responsibility to lead the salvage fleet to the uncharted waters of *Los Mimbres*.

A number of survivors and officers of the *Jesus, Maria y Josef* provided their depositions of the tragedy while in Cartagena. Some of the more significant comments are included in this text. They tell the story from a first-hand basis, as well as provide considerable additional details to help form a clear understanding of the events as they actually occurred.

Miguel de Nicoleta was the chief diver on the *Maravillas*. He was among one of the more fortunate to be rescued. On March 12, 1656, he told his story:

"The *almiranta* was struck at the starboard bow by the *capitana*. The bow section was stove in and the ship quickly filled with water. Although we anchored in the shallows in six fathoms, the ship began to break apart. It went to pieces, everything was lost. The waters are clear. The treasure lies on a white bottom of shell-sand. The seamen who picked up the survivors said they were even able to see some of the silver bars lying among broken timbers and sand. With the help of God we can save it. I will need at least thirteen divers with the necessary equipment. The work must be accomplished before the end of summer, otherwise it will likely be covered by shifting sand."

Don Diego Perez de Vargas Machuca, assistant pilot of the galleon *Jesus, Maria y Josef*, declared:

"When the *almiranta* fired its signal gun we attempted to veer away from the shallows. We suddenly found ourselves among breakers. The rudder struck a shallow reef and was knocked completely out of its gudgeon, falling into the sea. We quickly anchored in four and a half fathoms. It was a miracle the hull was not damaged. We fired guns and muskets all night, trying to inform the others of our peril. In the morning we saw a distant erect mast. Dozens of people were desperately clinging to it. There were many packages and personal belongings floating by. After seeing the mast collapse and disappear into the sea, I volunteered to take the small boat to try and help those in the water. This was clearly a risk. There was still a lot of wind and heavy seas. I retrieved six people who were struggling to hold on to floating debris. I rescued as many as I could safely carry in the small boat. One of the survivors, Gaspar de los Reyes, was also a pilot. When we returned to the *Jesus, Maria y Josef*, he helped crew the shallop. Together with the longboat we returned a second time and once again picked up as many as we could find, approximately forty people. Later, Gaspar and I sailed the short distance to the site of the drowned *almiranta* and took soundings and sun sights. Water depth was six fathoms (*brazas*). The hull is lying just north of *El Mimbre*, in line with the head of the breakers. The bottom is clean sand. We observed our height [read their latitude by measuring the altitude of the sun with an astrolabe] for several consecutive days. The first day our sun sight placed us at 27⅓° (27° 20′ N). On the second day we observed 27⅙° (27° 10′ N). It will be possible to recover some treasure if we hurry."[44]

March 15, 1656

Don Domingo de Vega, Knight of the Order of Christ, and my dear, thoughtful friend, prayed fervently with me while we floated together on the hatch cover. His testimony explained it only took fifteen minutes for the water to fill the hull of the doomed *Maravillas*.

"The *almiranta* turned to the left into the wind to try and obtain leeway from the shallows. Suddenly, the *capitana* also veered in the same direction. There was insufficient steerage space. The *almiranta* was struck instantly at the wash room on the starboard side. Water rushed in so rapidly the four pumps were not capable of controlling the flooding. In a quarter of an hour the galleon clearly was doomed.

"The ship came to rest on the shallows of the sand bank," de Vega continued. "The lower hull settled in six fathoms. The dark shadow of the sunken hull was obvious on the bottom, outlined against the brilliant white sand. The waters were exceptionally clear after the wind calmed down the next afternoon, so the sea was like a sheet of glass." As a matter of fact, he heard sailors among the survivors say they were able to see silver bars scattered around the wreckage because the water was so clean.

Gaspar de los Reyes, in his deposition of March 12, 1656, stated, "The entire armada was sailing on a northeasterly course about midnight when they came upon the sandbank of *Los Mimbres* at latitude 27¼° (27° 15′ N)."

Before Juan de Hoyos sailed away from his anchorage at the *Mimbres*, he summoned all pilots to make latitude observations. The average of the sights placed them at 27⅕° (27° 12′ N). He was anchored south of the *Maravillas*, but the ship's foremast was still visible. It fell into the sea the next morning.

7

All of Spain Prays

*Of course, Your Majesty, just in case the accident of shipwreck is far
worse than I imagined, I recommend the best pilot from Havana be
sent in a shallow draft vessel to the sandbanks called Los Mimbres to
be certain the treasure was not lost.*
Marqués de Montealegre

EL SANTO CRISTO DEL BUEN VIAJE was the first of Montealegre's fleet to reach Cádiz safely, on March 2, 1656. The arrival
created much rejoicing among the crew and townspeople of
this strategic Spanish port.

A report was immediately presented to Lorenzo Andrés Garcia,
attorney of His Majesty and general overseer of the *Casa de la Contratación* in Cádiz. It was the first time news of the tragedy and the
potential enormous treasure loss reached Spain.

Domingo de Parga, pilot of the galleon, prepared authorities for
the worst: "Because night was falling and the current was so strong,
we were in great fear of the many sandbanks and other reef dangers.
No matter how we attempted to tack toward the open sea, the winds
kept pushing us back. We saw the stricken ship, but were unable to
stand by or render assistance. My own vessel, as well as the *capitana*,
the *gobierno* and the *patache de la Margarita*, continued our journey."

On March 15, another courier raced to Madrid with news of the
capitana, *gobierno* and the *patache de la Margarita* arriving safely in
port at Cádiz. They still knew nothing of the remaining two galleons,
the *Maravillas* and the *Jesus, Maria y Josef*.

Interviews, interrogations and depositions immediately were ordered. The Marqués de Montealegre, commander-in-chief of the
fleet, was the first to testify.

When questioned about the lost vessels, the captain general admitted he was uncertain of their whereabouts. He described in great
detail the damage to his vessel, including the problems incurred after

the collision. While he gave full credit for their salvation to his own courage and belief in the Lord Almighty, he avoided questions relating to the condition of the *almiranta*. "In the confusion," he reported, "I am not certain it was the *almiranta* or another ship, possibly the *Jesus, Maria y Josef*." He was also unable to determine if she was in danger. Protected by the power of his position, he continued his testimony:

"Several pieces were fired and a light was placed at the *capitana's* main mast as a signal to determine if any other galleons were damaged," he stated, defensively.

"Our people were very frightened as everyone considered the possibility of shipwreck. The confusion was so great, very few of the crew were able to work. None of the officers were able to issue orders. The only decision that was made was to try to find safe water away from the dangers of the reefs. We were fortunate to have good wind in the sails, but were not certain of the direction of land. Fearing we were in the midst of the reputed *Los Mimbres* reefs, there was much bewilderment. So many were shouting, even our leadsman was confused. We had difficulty measuring our water depth. The night was very dark, but we believed land was to the southeast. Judging from the sounding lead, handled by Martin Perez de Galarza, *contador* of the armada, the water depth indicated five fathoms. We managed to leave our quandary and reach deeper water until the lead line failed to touch. It was only thanks to our trust in God and great luck that we safely emerged from the dangers of the collision and the reefs."

One seaman, however, shed a different light on the events. The same sailor who was working in the *almiranta's* spritsail rigging, was knocked from the ship during the collision, then miraculously and safely landed on the foredeck of the *capitana*, chose to not let the marqués off so easily. Taking the customary oath, he swore before the court.

"After I fell from the impact," he explained, "I rushed to the marqués to tell him the *almiranta* was taking on water at her bow. He could see it already reached the level of several rooms."

The marqués countered with, "Because of the darkness and confusion, I was unable to determine if the *almiranta* was severely punctured, or if the water was entering through faulty caulking."

Each time a different witness stepped forward under oath, the marqués' influence and persuasiveness overruled contrary testimony.

While some swore the *almiranta* was severely damaged and was last seen stranded on the sandbanks of *Los Mimbres*, others testified they hoped to see her sails as dawn arose the next morning.

When morning dawned on January 5, of course, there was no *almiranta* and no *Jesus, Maria y Josef* in sight.

After conferring with the *capitana*'s officers the marqués decided to attempt to retrace his route to the sandbanks of *Los Mimbres*. Most of the day was spent reversing course, all the while encountering heavy seas and high winds. As evening fell they saw a galleon in the distance, quietly resting on the horizon.

"About an hour before sunset we arrived near *Los Mimbres*, the site of the stranded vessel," Montealegre stated. "The same thing happened to us as occurred the night before. When the currents caught the galleons we were unable to maneuver away from the sandbanks and reefs."

The marqués continued, "We discovered the vessel was stranded on the bottom in the last bank on the north side of *Los Mimbres* with all masts intact. We attempted, but were unable, to contact the vessel."

No identification of the ship was made. The vessel was darkly silhouetted against the shallow seas. It was very quiet. No flags were hoisted and no guns were fired on board the mystery ship. The marqués was concerned about going closer to the vessel.

"Use caution," he told his duty officer. "We must not jeopardize our people or the treasure."

"It was probably the *Jesus, Maria y Josef.* Her people and cargo were transferred to the *almiranta*, now somewhere safely at sea," he rationalized.

In a letter to the king, the marqués stated his reasons for abandoning the grounded galleon.

"Although they made no sign at all, the masts and rigging seemed all right. I assumed they were out of danger, just waiting for a good wind to sail out of there. I had little time to send a launch as I feared for the safety of my own people. I was concerned about the high seas and winds. Considering the many problems the remaining ships faced, and because the channel was very narrow and difficult to maneuver in, I decided to continue my homeward trip.

"Of course, Your Majesty, just in case the accident of shipwreck is far worse than I imagined, I recommend the best pilot from Havana be sent in a shallow-draft vessel to the sandbanks called *Los Mimbres* to be certain the treasure was not lost."

The mystery galleon the marqués referred to was indeed the *Jesus, Maria y Josef*. The last visible signs of the *almiranta* disappeared forever beneath the surface of the sea at sunrise that same morning. But why was there no sign of life aboard the stranded vessel? After such a busy day of rescuing survivors, was there no watch? Was everyone retired from exhaustion? Were they at mass or having dinner? Why did not one person notice the distant sails? Perhaps the *capitana* really didn't approach as close as they indicated. With the darkening skies, perhaps their ship was not visible on the horizon, especially to the weary eyes of those aboard the anchored vessel. Still, this does not explain why the marqués did not fire a signal cannon or send a small boat to investigate.

The foreboding tidings soon reached the king in Madrid. The scribe of the court, Jeronimo de Barrionuevo, recorded for posterity:

"The *capitana* and *gobierno* emerged safely from the Bahama Channel. The galleon of Juan de Hoyos and the *almiranta* of Matías de Orellana grounded. Both vessels were shooting many guns indicating their distress. Several ships in the fleet wanted to help them but the winds and currents were a hindrance. In the morning they were not visible. Running before the wind the ships were pushed on their way to Cádiz. May it please God—all of this is a lie."

After reading the news, and after hearing it repeated, multitudes flooded the cathedrals and parish houses in prayer. Masses were said in Cádiz, Madrid and Seville, as well as throughout most of the kingdom. All prayers asked for safe harbor for the missing galleons.

"Despair is great," said Barrionuevo. "It is reported the two galleons were bringing twelve million in silver. Each carried several years' output of the mines. Many merchants will be bankrupted if they are lost. All of Spain is praying."

Spain did pray. But the truth was finally uncovered when the *Jesus, Maria y Josef* struggled into the New World bastion of Cartagena, delivering the survivors along with the dreadful news.

Several days earlier Marcus del Puerto returned to Cartagena with the Peruvian silver he picked up from Portobelo, including the salvaged treasure from the sunken 1654 *capitana* off Ecuador. He was one of the first officials to greet Juan de Hoyos, and to discuss the *Maravillas* tragedy.

"We lost our rudder and were left abandoned on the shoal of *Los Mimbres*," Hoyos told him. "Apparently the marqués was more concerned about his own life than the king's treasure, or our safety. The *almiranta* of Don Matías de Orellana sailed very close ahead of us. She disappeared during the night, shortly after we were forced to anchor. She went down on the edge of the sandbank. Almost everyone was lost, except for a few we picked up the next day."

Word steadily began to circulate in Spain, as well as *Tierra Firme* and *Nueva España*. More than 600 lives and five million in registered treasure were lost when the 900-ton *almiranta* was destroyed on *Los Mimbres*.

When news of the *Maravillas'* actual and verified loss reached Madrid, numerous inquiries were scheduled to determine the full truth of what caused the accident, and to determine if successful salvage was possible.

While the Crown chose to accept the report of the marqués, agreeing he was unable to assist Don Matías, it is interesting to look at the correspondence from the War Council of October 28, 1656, where reference that "the illness of the marqués will not allow him to make this next voyage" is noted.

As *Captain General Propietario*, the marqués was committed to leadership responsibility of each *Tierra Firme* fleet. We shall never know if his "illness" was serious or not. The king, once again, chose to believe him. He instructed the Council to appoint someone else to take the next fleet to America. He also ordered the normal salary be awarded to the marqués as *General Propietario* of the galleons.

The marqués' younger brother, Don Pedro Nuñez de Guzmán, may have helped to influence the king by speaking on his brother's behalf. His influence was most likely very strong, as he was named president of the *Casa de la Contratación* in Seville on November 15, 1654.

In any case, there is no indication the marqués made another voyage to the Indies. He carried the title of Captain General of the Armada until his death, nineteen years later, on March 6, 1675. He also served as a member of the Council of the Indies in 1657, and was named by His Majesty to serve on the Council of War.

Upon his death, his will empowered his brother, his brother-in-law, Don Francisco de Borja, his accountant, Don Juan Martinez and his chaplain, Lorenzo de Hechan, executors of his estate. His salary that year, 4,000 ducats, was prorated to the date of his death and paid to the estate. The title of captain general was not only honorific, but provided a tidy source of annual income, even in view of only one voyage to the New World, and despite that particular voyage's destiny.

His brother, Count of Villa Umbrosa, became the third Marqués de Montealegre, as his older brother died without having children.

Could the Marqués de Montealegre have done more to save the treasure of the *Maravillas*, the lives of Don Matías de Orellana and the other 600 unfortunates on board? What were his primary responsibilities as captain general of the 1656 fleet?

The duties of the captain general were officially defined as far back as 1574:

"It is the general, the supreme commander of everyone who goes in the armada, who has complete authority, the same as if he were king of the fleet. Because of this he must be very carefully chosen. He must be of high lineage, hardworking, well versed in seafaring requirements, liberal, generous with his staff and above all, loyal."[45]

Being appointed Captain General of the Armada to the Indies was a very high post and a great honor. The marqués was appointed for life, unlike others who were named on an annual basis to command the fleet. The captain general *propietario*, however, carried his title through his lifetime.

It was his responsibility to completely prepare, equip, provision and staff the vessels of his fleet. He issued the sailing directions and administered his personal hand in selecting the other primary officers, taking care to respect seniority.

His *capitana* was required to sail at the head of the fleet, flying his flag from the foremast during the day and burning a lantern at night. He was the leader. No other ships were to purposely pass him. The *almiranta* was supposed to follow the *capitana*, and was followed then by the *gobierno*, carrying the majority of the infantry.

It was the general's duty to confer at least twice a day with the admiral (though it was the admiral's responsibility to arrange an audience with the captain general). He was to check on his ships each morning and attempt to keep his fleet intact. If a ship was unaccounted for, it was his duty to attempt to locate it, always maintaining a constant eye for any clandestine trading.

The disastrous defeat of the Spanish fleet in 1628 off Matanzas, Cuba, by the Dutch Admiral Piet Heyn, created this policy. When the Spanish Captain General Don Juan de Benavides fled without fighting, a statement of policy was raised by Captain General Tomas de Larraspuru to the Count de la Puebla[46] in order to establish definitive procedural action if an enemy was encountered and there was much treasure on board:

"Should the captain general stand and fight honorably and risk losing his ship and valuable cargo? Is it his duty to assist any of the other royal galleons appearing to be in eminent danger? What about Spain's merchant ships? Should he come to their aid or should he give primary consideration to his own *capitana* and the king's treasure?"

The official policy statement was, without exception, that the captain general must consider the safety of his ship and his cargo. He must take such measures to insure his treasure will not fall into enemy hands. He must never allow a situation to occur to jeopardize all of the king's treasure, even if it is only possible to save a part of it. Of course, if he is able to come to the aid of another treasure galleon when there is no visible danger, it is his duty to help the other ship. As for rushing to assist a merchantman, at the risk of losing the *capitana*'s treasure to the enemy, he should not do so. However, if the opportunity prevails to assist any ship flying the flag of Castile, and he believes he can do so without undue peril, or laying himself open to a large enemy squadron, then he must fight to defend the authority of the flag and the reputation of the arms of the king.

8

The Homecoming

*The English had more than fifty guns per ship. There was fire and
smoke and destruction everywhere.*

April 7, 1656

At the castle of Bocachica[47] in Cartagena, Captain Marcus del Puerto
swore on the Holy Bible before Don Pedro Zapata, Knight of the
Order of Santiago, Governor and Captain General of Cartagena. He
verified his receipt of 381 silver bars on board his *capitana*, the *San
Francisco y San Diego*, of a total of 1,010 the fleet carried for His
Majesty. He further swore to defend Spain's treasure with his life, and
never surrender from dangers confronting him.[48]

Marcus del Puerto, then age forty-nine, was descended from a very
old family from Oñate in Guipúzcoa, in northern Spain. He pursued
a military career, as his forefathers before him.

He served as sergeant major (*sargento mayor*) since 1644, on
fleets headed to and from the Indies. The sergeant major was the rank
and file chief of the marine infantry (the king's soldiers), a very respected post. He enjoyed being the man responsible for successfully
completing projects and carrying out orders. He was usually stationed
on board the *gobierno*, with the *gobernador* as third in command of
the armada. His responsibility included supervision of the soldiers assigned to this galleon.

The sergeant major was often competing with the captain of infantry for authority. His rank was classified only as ensign though his
salary equaled that of a captain of sea and war. (The reasoning was
that a galleon captain would not be subordinate to an ensign's position.) Men like Marcus del Puerto rose quickly in rank due to superior
service to the king, such as distinguishing themselves in battle or
some type of high allegiance.

In October of 1652, Marcus del Puerto was the only sergeant major on a proposed list of nine captains. Three were selected to sail to the Indies on the next fleet. The Council of the Indies, acting on behalf of the king, did not choose him. A year later he was one of three proposed for a command in Panama. Marcus was named, but he did not accept. The reason was obviously because he was one of three proposed to command an infantry company on the *almiranta* of the *Tierra Firme* fleet of 1654. For reasons unknown he was bypassed once more and then again in 1655.

He was finally named *gobernador* of the small 1656 fleet rushing to *Tierra Firme*. His assignment was to bring back the million badly needed by His Majesty to help prop up the shaky Spanish economy as a result of the loss of the 1654 *capitana* and the *Maravillas* earlier that year.

On April 22, 1656, the *capitana*'s treasure register was modified by both Marcus del Puerto and Don Pedro Zapata. They acknowledged seventeen silver bars were taken from the inventory. They explained this was to cover expenses of preparing and fitting out six salvage frigates to search for the sunken *almiranta*, now lying on the bottom of the sea at *Los Mimbres* in the Bahama Channel.

Marcus del Puerto's *Tierra Firme* fleet sailed from Cartagena for Havana on April 27. Included in the armada were the *Jesus, Maria y Josef*, five other treasure galleons and six frigates loaded with diving gear and pearl-divers from Margarita Island. They were all eager to reach the site of the wrecked *Nuestra Señora de las Maravillas* to try their luck at treasure salvage.

Marcus del Puerto was optimistic the voyage would place him in great favor with the king. Returning to Spain with not only the wealth brought by his own fleet, but also with salvaged treasure from the sunken *almiranta* certainly meant he would be rewarded with the personal recognition he felt was long overdue.

The king's galleons put into Havana, Cuba on May 23. Under command of Juan de Somovilla Tejada, the salvage vessels sailed farther down the coast to the port of Matanzas. Supplies were loaded there, then the salvage frigates sailed for the shipwreck site of the sunken *Maravillas*. Del Puerto's armada remained at Havana.

Two months passed with no word from Somovilla or his divers. Marcus del Puerto occupied his time careening his ships. He oversaw caulking, painting, replacing worn rigging and ordering provisions in preparation for his Atlantic crossing back to Spain. His departure timetable became extremely tight. The hurricane season was upon them.

By mid-July, a council of the various captains was called. They debated whether they should leave for Spain immediately, or wait for reinforcements and the anticipated treasure salvage from the *Maravillas*.

The reasons to begin their voyage far outweighed the reasons to prolong the wait. The threat of deadly tropical storms grew more intense. They already had spent 200,000 pesos maintaining their ships and men in Cuba. If they remained longer there would be nothing left of the king's million. A total of forty-five bars of silver were removed from the king's register on the *capitana*, *almiranta* and the galleon of Don Juan de Hoyos to cover these expenses.

The fleet of seven vessels departed Havana on Monday, July 24, 1656, at approximately nine o'clock in the morning.

The galleon of Don Juan de Hoyos, the *Jesus, Maria y Josef*, was the largest ship in the fleet. Consequently, it carried the greatest number of passengers and approximately one-third of the king's treasure.

Included on the passenger list of this galleon was the very notable Don Diego de Villalba y Toledo, former Governor and Captain General of Havana, now returning to Spain. Because of his previous military experience, extensive by any comparison, Captain Hoyos requested he serve as chief of artillery on the voyage.

July 24, 1656
Havana Harbor

Along with three other priests, I was sailing aboard the *almiranta* of Francisco de Esquivel. Our fleet commander, Marcus del Puerto, requested I say a mass and lead everyone in prayer prior to weighing anchor. I was overjoyed to have the opportunity to bless the fleet and to once again, publicly, thank the Lord Our God for His great mercy. I was especially grateful in view of the tragedy and discomfort I endured earlier this year. Though I continually fulfilled my personal vows of thanksgiving, this was an opportunity to also bring many others to prayer for thanks.

"Heavenly Father, please be with each and every one of us as we embark upon Your great ocean. Spare us from the potential damage of stormy seas and hidden reefs; of potential injury from heartless enemies and evil pirates; of destructive boredom and faithless moments. Deliver us safely to our Motherland and to our loved ones who wait for us, and who also pray for our safe return.

Del Puerto's Seven Ships and Their Complement

Capitana *Gobernador* and Captain Armed with 26 guns - 200 people on board	*San Francisco y San Diego* Marcus del Puerto
Almiranta Captain Armed with 30 guns - 200 people on board	*San Francisco Javier* Francisco de Esquivel y Zárate
Galleon Captain Armed with 28 guns - 400 people on board	*Jesus, Maria y Josef* Juan de Hoyos
Galleon Captain Armed with 20 guns - 200 people on board	*Nuestra Señora de la Victoria* Juan Rodriguez Calderón
Urca merchantman Captain Armed with 26 guns - 200 people on board	*Profeta Elias* Juan de la Torre
Urca merchantman Captain Armed with 24 guns - 200 people on board	*Nuestra Señora de Rosario* José de Paredes
Patache (aviso)	Private vessel owned by José de Pimienta

"Because so many of our friends and shipmates, brothers and sisters, were lost on a similar voyage seven difficult months ago, we pray You will grant us the serenity of a safe and peaceful journey."

Among the most significant passengers on board was the noble family of Don Francisco Lopez de Zúñiga, the Marqués de Baides, who is also the former governor of Chile. Along with his wife, three daughters and three sons, he was returning home with all their personal belongings and family wealth. The youngest son is an infant, born recently in Cartagena. The marqués arranged for his oldest daughter to be married to the son of the Duke of Medinaceli. The wedding is scheduled shortly after our fleet reaches Spain. The second daughter is engaged to Don Juan de Hoyos, the commander of the *Jesus, Maria y Josef*. There is gossip about, saying the family was originally to sail on de Hoyos' ship. Perhaps because the marqués, in a second thought, felt it was not proper for his daughter to be in such close quarters on so long a voyage with the man who is not only her fiancé but also captain of the ship, plans were changed at the last moment. The family, together with a servant who tends the infant, and all their possessions, were transferred to the *almiranta*. They are eagerly anticipating their long awaited return to Spain. The two oldest daughters are agreeably excited about their forthcoming marriages.

The small fleet's passage through the Bahama Channel[49] was swift and pleasant as we were propelled by a moderate southwesterly breeze. The only incident of any significance occurred about two days out of La Havana. A short time after midnight, I was awakened by a distant cannon shot. It was followed by another. Orders were shouted on board to drop sail.

It appears Juan de Hoyos and another *nao* bumped against some of the shallow sandbanks projecting seaward from the *Cabeza de Martires*.[50]

The *nao* managed to find deeper water, but the *Jesus, Maria y Josef* was stranded on the hidden shoal. Throughout the long and dark evening, sailors attempted to push the vessel clear by using long poles. They also kedged and warped with the smaller anchors.[51] The rest of the fleet dropped their sails and hovered nearby to wait for daylight. The ship captains were distressed over this delay. Don Juan de Hoyos was especially frustrated as he felt he already experienced his share of groundings in the Bahama Channel. The tide finally flooded about mid-morning. With the long poles pushing, the deep-drafted and heavily laden galleon finally floated free.

As soon as the vessel safely cleared the shoal with the incoming tide, the fleet continued its northward journey.

We reached the latitude of *Los Mimbres* where the great *almiranta* was lost almost seven months earlier. All the passengers and most of the crew gathered in the ship's forecastle for a special mass celebration. Everyone aboard our ship somberly reflected upon the horrendous tragedy to the hundreds of friends and countrymen who suffered their dreadful deaths by drowning.

Most of the fortunate forty-five who were rescued along with me swore they would never put to sea again. Those of us who were determined to reach our homeland had no other choice. We prayed constantly for a safe journey.

Though as in answer to our prayers the weather cooperated. For several weeks we enjoyed the wind abaft our beam.

Just past the isles of Bermuda, at a latitude of about thirty-nine degrees, the chief pilot ordered an easterly heading. We experienced several days of rain squalls accompanied by gusts of strong wind. Thankfully, there were no hurricanes.

Several of our captains cornered a Portuguese ship loaded with hides and 1,500 sacks of wheat off Terceira in the Azores. It was a small coastal vessel with only a few crew.

The Spanish sea captains were told that English ships, under command of General Robert Blake, were patrolling off the Andalusian coast of Spain. There was justification for considerable concern as to the whereabouts of the enemy, especially with the arrival of treasure fleets approaching Spain's coast.

Marcus del Puerto questioned the captain of the Portuguese vessel about the location of the English ships. He was informed, "The Spaniards beat them off the coast a month ago."

Their fears of impending danger allayed, the treasure fleet bore up for Cádiz.

In fact, the English fleet sailed from Plymouth on March 18, 1656. They were forced to put into Torbay due to adverse winds. By April 12 they reached the Bay of Cádiz. After scouting and observing they learned to their dissatisfaction that the treasure fleet from the Indies had already arrived. Consequently, the English captains realized they may be cruising offshore for many monotonous and weary months while waiting for the next returning *plata flota*.

Their friendly alliance with Portugal provided the English with intelligence opportunities and information as to the movement of the Spanish fleet. The Portuguese connection also gave them access to convenient sheltered harbors, fresh water and limited provisioning at Lisbon and Lagos. One of the logistical nightmares for Generals Blake and Mountagu (Montague) was the victualling of their large fleet. Supply ships bringing provisions from England were not on regular schedules. Bad food led to bad morale. Furthermore, the navy seemed to struggle constantly with the government for operating funds. Because of slow pay many purveyors were reluctant to release supplies.

Throughout the summer of 1656, English squadrons harassed Spanish ports and shipping. They fired on and destroyed several vessels at Vigo Bay and Redondela. They attacked and burned Spanish shipping in the Mediterranean around Málaga. When there was nothing else for them to do, they stopped and searched independent merchantmen who were trading with Spain.

By mid-August 1656, General Robert Blake left Captain Richard Stayner in charge of eight frigates, ordering him to cruise offshore Cádiz. The general then headed to Portugal. His counterpart, General Edward Mountagu, sailed to Asilah under orders from Lord Protector Oliver Cromwell. His assignment was to endeavor negotiating a treaty with the Barbary States to eliminate or reduce the raiding and pillaging against English shipping.

On September 18, the inbound Spanish fleet sighted Mount Higo. They sailed within sight of the coast the entire afternoon, passing Ayamonte, Huelva and Arenas Gordas. At sunset they sighted the convent of Our Lady of Regla. The *capitana* fired a salute to the Virgin with three pieces of artillery. The other ships did likewise.

Just before darkness the *flota* saw lamps flickering from Sanlúcar de Barrameda. The *patache* was ordered to gather all letters, reports and official documents for His Majesty. They intended to be first to reach port in the morning, bringing advance news of the arriving squadron.

Marcus del Puerto wrote a lengthy dispatch to King Philip IV, summarizing his voyage and all the events requiring his attention, at sea as well as in port. He even mentioned what he did in the River Cinu when he was sent there to rescue a galleon under construction. Concern spread over the possibility the English fleet might destroy it. He actually confided his feelings in the letter, "If the nearby English ship found and engaged us there, my crew would probably have jumped ship and swam to shore, rather than fight."

He provided an accounting of the cargo of royal treasure his fleet carried. It included 857 bars of silver from the original 1,010. Of these, 352 were aboard his *capitana*; 322 were officially registered to the *almiranta*; 183 were on board the galleon of Juan de Hoyos. He also reported 840,642 pesos, "separate from the king's million."

Marcus del Puerto was blunt concerning other issues in his memorandum to the king. He requested generosity in paying his officers and men. "Since they have been at sea for a very long time, the other ship captains have performed well and should be rewarded, as should the master pilot of the fleet, Gaspar de Tendilla. I shall send a detailed report as soon as I drop anchor in Cádiz."

Darkness enveloped the returning galleons when six sails were sighted in the distance toward the Southeast. The Spaniards assumed they were local fishing vessels trawling along the coast.

The *capitana* hove to, putting its prow toward the sea with slight sail up. Marcus del Puerto lit his sterncastle lanterns. The other ships followed suit, also lighting theirs.

Juan de Noriega, pilot of the *Jesus, Maria y Josef*, stood on deck and murmured, "What's the chief pilot doing? Is he navigating in twenty *brazas* (fathoms) in order to find himself in the morning at port? Or does he plan to enter Cádiz in the darkness of tonight?"

The Spaniards began their tack toward Cádiz before sunup on September 19. They were only three or four leagues offshore their final destination, their long voyage nearly ended. The westerly wind came around during the night, now blowing from the northeast.

When dawn broke, they sighted the six sails drawing nearer. Were these the friendly fishermen seen the evening before? Were they here to escort the returning heroes and their treasure into Cádiz? Perhaps they had been alerted by the cannonade salute the previous evening.

As daylight improved visibility, tensions began to mount. The approaching ships carried too much sail to be coastal fishermen. Suddenly it was too late to escape. The "fishing vessels," seemingly small to the bulky and heavily laden galleons, were identified as sleek, fast and heavily armed English warships.

In one awakening moment it became clear these were enemy ships. One of the frigates to seaward attacked the *urca* of Juan de la Torre, lagging behind about one league to leeward. With the help of another frigate, the attackers fired close charges of artillery. They then boarded her, and with great force quickly overwhelmed the ship. Juan de la Torre struck his colors, surrendering, and was taken in tow.

HMS Tredagh of Captain John Harman, boasting a powerful armament of fifty-six guns, had captured the unsuspecting *Profeta Elías*. This first incident marked the beginning of a day of sorrowful events for the ships of Spain.

It was about seven in the morning when four of the swift frigates came in from the east. Under full sail, they moved to gain the windward side of the *capitana*, the *almiranta* and the two galleons, now sailing in a star formation. The *capitana* in the lead, Juan de Hoyos' galleon was to the leeward. Calderón's galleon followed the *capitana* while the *almiranta* sailed behind Juan de Hoyos, perhaps a cannonshot away. The *urca* of Joseph de Paredes and the aviso from New Spain (José de Pimienta), along with the captured Portuguese prize, all faster vessels, stood inshore toward the Santi Petri River.

There was obvious consternation amidst those onboard the *capitana* of Marcus del Puerto. Should he stay and fight? Or should he run for Cádiz to save the portion of the king's treasure he carried? Being in the lead and under full sail, he had a clear edge on the English.

Calderón suddenly realized what was happening. Having received the first major bombardment, he returned fire. As he observed the English men-of-war move to cut off the *capitana*'s course, he made a monumental decision.

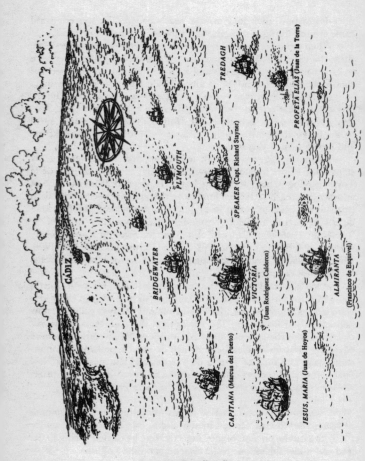

A Surprise off Cadiz

The Spanish ships were sailing in a star formation, the *capitana* in front, Juan de Hoyos to leeward, Calderón following the *capitana*, and the *almiranta* behind Juan de Hoyos, perhaps a cannon shot away.

"Left rudder and prepare to engage," he commanded. "Shift all sails to come about! Fire as you will and let them have a taste of the might of Spain! We must save the *capitana*. Then we must save ourselves!"

The English warship endeavored to cut off the homeward route of the *capitana*. But Calderón successfully maneuvered to intercept and engage the fast-approaching man-of-war, blocking its advance toward the *capitana*.

He steered directly for the Englishman, about three cable lengths away. Sailing on a reach that put him directly in front of the onrushing frigate, his bold action caught the English off guard. As the two vessels raced toward each other, a collision appeared imminent. At the very last instant the English frigate swerved to port. Both vessels raked each other with ferocious broadsides at point blank range. Masts splintered and spars cracked. Men screamed out in pain.

Hoping to prevent the warship from maneuvering, Calderón luffed up in an attempt to make his turn and come back along the Englishman's lee. For a few long moments the galleon was temporarily becalmed. Soldiers began firing muskets and small arms while gunners concentrated on cleaning and reloading the heavier artillery.

Calderón's galleon soon found wind again. Its sails filled and tightened as it came around to starboard, for another round with the sleek frigate. The English ship also turned. It held its position, ready for round two of the fight. Both vessels unhesitatingly approached one another on opposite tacks.

The two combatants were separated by only a hundred yards. Calderón steadied his gunners for another broadside, all the while shouting encouragement. Suddenly a thunderous blast hit his ship from astern. Another English warship bore down on him from the rear. The main topsail came down in a shattering crash. A number of his officers lay injured—or dead on the quarter-deck. Still he persevered. He pounded the first Englishman with another broadside as the two moving targets nearly collided.

The Spaniard realized his predicament. As the smoke cleared, Juan Rodriguez Calderón surveyed the damage to his ship and to his men. The galleon's rigging was torn apart, the sails now in tatters. There was much confusion on deck amidst the bodies lying about.

The English ships approached again. Calderón tried desperately to regroup the few uninjured souls remaining.

A witness later testified, "The actions of Captain Calderón were heroic and made it possible for the *capitana* to escape."

Finally one of the English ships cornered Calderón's galleon. Another frigate took a position immediately behind it. They continued firing at nearly point blank range.

Juan Rodriguez Calderón fought on all sides and with great effort, but to no avail. The English managed to come alongside the despairing vessel. An English party attempted to board the galleon at its forecastle, but were repulsed with swords, shields and pikes. The big frigate was forced to swerve aside and disengage.

The warship soon returned, its crew arranged along the starboard side with small arms to assault Calderón once again. The Spaniard realized the severity of his plight. Out of 122 soldiers originally on board, only thirty-one were now able to fight.

Calderón, determined to use every opportunity he saw, made one more gallant decision. As the English came alongside for a second try at boarding, Captain Calderón set his vessel on fire. He then ordered his boatswain below deck with heavy sledges and crowbars. They opened a wide gap between the seams below the ship's waterline enabling the galleon to sink quickly.

As the fire aboard the galleon intensified, Calderón and several others saved themselves by jumping aboard the English frigate just as it was drawing away. Those remaining threw themselves into the water to face their death by drowning, or be picked up by English longboats.

Calderón was taken prisoner, but later released in Portugal. In the official inquiry of the highest court representing the King of Spain, Juan Rodriguez Calderón received a commendation for valor.

Jeronimo de Barrionuevo spoke for Captain Calderón. "A very valiant man of thirty-six years. Hearty, robust, dark, tall and well-proportioned with broad shoulders. I have personally spoken with him. He described his actions in the calamity with total modesty. His gallantry stands out gloriously among thousands of men."

All spoke well of Juan Calderón. His ship sank before the English could steal anything.

The name Calderón is widely spread throughout Spain. Its origin can be traced back to Fortún Ortiz Calderón, private secretary of the Lord of Biscay, a "rich man of Castile."

The cargo on Calderón's ship, the *Nuestra Señora de la Victoria*, is stated to have been 600,000 pieces-of-eight *reales*. Several reported there was much more than this on board.

By nine o'clock, the Spanish raised all possible sail. Their port of Cádiz was in sight.

Several of the English squadron found themselves too far leeward to take part in the initial engagement. Now, *HMS Speaker*, a second-rate ship of the line carrying sixty-four guns and skippered by Captain Richard Stayner, moved in for the kill. He was accompanied by the *Plymouth* with fifty-four guns, the *Bridgewater* with fifty-two cannon, and the sixty-gun *Diamond*, captained by Gilbert Gott.

According to the testimony of Juan Noriega, pilot of the *Jesus, Maria y Josef*, the English sails were identified when they were three leagues from Cádiz. "We were sailing on a course in a line northeasterly to southwesterly with the holy church of the said city."

As the *almiranta* fought the enemy she continued her course toward Cádiz. Six hours of intense battle ensued. By midday, just as the English prepared to board the *almiranta*, Admiral Esquivel set her on fire. The wind freshening, the flames quickly consumed rigging and sails.

One of the English warships had come alongside the galleon with intent to board. It was an effort alone for the English to free themselves and disengage their vessel from the burning inferno. Suddenly, red hot flames reached the powder room of the galleon. A terrific blast shot out, horrifying fishermen and spectators witnessing from the shores around Cádiz.

Antonio de Quintana relived the traumatic experience in his testimony. "The first large English frigate reached the ship upon which this witness sailed. We fired a great artillery charge at the vessel. They fended off with a huge charge of their own, remaining a bit astern of us. Soon another three English ships came as reinforcements. The *almiranta* defended herself against all of these, firing many times, fighting and resisting with great valor. The English had more than fifty guns per ship. There was fire and smoke and destruction everywhere. Still, the *almiranta* resisted."

At the first sign of trouble, the Marqués de Baides immediately volunteered to assist in the defense of the *almiranta*. He appeared from his cabin carrying a wide sword and wearing his shield. By his side was his oldest son, Francisco Lopez de Zúñiga, carrying a smaller

sword and shield. The son was ordered to the port side of the ship to
assist the infantry. The marqués took a position on the starboard side.

Captain Antonio de Quintana appeared to be everywhere at
once. He fired artillery on one side, then was seen loading guns on
the other. "It was necessary for him to move with such dexterity because he did not have the necessary people to adequately manage each
piece of artillery," said one witness. Quintana made certain the artillery was perfectly positioned. He shouted encouragement to each
gunner, complimenting their marksmanship and patting them on the
back. Then he went on to the next battery.

After more than six hours of desperate battle, the main topsail of
the *almiranta*, including all its rigging, came down in a smoking
nightmare. More than 100 men lay dead on the decks. Counting even
the wounded, only a few dozen were still standing. Forty of the approximate one hundred ninety people on board survived. Most of
them suffered wounds.

There was little powder and no fuses remaining. The vessel was
badly blasted from the artillery fire. The rigging was shattered and
useless.

Admiral Francisco de Esquivel realized the great strength of firepower the enemy possessed versus the minute amount remaining in his
favor. Since most of his people were dead or wounded and he was unable to manage his vessel, he ordered his men to ease up. He called to
his sergeant at arms to beckon the closest English ship to come alongside. His hope was to take at least one of the enemy down with him.

The English frigate slid next to the faltering galleon. Her sailors
lined the rail in preparation of boarding. Francisco de Esquivel went
below deck, to the poop. He personally set his ship ablaze with powder cartridges.

The *almiranta* immediately began to burn intensely. The English, realizing they were tricked, became alarmed lest they be trapped
and burned alive in the blaze.

The wind freshened and the fire leaped up the main mast. As the
topsail came crashing down, some Englishmen who were climbing
aboard the *almiranta* were crushed. They burned along with many
Spanish sailors.

Because the master of his vessel and his pilot were both dead,
Esquivel placed his infantry commander, Antonio de Quintana, in
charge of plans to abandon ship.

Quintana immediately began assisting the wounded, helping them off the burning vessel. He also dumped all the water buckets overboard so the English were unable to extinguish the flames.

The few people who remained alive aboard the ship threw themselves into the sea. Admiral Esquivel, his face and arms badly burned, jumped into the water.

The *almiranta* and everything she carried burned fiercely. The enemy was unable to get any of the treasure. In fact, the English frigate barely managed to cut herself free before the galleon exploded.

Quintana was one of the last to leave the ship. He made his way to the prow, preparing to jump into the water, when he noticed a terrified black woman, holding an infant in her arms. The baby was the year-old son of the marqués. He took the youngster from her, and holding him tightly in his arms, leaped into the sea. Quintana swam toward an English longboat where he and the baby were helped aboard. From there he witnessed as the baby's governess jumped from the burning galleon. However, he did not see her surface.

Then he spotted Francisco de Esquivel, wounded and near drowning as he clung to a line trailing from the galleon. Quintana excitedly explained to the English seamen that this was the admiral. They rescued Esquivel, but only after his insistence and forfeit of the cherished gold reliquary he wore around his neck. The action-thinking and performance of Admiral Francisco de Esquivel during the entire ordeal were incredibly heroic. His courage served to motivate everyone on board the galleon.

In his report to Generals Blake and Mountagu dated September 24, 1656, Captain Stayner described the sinking of Esquivel's *almiranta*.

"The *Bridgewater* had trouble clearing herself of the burning ship. She was board by board with her. She was their Vice-Admiral, having in her some store of plate. The enemy, seeing themselves unable to hold out, fired their ship themselves. Most of their lives were lost, as were some of our men who were on board."

September 19, 1656

I cannot say enough about this man, Quintana. I owe him my life. He was a hardworking and loyal soldier. He was a gentleman of courage. He was the only son of Antonio de Quintana Talledo and Maria de Sopeña Somano. The house of Quintana originated in the Valle de Ontón, in the province of Santander in the north of Spain.

I was moving between decks hearing confessions of the wounded when I encountered a seaman who was hit by a musket shot. As I held his hand, a cannon ball passed by, splitting him in half. His intestines spilled on my legs and feet.

A short while later, more English ships closed in, bombarding us unmercifully. The cruel battle intensified. A wounded soldier called for me. He put his lips to my ear to offer his confession. Before I could understand what he was trying to say, an enemy shot hit him. His head was completely severed. The headless body leaned against me, blood spurting from its neck onto my face.

Another young man, this one from Cartagena, was as brave as anyone on board. He cursed with each and every breath. Fighting valiantly, he branded the English as enemies of Jesus Christ. Swearing at those preparing to board, he dared them to meet his sword. His courage (and curses) rallied our men until his last moment. He was shot in the head, then fell to his death.

Below decks the situation was equally bad. Horror, confusion, blood and smoke billowed all around. Those still alive believed they must surely be in hell. Desperation, pain and suffering prevailed. Mariners, their arms and legs severed, dragged themselves to the water buckets. The slippery stream of blood and bodies of the dead and wounded laying virtually on top of one another made it difficult to move about the ship.

The burning smoke choked our lungs while the stench of death was suffocating. Voices straining to be heard above the sounds of battle seemed alien and unearthly to the ears of this simple priest.

"They are attempting to board on the port side! Repel them!"

"Damnation! We've lost our rudder and topsail!"

"Water! Help me! I'm on fire!"

The moaning and screaming was like a nightmare breaking our hearts and tearing our spirits. Those of us still alive were worse than the dead. No one can possibly know the trauma of this unless they personally experience it.

In the thick of all this, my thoughts turned to Francisco de Esquivel, Knight of Santiago, like his father and older brother, Diego. Originally from Vitoria in the province of Alava, in the northeastern Basque country of Spain, he previously served as a captain of infantry in Cuba and in Cartagena. He conducted himself as only a true and noble knight could. Throughout the grim melee, his words and actions countered his youthful thirty-five years. Fear encompassed and paralyzed all who were caught in the middle of this battle, including, admittedly, myself. But Esquivel did not quiver for even one second. I observed as he shouted numerous and precise orders. He moved about the smoking inferno of our ship as deliberately as if it was his required daily exercise. There was a soldierly quality about him evoking previously concealed martial spirits, as though it was a part of his nature. His fortitude and stamina encouraged and motivated everyone.

The young admiral took it upon himself to set fire to the king's *almiranta*. Before going below to the gunpowder room, he ordered everyone who was ambulatory to abandon ship by whatever means possible. The waist of the galleon was a madhouse of confused people. They ran, pushed and stomped over the dead and wounded bodies in a frantic effort to find an escape route. The options were to jump into the sea where uncertain fate waited, or remain on deck, the latter an invitation to certain death.

After Admiral Esquivel set the ship on fire, the ashen-faced marqués came to me for confession. When he finished, he asked me to kindly console his wife and children who were in their cabin below the quarter deck. I hurriedly ran to them to do so. When I returned to the main deck, I found the ship burning fiercely. Some English already had boarded with weapons and were attempting to break open any chests and boxes in sight in their desperate search for treasure. Those of us still physically able were jumping into the water amidst four or five English launches moving about.

One of the smaller boats approached our bow. I tried to throw myself into it but missed, splashing into the sea instead. Unable to swim, I grabbed desperately for the gunwale of the launch, whereupon I was promptly whacked on the back of the head with an oar.

I lost consciousness for a brief moment and began to sink. I recall swallowing a lot of water, the salt burning my throat and nostrils. I agonized over my imminent death as I continued thrashing the water. Suddenly one of my hands grasped something.

It was the foot of Admiral Esquivel. He was clinging to a line hanging from the stern of our galleon. Submerged in water up to his neck, his face was burned and he suffered a bad head wound.

God then appeared in the form of the gallant Captain Quintana. He extended an oar from his launch to his admiral and to me. Because of our wounds and weakness, getting into the boat was difficult. Quintana extended only one hand, his other arm tightly clutching the infant son of the marqués. He was also wounded, a musket shot in his back. Finally an English seaman, cursing and swearing, grabbed me by my tunic and pulled me into the boat. He also saved Don Francisco de Esquivel.

The reality of it all hit me only after I was safely in the launch. I put my hand on my stomach, leaned over the side and vomited.

The marqués' two daughters, also in my boat, came to me directly. They cried bitterly. I realized I could not think of only myself.

I huddled as close to them as possible in the crowded boat. Leaning forward and stretching my arms toward both girls, I clasped their hands. Those desperate sobs, coupled with my own fears, made me choke and tremble.

When our longboat reached the English frigate, ten sailors from the heretic mob met us as we were ushered aboard near one of the stern chasers. Like wolves they attacked us. They tore the jewelry the girls wore from their bodies. With no morality or concern, they put their hands on the young girls' breasts, and grabbed their buttocks.

Then they turned on me. I was sopping wet. My mouth and nostrils burned from the salt water ingested. I trembled from an equal mixture of fear of my destiny and discomfort from my condition. My dripping clothes stuck tightly to my skin. In their search for jewelry or other valuables I might be carrying, they ripped my clothes completely. They stripped me with such fury I felt dismembered. Having them ravage my body was like being skinned alive. They left me totally naked, with only the flesh I had when I entered this world.

They went about bullying me. I was very embarrassed about being naked in front of all those people. The youngest daughter of the marqués, Catalina, removed her slip and threw it over my nakedness. An English sailor then approached. He hit and kicked me repeatedly. Throwing me down, he pulled the slip from me, leaving me naked once again. We were then taken to a chamber.

At the same time the *almiranta* exploded, Juan de Hoyos was engaged in the battle of his life. His *Jesus, Maria y Josef* was being pummeled by English ships on both sides. Even with the heavy barrage of cannon fire, Juan de Hoyos continued flying full sail for Cádiz. The English pursued like hound dogs who trapped but could not stop a tired rabbit.

Sergeant of Artillery Juan Gomez Valdes swore under oath: "As the ship sailed under full sail to the windward of all the other Spanish ships, Juan de Noriega, first pilot of the vessel, leaned over the port side of the poop deck. He told Don Juan de Hoyos it was dishonorable to enter the port in flight with the *almiranta* burning and still engaged with two enemy ships.

"At this point an argument broke out between the pilot and Matías Moreno, the ship's guardian. They insisted they should pursue their course, the same as the capitana. If they did so, they would succeed in saving the silver. The pilot responded they would never be able to reach San Sebastián de Cádiz. Rather, they should stay and fight in an attempt to help the *almiranta*. After hearing this, Don Juan de Hoyos told the guardian to stay out of it and ordered him back to his station. Turning to the pilot he said, 'The *almiranta* is fighting and we shall assist her!'

"This witness then heard the pilot command, 'Strike those sails robbing the captain of his reputation.'"

The instant the English realized the galleon of Juan de Hoyos was slowing, they moved quickly. The first broadside killed the chief boatswain and many of the Spanish gunners. The second blast badly injured Diego de Villalba, the chief of artillery. Bleeding from a fragment in his back, but with sword in hand, he shouted, "Let us fight for God and king, and we shall die with honor!"

Another broadside of English cannonade knocked down a mizzen boom striking Don Diego in the head. He fell senseless on the main deck, not even able to squeeze the hand of a Franciscan friar who ministered to him.

The English surrounded the galleon. They continued to fire both cannon and musketry. Each volley saw a number of Spaniards fall. Those of the crew still on their feet were totally disorganized.

Juan de Hoyos' galleon, the largest ship of the fleet, had many passengers on board who begged him to surrender. Their concern was to save themselves, even if it meant losing their own as well as the king's treasure.

The clamor for surrender reached its peak right after Juan de Hoyos was struck. Hit in the face and chest by cannon ball fragments, his jaw was broken and several teeth were knocked out. He was taken below for medical attention, but soon reappeared on deck. Shortly thereafter he was shot in the left shoulder, over his heart.

"Quarter, Quarter," yelled the passengers. A white tablecloth was then hoisted.

Three English longboats came alongside and boarded her. Some Englishmen even came swimming! Once the ship surrendered, more than sixty sailors, cabin boys and pages came out of the boatswain's locker where they were hiding.

The English began searching the ship. They even took the red cape from the captain's body he wore for warmth after being treated for his injuries. He was helped from the galleon by his English captors. Many believed his wound was fatal.

At inquiries held later, many witnesses condemned the decision to drop the sails. They swore under oath the galleon could have followed the course of the *capitana* and pressed on into Cádiz. But once the vessel stopped it was doomed. There was no escape. The galleon's ability to fight was questionable.

"Some witnesses say the galleon carried many chests, boxes of sugar and other cargo among the guns on the gun deck. During the fight only seven cannon were free and operable on the starboard side because of the congestion packed on and around them. Swill for the herd of pigs aboard was stacked between the guns on the port side, making most of them inoperable."

There are many documents questioning the degree of resistance of Juan de Hoyos. Some say he fought a long while before surrendering. Others say he fired only three shots before he dropped the flag of Spain and replaced it with the white table cloth of surrender. Could he have beached the *Jesus, Maria y Josef* on the shores of Cádiz? Whether the huge cargo of treasure could have been saved will never be known.

During the battle, the Spanish on shore at San Sebastián sent out twenty longboats with oars and 1,000 armed men. The wind velocity soon increased. Once they reached a mile offshore, many of the boats took on water from the choppy seas and were swamped. Other than firing a few pot shots, the small galleys were no match against the large frigates.

The *Rosario* of José de Paredes escaped, but later grounded in the Santi Petri River. José de Pimienta didn't even attempt to make port. He chose to beach his vessel on the shore near Cádiz. The *capitana* of Marcus del Puerto, after picking up a few survivors from Juan Calderón's galleon, and seeing the *almiranta* on fire, quit the battle and raced for Cádiz. She safely landed 352 silver bars, chests of pieces-of-eight and gold *escudos*. Eight of her crew were killed in the vessel's brief exchange of fire with the English.

"Marcus del Puerto initially turned to help the *almiranta*. Realizing the ship was on fire, the *capitana* turned again and continued to Cádiz," one survivor later told a court of inquiry.

A contemporary writer stated, "Spain recognizes a total loss of 14,300,000 pesos of eight *reales* of silver and 272 pieces of artillery for the king. Fourteen hundred men are also dead.

"The lost battle disarmed the people of Cartagena at a most unfortunate time. Many of the infantry aboard were soldiers assigned to the fortress there. This should have been prevented. The tragedy provided the English with 4,000,000 pesos, two ships, fifty-four pieces of artillery and the reputation of having taken all of this within view of the homes of Cádiz."

Of all of the lost treasure and personal saga, the tragedy experienced by the family of the Marqués de Baides is one history should remember. The entire family and all of their worldly possessions were on the *almiranta*. The marqués, his wife and one of his daughters died when the galleon exploded and sank. The oldest son, Don Francisco Lopez, sixteen years old, his younger brother, Don José Zuñiga and sisters, Doña Josepha and Catalina, and the year-old son were saved. The boys were imprisoned for a while by the English.

"Amongst the survivors was a boy of sixteen. A most pregnant, ingenious and learned youth," said Admiral Mountagu.[52] "His is the saddest tale I have heard or read in my remembrance. He was the eldest son of the Marqués de Baides, Governor of Peru (actually Chile). He embarked upon the galleon with all the fortune he gained in the colonies. The whole of his family was on the ship. In the fire, the marqués' lady and one of the daughters fell down in a swoon and were burned. The marqués had opportunity to save himself, but seeing his wife and daughter, whom he loved exceedingly, said he would die where they died. Embracing his lady he was burned with them."

The English account of how the marqués died differs radically from Padre Diego's:

September 19, 1656

After regurgitating all the water I swallowed, I turned to look at the galleon. From the launch I could clearly see the marqués and his wife nearly engulfed in flames. They were waving their arms and begging for help. The more they yelled, the more we cried for them. Finally, with their clothes ablaze, they jumped from the ship. The English coxswain refused to bring our boat closer to them. However, another English boat approached. We watched in horror as a sailor rammed a lance through the heart of the pleading marqués.

Two of his daughters were in my boat. Josepha, eighteen years old, and Catalina, age nine. They sobbed bitterly as they watched the execution of their parents. The more they cried, the more my own pain and compassion grew. Neither child imagined this awful day would be the last in their parents' lives.

The body of the marqués gently washed ashore at San Sebastián a day after the battle. He was badly burned, one leg was broken and a gaping hole showed through his chest where it was pierced by the lance. The Capuchin fathers picked him up tenderly from where he came to rest among the coarse, khaki sand and rocks on the beach of Cádiz. They buried him without pomp because the body was too mangled to be placed inside the church. However, a memorial service was provided in his name. The Count of Molina[53] provided the service after his burial and the entire city attended. The marquesa was buried at Rota. This lady deserves to live in God's eternity because of her many virtues.

Don Francisco Lopez de Zúñiga, the Marqués de Baides, Count of Pedrosa, Knight of Santiago and Lord of nine small towns of Tobar, was dead less than a month after his fifty-seventh birthday. Having leaped from the flaming galleon into the sea, his loving wife in his arms, he was killed by the passionate thrust of an English lance.

After he had served sixteen years as Grand Master of the Camp in the wars of Flanders and Germany, King Philip named him Governor and Captain General of Chile, succeeding Don Francisco Laso de la Vega.

"Many Indians and Spanish were freed from bondage with his aid, and great were the acts of kindness he did for them. He was feared by his enemies and loved by his friends. He was generous in giving to them, from funds of the Royal Treasury as well as his own money. With the citizens he was favored. To the soldiers he was affable. For God he was devout. The Marqués de Baides, and equally his wife, set a fine example for everyone during their lifetimes," one contemporary biographer stated.

His oldest son, Francisco, became the sixth Marqués de Baides upon the death of his father. Francisco's younger brother, José, entered a religious order and was sent as a missionary to Chile. He pursued his theological purpose with an apostolic fervor.

"The great valor of the marqués and his son, Esquivel, as well as Quintana will forever be an honor and glory to the Spanish nation," Jeronimo de Barrionuevo later stated.

9

To the Victors Go the Spoils

The silver was loaded on eight and thirty carts, then conveyed to the Tower of London amid ringing of bells and firing of cannon.

September 20, 1656

The marqués' daughters and I were taken to a strange, dark cabin aboard the English warship and locked inside. Captain Quintana, bleeding badly from his wounds, was taken to their surgeon. The girls cried so hard I was unable to console them. My nudity probably concerned me more than it did the girls, but the culminating shock of the entire calamity absorbed us all.

The oldest, Josepha, wailed openly to her small brother who was cradled in her arms. "Where are your parents who love you so much? Where are they?" She screamed and moaned, "They are dead! They are dead!"

"Where is the nanny who nurses you? Where is she? How can I possibly care for you? How will I ever bring you up?" She lamented.

"It is not enough what I have been through already? Now I must watch you, poor baby, die of hunger. It would have been better for us to have perished on the *almiranta* than to end up like this!"

Her emotions, so sincere and delicate, left the younger sister and me touched to silence. The three of us were sitting there sobbing and alone with our feelings when the door flung open. We were amazed and delighted to see the baby's nanny. She was dripping wet, and like me, totally nude. The baby unhesitatingly threw himself into her arms, cooing and warbling his joy at seeing her again.

She explained how she took off her clothes to jump into the sea when the fire became intense. She managed to swim to the galleon's mainmast, shot loose and floating nearby. Two Spanish seamen pulled her onto the long timber. Soon afterward an English dinghy picked them up.

I was told the English have no tolerance for priests and might just as soon cut their throats as look at them. I was very nervous when any of them came close or, heaven forbid, summoned me. But this was exactly what happened next.

Without even a knock on the door, they burst into our quarters. Squeezing my neck, they forced me to walk in front of them, slapping me as if I were some pig being herded into the slaughter pen. I was certain the enemy's intent was to kill me. With prods, shoves and curses they ushered me into a spacious cabin.

A table in the center of the room displayed numerous weapons of death. I saw scimitars and swords, machetes and knives. Standing ever so erect by the side of the table was a soldier twirling a hatchet. I knew this was the place of my execution when I noticed the hatchetman wiping the blade with his shirttails.

Casting my eyes to heaven, I begged mercy from the Lord, offering Him my death in satisfaction of my sins at the same time. All of this was very difficult and uncomfortable as I was still naked. The Englishmen stared at me, mocking my vulnerability. Suddenly they grabbed me and shoved me down a passageway into the blinding sunlight on the main deck. I was certain they would detach my head from my body.

"Sit here!" They ordered. I obeyed, continuously repeating Acts of Contrition, for I sincerely believed I was upon the time of my execution.

I squatted nude near the forecastle for a period seeming to last several hours. I felt much like a freak being displayed to amuse and entertain the onlookers. In the midst of this vessel of heathens, you can imagine my amazement when one of the men approached me and introduced himself as the chaplain of the frigate. Speaking partly in Spanish and partly in Latin, he presented me with some simple clothing. I expressed my sincere gratitude to him. The young minister was only twenty-six years of age, but extremely intelligent and alert. He was most interested in conversing about my religion. He asked numerous questions about our words of absolution. I twice repeated our Catholic sacrament of penance to him.

We sat on a cannon and talked under a faint light from a distant lantern until well after midnight. I reminded him I had not eaten for thirty hours. He left, but soon returned from the ship's galley with a hard biscuit, a piece of cheese and a wooden jug filled with water and vinegar. I devoured the food, then rested my head against the gun carriage and slept the entire night.

We met and spoke several times during the following days. I actually participated in one of his Protestant prayer services, but few of the crew showed interest or paid the least attention.

I carefully observed other behavior of the English crew. While my profession is far from being a soldier or seaman, I watched the English military men carry out their shipboard duties with an unrecognized discipline. As a warship, the frigate showed absolutely no clutter of goods or bulky merchandise stored anywhere on deck. Their artillery was clear of any nearby obstacles possibly restricting the operational movement of gun carriages and tackle. The gunners appeared highly experienced. Batteries were well manned and self-sufficient, able to operate without close supervision. They used refined powder and stocked huge stores of all types and sizes of cannon balls and musket shot. In comparison, our *almiranta* included only a few officers who were well enough versed to handle the heavy guns. Although our men fought valiantly, it was obvious they were no match against these professional warriors.

I soon learned we were to be put ashore at Lagos, Portugal.

September 27, 1656
Lagos, Portugal

I sent a message[54] to Count de Baldo Reis, Governor of Lagos and the Kingdom of Algarve, asking him to mediate an immediate release of the wounded and the women, especially the Baides girls. The governor expediently came to our aid. There was, however, an undue and unnecessary delay on the part of our captors in releasing us. The English apparently intended to hold some of our key officials for ransom. After two days of forced waiting on the crowded frigate, the Governor of Lagos angrily sent word to the English captain. He threatened to cut off all fresh water and other important victualling supplies. He even stated that, if necessary, he was prepared to go to war against England if they delayed our release any longer. Within a short time the count's personal launch appeared alongside, manned by eight oarsmen, two captains and several soldiers. They assisted on board the Baides girls, the nanny and infant, Miguelico, Captain Quintana and myself. The eight days we were held captive were the longest of my life.

The beach at Lagos, Portugal, was crowded with onlookers when we were transferred to shore. I was as naked as the day I was born when the English shoved me from the boat. Many others were stripped of their clothing also. This insolent lack of compassion displayed by the English sailors brought sympathetic condolences from the local Portuguese people who cursed not only the heathen sailors, but also their own Portuguese government for allowing the English to operate in their country.

The ill-feeling of the Portuguese against the English was further confirmed the same afternoon when English officers came ashore to purchase local bread and wine. The merchants refused to sell to them. The Portuguese were more than happy to feed us, however. I begged a tunic from a nearby monastery. The same abbey became a haven for many of our wounded.

We were taken to the home of a fine gentleman of Lagos, Don Pantaleón Diaz de Acosta. We were graciously received by his wife, who presented both Josepha and Catalina Baides with black mourning dresses. This was a most considerate gesture of compassion and friendship. Their home also provided a perfect place of temporary residence for the girls as the Acostas had two daughters of similar ages.

Almost everyone in Lagos was required to house some of our dislocated people since their hospital facilities were unable to handle the many wounded and sick. Don Nuño de Mendoza, the eldest son of the governor, recommended every citizen take a sick Castilian into his home. "Spare no expense. Do whatever is necessary to heal and succor the ill and unfortunate neighbors of Portugal," he stated.

Reporting later from Madrid, Jeronimo de Barrionuevo noted a conversation with a soldier from Juan de Hoyos' ship who had just re-

turned from Portugal. Having been released by the English at Lagos, the
soldier said, "The ship was so overloaded there was no way to use the artillery. The *plaza de armas* (center section of the galleon where the musketeers normally would have been fighting) was so full of merchandise
and crates it was impossible to even stand there."

It was also confirmed that only a few guns on the upper deck and
at the sterncastle were operable. Artillery on the gun deck (one deck
beneath the main) was enclosed by the pig pen. This was also stacked
to the overhead with cargo, including the captain's wine and liquor
supplies and many boxes of merchandise and baggage. In the midst of
this gun deck there were also many passenger privacy enclosures.

When the enemy ships were identified, a strenuous attempt was
made to free the cannon: "Although everyone exhausted themselves
in the effort, the deck was still badly cluttered. It was impossible to
work the gun carriages efficiently. The lower deck was totally overloaded with one thousand boxes of sugar, hundreds of rolls of tobacco and bundles of indigo."

Because of the numerous conflicting testimonies regarding the
cluttered decks, how many guns were available and how many cannon
were actually fired aboard the ship, more depositions were taken and
more hearings were held. The primary accusation was: "Hoyos surrendered his galleon before the English attempted to board it." Tech-
nically, this was a true statement.

To imply that the captain, a Knight of Alcantara, did not display
his "best" effort in the battle would be a misrepresentation. A musket
ball ripped off part of his lip, knocked out several teeth and broke his
left jaw. In spite of this wound he put a handkerchief in his mouth and
continued to issue orders. He encouraged everyone to fight or die for
victory. He even offered one hundred *doubloons* to any gunner who
sank an English ship or shot away a mast.

An hour later a spar shattered from a close range cannon shot.
The blast sent a large wood splinter through the left side of his chest,
breaking several ribs and opening a deep gash. He was taken below
decks to be treated by the ship's surgeon. Before leaving the bridge,
he placed Don Diego de Villalba in command. But Villalba was soon
injured as well, and left unable to command.

When Don Juan de Hoyos was told of Villalba's critical wound,
he insisted on being taken back on deck. Though weak and shaky
from the trauma and loss of blood, he leaned on the shoulder of a

corporal and, with sword in hand, shouted encouragement. By then, however, his voice was weak and his cause was lost.

He realized his situation was critical when he learned twenty-two gunners were dead and many more sailors already left the deck. As gunners began to fall, a number of fighting posts were abandoned. Sixty crew members hid in the forward rope and sail locker.

Hoyos ordered the ship be set on fire. Don Miguel de Salzedo exploded three cartridges, "but badly burned only himself," a witness later testified.

Hoyos then ordered every possible sail raised and the galleon headed for the beach at Cádiz. But there was little left of the working rigging. The sails were in tatters. Only terrified passengers and dead crewmen remained available to hoist them.

His galleon was surrounded by four enemy ships of superior fire power, one on each side, fore and aft. They continued to pummel him with shot and shell. One hundred thirty men were dead and many others wounded, or disappeared. His passengers were screaming for quarter.

Barely able to hold his head up, Hoyos did what he must. He surrendered.

A large number of Spanish naval officers, crown officials, and *hidalgos* were detained on the English ships anchored at Lagos. It was rumored they were to be taken to England to be interrogated, then ransomed for their freedom. Because of the serious wounds of Juan de Hoyos, I pleaded with the young English Protestant chaplain, the only one who had shown any compassion.

"Hoyos must be transferred to shore," I begged. "Please get him to the hospital on land before he dies in your sick bay."

It took another day before this humanitarian removal of Captain Hoyos occurred. His limp body was lowered by a rope sling to a waiting boat with four Portuguese oarsmen pulling. Upon reaching shore the men dragged the boat up on the beach. They lifted him very carefully and, gently cradling the captain in their arms, carried him to the Lagos hospital.

Two days later I was summoned by the surgeon to confess de Hoyos because he had rescued me nine months earlier on the desolate shoals of *Los Mimbres*. Upon entering the hospital, I found him in a dreadful state. He was very pale, his eyes were closed and he was unable to speak. Not only was part of his face shot away, but there was a large gaping hole over his heart. So large, in fact, one could have placed five fingers into it. When the doctor scraped the wound you could clearly see his ribs and the envelope of his stomach and heart. All of these organs were filled with pus.

I took his hand and declared his sins conceded. I felt him squeeze my palm with what little strength remained, and I said a short prayer.

Juan de Hoyos died a short time later.

Juan Guttierez y Fernandez de la Guerra Gayón y de Hoyos was knighted in the Order of Alcantara in October 1641. During the 1630's, he contracted to build several ships for the Crown. He was later forced to back out, as were others not paid by the Royal Treasury. In 1651, Hoyos sailed for *Nueva España* as master of the *nao, La Purificación de Nuestra Señora y San Juan Evangelista y San Antonio*. From 1653 to 1654, he sailed in the New Spain fleet of Don Diego de Portugal. This was prior to his association with the Marqués de Montealegre. The actual date of Juan de Hoyos' death was October 22, 1656.

Those of us who were close to Juan de Hoyos believe he lost his life because of his true love for Josepha. She was on the *almiranta* when Hoyos slowed to assist that galleon. This enabled the other trailing English frigates to catch him. His love and concern for his bride-to-be is likely the reason he received his first wound, a musket ball through his jaw.

Josepha was able to visit him for a brief moment before he closed his eyes for the last time, and took his final breath. She held his hands, her head resting on his bandaged chest as her tears ran upon him. It is said his final words to her were, "If I must die before my time, I go in comfort knowing you are alive and well, my love. My love for Spain is matched only by my love for you."

As I reflect on the last hours of Captain Hoyos, I cannot help but weep for him. He was forty-six years old when he died at the Lagos hospital. He and Josepha had so much to look forward to. He was a descendant of old and noble ancestral houses of pure and well-known blood. The son of Don Diego Perez Gayón and Doña Maria de Hoyos, Juan was one of the first knights in the family. Several of his brothers came to be knighted also. His family was from the small town of Sanctibañez in the Cabezón Valley in Asturias. Following the disaster at Cádiz, there was much controversy and speculation about the actions and battle behavior of Juan de Hoyos. Personally, I remember him as a kind and good person.

The last report written by Juan de Hoyos was found in *Contratación 5122, pliego 10*. In the letter he relates his sadness to His Majesty in having to report the loss of the *Maravillas* and Admiral Don Matías de Orellana.

"It makes me most disconsolate to have to report the untimely end of the *almiranta*, its people and treasure. I realize it is my obligation to give Your Lordship the facts. The regrettable memories accompanying this letter are all this galleon carries for the account of Your Majesty, other than the few individuals who were saved."

The defeat of the Spanish fleet in sight of its final destination was an unexpected humiliation for many of those in high positions of authority within the kingdom. Consequently, months were spent in accusations, interrogations and fault finding.

Fernando Duro, in his *Armada Española* (V. p. 24), adroitly expresses his dissatisfaction with those in the Spanish Government who continued to degrade the tragic situation.

"The painful impression in the Court of Spain made by the news of the disaster off Cádiz resulted in unjust and injurious charges and untrue accusations being made against those who suffered the most in the tragedy of battle. It was not enough for the ones who sacrificed their lives to have their honor preserved."

There was an official posthumous inquiry undertaken at the insistence of Don Francisco de Hoyos Guevin, a Knight of Alcantara and a cousin of Captain Don Juan de Hoyos. Its intent was to suppress, once and for all, any unjust criticism and to clear the family name.

A Tribute to Captain Hoyos by an Anonymous Poet of His Day

A Don Juan de Hoyos	*To Don Juan Hoyos*
enamorado de la hija	*who was in love with the daughter*
del Marqués de Baides	*of the Marqués de Baides*
En defensa de su dama	*In defense of his lady*
Don Juan de Hoyos se empeño	*Don Juan de Hoyos fought to the end.*
En su nombre tropezó	*In the name of her he fell*
Mullida estaba la cama.	*But the bed was so very soft.*
El Inglés puso la llama,	*The English had lit the flame*
El amor avivó el fuego,	*and sweet love stoked the fire.*
Hallóse en el agua ciego,	*When he found himself, blind, in the water,*
Majáronsele las alas	*The wings drenched by the waves*
Y en viendo que llueve balas	*Under a thick range of bullets*
Se dió por perdido luego	*He knew too well that all was lost.*
Por las Indias de Castilla	*For the Indies of Castile*
No daré una blanca ya	*I shall not give a blanca[55] now,*
Que el Inglés acá ni alla	*Since neither there or over here*
No deja pasar barquilla.	*Can one boat escape the English.*

De la plata es la polilla,	He is the leech of the silver,
De España la confusión,	He is the confusion of Spain,
Borrón de la religión,	The eraser of religion
Asombro del que navega	And the terror of the seaman,
Gallo que turba y que ciega	The rooster who disturbs and blinds
Hoy solamente al león.	The lion, but not for long.

I left Lagos on the first of October in company with some of the released prisoners who were returning to Spain. We headed for the small port city of Castro Marin near the mouth of the Guadiana River, the separation line of the two countries, Portugal and Spain. After the sounding of signal trumpets we were rafted to mid-river, transferred to a Spanish launch and taken to Ayamonte on the Spanish shore. Then we were escorted directly to the governor's house where we were debriefed. I proceeded to Seville the following day to seek out a long-time Baides' family servant, Pedro Gonzalez. He was sent back to Spain two years earlier to make preparations for the return of the Baides family.

Upon reaching Seville on October 6, I rushed a letter to my sponsor, Don Juan Gonzalez de Uzqueta in Madrid, informing him of my ordeals and penurious plight. While awaiting his response, I spent most of my time in prayer and in relating my adventures and the traumatic events of my journey, especially the atrocities committed by the English. I also located Pedro Gonzalez in Cuenca where he was recently married. I delivered a letter to him from the oldest daughter, Josepha. She requested he come to their aid and assist what remained of the distraught family in returning to Seville. They were to be brought to the home of their uncle, the Marqués de Baldencina.

Within several weeks, I received a letter of credit for fifty ducats from my generous protector. I also received an invitation to Madrid where I was to be presented to the Court. In the meantime, Pedro Gonzalez arrived. I assisted him in preparing a chest of clothing and acquiring a carriage for the trip to Ayamonte to receive the girls. He also took some maids to accompany the sisters and lend a helping hand to the nanny. Another servant accompanied us for cooking and to assist with other chores of transport. On November 1, I departed for Madrid by way of Andújar. The long awaited visit with my sisters was finally a reality I could anticipate.

News of the battle off Cádiz and the great victory against the Spanish reached England on Wednesday, October 1, by way of reports from Generals Blake and Mountagu, delivered by Captain Robert Storey of the frigate *Hampshire*.

Jubilant over the conquest of the two galleons and the sinking of two others, Lord Protector Cromwell organized a spectacular victory celebration. The event was endorsed by Parliament and widely circulated throughout the land. Writers and poets participated, adding their words to the occasion.

Later in the month, General Mountagu arrived in Portsmouth with the spoils of victory. He received a hero's welcome by all of England. "The silver was loaded on eight and thirty carts, then conveyed to the Tower amid ringing of bells and firing of cannon."[56]

The metals were turned over to the National Treasury. Public imagination and the lies of the government immensely inflated the value of what was taken. Three, five, even as much as nine millions of pesos were the rumored amounts.

Thurloe wrote to Cromwell: "This is much less than what we hoped for. What we have taken is, in fact, less than what we thought was taken in the beginning. There were almost 1,000,000 sterling in each of the ships. After looting, there was not more than 250,000 to 300,000 sterling left. There are some sailors who went away with 10,000 sterling. This is the universal custom of the seamen. It always happens in the heat of battle. Afterwards it's impossible to recover what was taken."[57]

The Spanish view was expressed by Fernando Duro: "Among the list of tyrannical acts of Cromwell, few can compare with the grandiose entrance into London of the carts loaded with the silver, preceded by music and flags as in a triumphal procession. This opportunity was what he purposely waited for prior to officially declaring war on Spain. This event afforded him much popularity and raised public enthusiasm for his deed."[58]

Barrionuevo, chronicler of the Court, reported to Madrid that Londoners were having huge parties and binges over the spoils seized from Don Juan de Hoyos.

He also spread the word about a tale brought back by one of the Spanish prisoners who was released in Portugal. The story said that General Blake had, on the walls of his great cabin in the stern of his flagship, a canvas painting of Cromwell seated in a regal chair. At his feet was pictured His Holiness, the Pope, who was kneeling with his crown on the ground. Cromwell's right foot was placed upon the crown, as though he rested it there. "This is a true statement from various prisoners who have thus affirmed it. From the nature of the fight, the loss of the vanquished was far greater than the gain of the victors. It was first estimated the loss of Spain amounted to nine million pieces-of-eight.

The captured silver and merchandise were said to be worth half this sum."[59]

Although Richard Stayner was in line to be knighted, the day belonged to Edward Mountagu, as is indicated by the following verse:[60]

> *Others may use the ocean as their road,*
> *Only the English make it their abode,*
> *Whose ready sails with ev'ry wind can fly,*
> *And make a cov'nant with th' inconstant sky;*
>
> *With these returns victorious Mountagu*
> *With laurels in his hand, and half of Peru.*
> *Let the brave generals divide that bough,*
> *Our great Protector hath such wreaths enough.*
>
> *Let the rich ore forthwith be melted down,*
> *And the state fix'd by making him a crown:*
> *With ermine clad, and purple, let him hold*
> *A royal sceptre, made of Spanish gold.*

While tons of silver bullion and specie was hardly "half of Peru" as the poem indicates, the treasure, and even the feat itself, lent considerable support to the views of the Admiralty commissioners in England's war with Spain.

However, the evidence shows not all the captured Spanish treasure went to the coffers of England. To the contrary, an amazing amount was schemingly and carefully misappropriated by both English and Spanish sailors.

Spanish documents placed the loss of silver and gold aboard the captured galleon of Juan de Hoyos and in the *urca* of Juan de la Torre between 4,000,000 and 6,000,000 pesos. Apparently, the English did not get to keep it all.

In a letter dated May 5, 1657, the oldest son of the Marqués de Baides told the King of Spain he was acquainted with Joseph de Leica, silvermaster aboard the galleon *Jesus, Maria y Josef*, under the command of Juan de Hoyos. Señor de Leica was taken prisoner by the English. He confided to the teenage marqués that the English did not get anywhere near the total amount of treasure aboard the captured galleon.

According to the young marqués, the silvermaster, upon his capture, began "bargaining and communicating" with the English. His primary interest was to persuade them to release some of the personal items belonging to individuals who were taken prisoner. By agreeing to grease the palms of several of his captors, he was able to smuggle off the galleon "silver, gold and jewels belonging to many persons."

The treasure was removed from the galleon on various nights in small boats navigating among the ships anchored around Lagos, the port the English sailed to after the capture. Many bars and chests of silver were whisked away. No more than 935,000 pesos fell into Cromwell's hands.

When the English generals finally got wind of the scheme there was not a trace or clue as to where the pilfered valuables were deposited.

Although an inquest was held by the English and some depositions taken, the clandestine matter was quietly quashed in typical military bureaucratic fashion, lest their superiors back in England learn about this embarrassing episode. This is also evidenced by reading between the lines of a report later dispatched by General Mountagu.

"There have been some miscarriages by our ships in taking the ships of Spain . . . General Blake and I have used the best art available to prevent embezzling. I have positioned as honest a commander as possible in the galleons. I ordered all our ships not to send any of their boats on board, nor on shore, without a special order from me."[61]

Joseph de Leica also received credit for negotiating the ultimate release of some 350 captured Spanish mariners who were put ashore at Lagos, Portugal. The amount of ransom paid for their freedom was never officially disclosed. The letter from the young marqués stated there were some who believed two-thirds of the galleon's cargo was pilfered as he described. He hoped His Majesty would justly honor the silvermaster and show him mercy.

The amount of treasure lost when the *almiranta* exploded and sank, and in the galleon of Calderón when it was fired and scuttled, probably approached a figure of at least 2,000,000 pesos, possibly as much as 4,000,000. We will never know for certain as their registers either did not survive, or were never officially recorded.

As the English rejoiced, the Spanish began their inquiries. Extensive hearings were held and numerous charges brought against Marcus del Puerto and other captains for losing the king's treasure. Testimony of survivors from every caste was tediously heard. Depositions of every conceivable sailor or eyewitness were meticulously taken.

A French passenger testified the English took 4,000,000 pesos of booty from the galleon of Juan de Hoyos. A sailor from Cartagena believed the Hoyos galleon carried at least 3,000,000. The pilot of the *Jesus, Maria y Josef* stated under oath he saw 265 bars of silver and ten chests of *reales* taken from the galleon and stored in the English ships.

Probably the most accurate assessment came from Captain Richard Stayner in a report to Admiralty.

"The ship I took, being very rich and so much torn, it was very hard for us to have saved her. I have, by the advice of the rest of the commanders, taken out as much plate as we could for the present, between 700 and 800 bars of silver. I conceive this will be about sixteen tons or thereabouts. I am credibly informed she is worth much more, but what it is we know not yet. We shall have hard work to preserve the ship. The wind being contrary, I intend to fit ourselves here (in Lagos) and also the prize so we may possibly save her. In truth, I have undergone extraordinary trouble already to preserve her, and also what is in her. We have 800 prisoners on board."[62]

Finally, at the end of all these deliberations, the Spanish *Junta* exonerated Marcus del Puerto and recommended commendations for bravery to Francisco de Esquivel of the *almiranta*, Antonio de Quintana, Artillery Officer of the *almiranta* and Juan Rodriguez Calderón, Captain of the *Nuestra Señora de la Victoria*.

Following the death of his father, the newly designated sixth Marqués de Baides remained a captive of the English fleet. They did not release him at Lagos, as they did his surviving sisters and the other prisoners. The governor of the Portuguese port of Lagos, where the Spanish prisoners were released, was related by marriage to the Marqués de Baides. He refused to allow the English to retain the daughters of the marqués and take them to London. The two sisters were released and cared for in a local home and later a nearby convent before being returned to Spain.

The newly designated marqués was an intelligent and enterprising young man. He used all of his personality and resourcefulness to entice and impress his jailers. Perhaps this is why they kept him prisoner. He was ahead of his years in intellect and in knowledge of the motives and methods of the Spanish Crown. He conversed with his captors openly and freely on many subjects. Some of the English sea captains were suspicious of him, but others were most impressed. The English also held his younger brother, José, a prisoner.

General Mountagu transported the treasure to England using the *Naseby*, *Andrew*, *Rainbow* and *Resolution*. They were thirty days arriving at Portsmouth from Portugal due to stormy seas. Two other English ships were lost off the coast of France, but they were not large vessels, so the fleet continued to their intended anchorage at Portsmouth.

England's Lord Protector, Oliver Cromwell, was notified of their arrival. After eight days, two members of Parliament and six commissioners came from London to welcome them and inventory the silver. They also brought greetings to Edward Mountagu, who was personally summoned by the Lord Protector. He was to receive a hero's reception when the cargo of treasure was brought into London.

General Mountagu personally escorted the two surviving sons of the late Marqués de Baides from the port of Portsmouth to London. After being paraded through the towns and villages of the English countryside, along with the carts transporting the silver bars and chests of coins, the boys were carried to the Court. The two teenage blue bloods were then taken to the palace where they were lodged with the general and his family.

Among the other prisoners brought to England were Don Diego de Villalba, the former governor of La Havana, the Marqués del Plato and their six servants. They were lodged in the house of John Tarrant, the postmaster. They apparently received very fine fare during their stay since English Calendar of State Papers later reveal the request for payment of 126 pounds of sterling "for the entertainment of the Governor of Havana and the Marqués del Plato." There were also ten Spanish officers and 112 soldiers imprisoned, many held at Chelsea College.

On the same night Mountagu went to receive his accolades from Parliament, the oldest son of Cromwell, Richard, visited with the two Spanish captives. He brought a message of sympathy and good wishes, assuring them they would be well cared for.

The next day tailors arrived with an assortment of clothing. The Spanish teenage squires were to be well dressed so they might be presented personally to the Lord Protector.[63]

In company with General Mountagu and the oldest son of Oliver Cromwell, they were received in the Hall, along with Cromwell's wife and daughters.

"After having looked at me for a long while, he (Cromwell) gave me tender words of condolences for the death of my parents. With tears in his eyes, he said they would cause me no further sorrow," reported Don Francisco Lopez in a letter he wrote afterwards.

"After returning to my room I received a note from Cromwell saying my brother and I were no longer prisoners. We were granted permission to see the city as well as the kingdom. A carriage and servants were provided for our convenience."

The teenage Spaniards were entertained by the London elite and shown particular attention by the Duchess of Richmond. The daughter of the Duke of Buckingham, she was once honored by King Philip IV in Spain.

Soon afterward the boys began touring the English countryside with none other than the famous Edward Mountagu as their host and guide. A highway carriage with six horses, and a sufficient complement of provisions and servants catered to their every need.

The two brothers spent three months visiting the Cotswolds and Cornwall. They even reached the boundaries of Scotland before returning to London. When they arrived, Cromwell received them with affection. He provided extensive passports enabling them to return to Spain without hindrance.

Before they departed, paintings were made of both Don Francisco Lopez and Don José Zúñiga. "The portraits were placed in the hall of the palace where so many famous men are displayed," Don Francisco stated.[64]

They sailed on March 19 with the fleet assigned to reinforce the vessels off Lisbon. Previous negotiations arranged for the Baides brothers to be exchanged for General Blake's cousin, Captain Cedric Blake, who had been seized almost two years earlier and imprisoned by the Spaniards at Fuentebravia.

On Sunday, March 24, Don Francisco and Don José were landed at Cape Finisterre. They received a royal salute from the same English ships that took them prisoner six months earlier. The teenagers made their way to Valladolid to visit an aunt prior to going to Madrid. There they had an audience with His Majesty on April 27. The king expressed his highest respects for their father, the deceased marqués. He also heard their plea for a pension to be established for the rest of the Baides family, now orphaned by the tragedy. This was a reasonable request since most of the family members' possessions were lost in the burned *almiranta* of Francisco de Esquivel.

Furthermore, the king already awarded 2,000 ducats to the

young orphaned daughter of Don Matías de Orellana, Admiral of the *Nuestra Señora de las Maravillas*, who died when his ship went down on the Little Bahama Bank. The pension was expected to cover the care and education of Doña Beatriz de Orellana at the Convent of Santa Isabel, where she was being raised. King Philip later committed funds to not only support the child's education, but also to provide a dowry for her if and when she married. There was also an Order of Knighthood conveyed in her behalf to the gentleman who married her. Part of this award constituted 38,376 *reales*, the payment her father would have received had he returned. The award was calculated on the basis of one year, eight months and twenty-eight days, from June 3, 1654 until the end of February, 1656. This is the date the voyage of Don Matías de Orellana was scheduled to be concluded.

On November 20, 1656,[65] His Majesty also made a gift to Don Francisco de Esquivel, the admiral of the fleet of Marcus del Puerto. It consisted of a paid military position for the person who would marry one of Esquivel's daughters, and a nun's dowry for another daughter.

Following the recommendation of the Council of War in Madrid, the king awarded knighthood in the military Order of Santiago to Antonio de Quintana. He also named him General of the *Armadilla de la Guardia de Cartagena*.[66] This was a small fleet whose purpose was to defend the important port against pirate and enemy attack.

Marcus del Puerto was confined to the Royal Prison of the Court for more than a year, waiting for his fate to be determined. In 1659, after being cleared of any wrongdoing in the battle of Cádiz, he was named a Knight of Santiago by the king. He was fifty-one years old at the time.

The explosion aboard the *almiranta*, *San Francisco Javier*, blew out much of the bottom of the ship where the ballast, bullion and other heavy cargo were stored. This portion of the hull sank like a rock. The upper decks, masts, sails and rigging drifted ashore in flames. The charred remains finally came to settle in about twenty-five feet of water a mile offshore of the ancient gates of Cádiz.

"According to the underwater examination that has been made of the hull of the *almiranta*," stated a diver's report, "it has been discovered the ship had been opened from the prow to the silver storeroom by the explosion of the powder magazine (situated just above the silver storeroom). There was nothing in it, not even the ballast, from the silver storeroom to the bow. Due to the explosion, the *almiranta* went down by the bow and submerged as far as the mainmast, where she drifted ashore all ablaze. The silver the *almiranta* carried spilled and deposited on that spot."

Lorenzo Andrés Garcia, the managing director of the *Casa de la Contratación*, wrote to headquarters in Seville.

"The smoldering hull of the ship was seen near the beach on Wednesday night, September 21. I sent the galleys to make sure no one would come near the wreck. I also sent some calvary to guard the area. When I reached the beach of Cádiz myself, I saw what was left of the hull still on fire. As I write this report at five in the morning, some 15,000 pesos in worked silver have been recovered from an upper cabin, and the seamen have just brought ashore three boats full of leather."

The treasure room of the *almiranta* was found locked with the original padlock, but upon further inspection divers discovered the front and bottom of the treasure store room had been destroyed. When the powder room blew up, the entire forward lower section was blown away, resulting in the loss of all the ship's ballast and silver.

"The sailors of some of the galleys have taken some things (before my arrival). They claim they had to do it for fear the English would come with their small boats and take it for themselves. It may be possible to recover some bronze artillery pieces and leather goods, and perhaps some silver might be found underneath," Lorenzo Garcia stated.

The Spaniards quickly undertook salvage efforts with the primitive diving techniques available to them. One group worked the shallow water site of the burned hull. Others contracted with representatives of the king to attempt to recover the bullion that was lost in deep water.

"Diego de Castro, Antonio Ganancia and Francisco Martinez, all residents of the city of Puerto de Santa Maria, put to sea in three *tartans* (lateen rigged, single-masted boats). They busied themselves, dragging their nets and grapnels to see if they could locate the silver of the *almiranta* that was lost within sight of this port."

These hopeful salvors had been told that the explosion in the powder magazine occurred a "league and a half from San Sebastian in twenty *brazas* of water in a range with the morro of the castle and the tuna fishery tower."

With the help of witnesses who had placed markers in the vicinity of the great galleon's sinking, the potential salvors worked diligently in their little boats when the weather and enemy corsairs permitted. Weather was their main hindrance as a strong southerly wind persisted.

"The tartans raking for the silver that scattered from the *almiranta*'s storeroom when it exploded continue in their diligence. This Friday they found some sticks of reinforced rope and other pieces of burnt rigging. However, until now they have found no silver."

After fifteen days, and while dragging in twenty-three fathoms, the nets of Diego de Castro snagged the wreckage. With much hope and anticipation, the shipwreck site was carefully marked with sightings on shore.

"There was much weight in the net, but with the help of people from the other *tartans* we raised it about three fathoms off the bottom. It remained suspended there until we could arrange ourselves and our boats to get a better purchase. As we struggled to hoist the extreme weight, the ropes parted and everything they contained settled back to the bottom's clean, fine and hard sand texture."

The weather worsened. The last effort of "deep water" salvage was merely a hopeful recommendation that, "Perhaps we can return next summer with our oyster rakes and sturdier nets."

For their efforts, the owners of the tartans were paid 4,015 *reales* of silver and 6,050 of vellon copper coin. Diego de Castro and his mates were paid 400 *reales* of silver for locating the deep water galleon wreckage.

In the meantime, the shallow water divers were busy. Within a week, they had stripped the singed wreckage of almost everything they could reach. For their underwater efforts they were paid 128 *reales* for the week's work.

An accounting of what was removed that first week:

Silver pieces-of-eight *reales*	4,921 pesos, found in the floorboards of the hull
Gold	*Doblones de dos* (two *escudos*) 452 two-*escudo* pieces found loose and valued at 1,808 pesos
Silver pieces-of-four *reales*	21,085 four *real* pieces valued at 3,573 pesos. (These were probably four *reales* from Potosí.)

Cacao	Six and one-half *arrobas* (165 pounds) valued at eight *reales* a pound
Tobacco	Twelve and one half *arrobas* and 1,450 hands of tobacco valued at 2,335 *reales*
Sarsaparilla	Nine and one half *arrobas* valued at 475 pesos
Tortoise shells	151 dozen valued at three pesos per dozen

Heartened over the first week's salvage success, the Spaniards pushed their divers to the limit. Winter weather soon would be upon them. They absolutely had to penetrate more deeply into the wreckage of the burned *almiranta*.

The scene at the wreck site was a frenzied one. Longboats and sloops of every description hovered in the vicinity, or shuttled salvaged goods to shore. The divers and their tenders had to be maintained, fed, kept warm and serviced from the beach. There was never enough rope and tackle for lifting objects, crowbars for breaking into locked doors, axes to cut away rigging worth saving, or bags, barrels, and cartons where retrieved items could be stored. To make matters worse, the chilly seawater temperature took its toll on the divers who constantly shivered from fatigue and exposure.

A mile away on land, soldiers guarded the salvaged cargo and accountants tallied the treasure totals. It was imperative for complete records to be maintained to be presented to officials of the *Casa de la Contratación* in Seville.

After several weeks, the list of salvaged goods and treasure was impressive. However, most of the items were personal belongings of the Marqués de Baides and other wealthy individuals who lost property in the disaster. Any personal property identified by family members would be returned to the owners.[67]

Salvaged goods from the burned hull of Francisco de Esquivel's *almiranta* were brought ashore in small boats and landed on the *Playa de Vendaval* in front of the entry gates.

The local fishermen, indeed anyone with a boat, were recruited to assist in the important undertaking. Even the personal and well maintained "green boat" of the Count of Molina was utilized. Small boat skippers were paid at the rate of eight *reales* a day, and crew members were paid six *reales*.

By November 12, most of the treasure, goods and products not damaged by salt water, and reachable by the divers, had been retrieved and either turned over to the Royal Treasury, claimed by owners, or auctioned. Even the hull of the galleon was sold to Francisco Ronsem for 200 pesos.

A gratuity of 420 *reales* of silver was given to the infantry captain and his soldiers who diligently guarded the salvaged items, and 892 *reales* were paid to Captain Diego Monaro, "for the extraordinary work he performed for twelve days assisting in the storage shed and as commander of the soldiers." Another 1,040 *reales* of silver were paid to divers and their assistants who worked on the *almiranta*'s hull. Sebastian de Poco received 324 *reales* for feeding those who worked on and around the sunken ship.

A final accounting of the auctioned merchandise was as follows:

Value of salvaged goods	78,601 *reales* (9,825 pesos)
Expenses that were paid	9,385 *reales* (1,173 pesos)
Balance remaining[68]	69,216 *reales* (8,652 pesos)

"Esteban Perez de León, constable of the *Casa de la Contratación*, transports under his command, from the Castle of Puntal of the City of Cádiz to the City of Seville, the boxes, cases, trunks, chests and bars of silver removed from the hull of the *almiranta* of the squadron under the command of Marcus del Puerto, which, after having been burned by the English, came upon the coast of Vendaval, before the gates of the said city. All these things are to be delivered to the presidents and judges of the House of Commerce, and what is contained in each piece has been inventoried as is evidenced in my declarations."

(signed) Juan Matías Perez

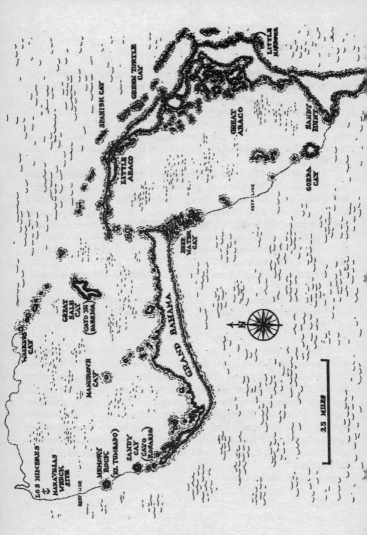

Northwest Bahamas
Grand Bahama and the Abacos

10

Treasure Salvage on *Los Mimbres*

It is extremely difficult to reach the silver in the forward strong room. The large starboard hatch cover is lying over it, together with many ballast stones, jagged timbers and artillery.

DURING THE SUMMER of 1656, the clamor for recovered treasure was fast becoming a daily ritual of the Spanish hierarchy. It was not only greed for additional riches. The absolute need to replenish the Royal Treasury coffers was an ever present necessity in order for Spain to maintain its status as a world power.

At the New World ports of Cartagena, La Havana and San Juan de Puerto Rico, administrative priorities were heavily focused on salvage of the valuable *Maravillas* treasure.

Word of the highly successful salvage work being accomplished along the desolate coast of the *Audiencia de Quito* spread quickly. Enormous quantities of silver bars and coins were being brought up from the *capitana*, lying on the bottom of the ocean near Chanduy since its sinking two years prior.

With Spanish treasury administrators being pressed to perform magical feats of deficit balancing, the need for successful treasure salvage on the Little Bahama Bank became a hot priority. As government sources emphasized the reality of His Majesty's need for money, local citizens of Spain's major cities were incited by the contagious enthusiasm to aid their country in any way possible.

Risk your life, but go was the guiding principle. "Go after the lost treasure! Recover as much as possible during the good diving months of summer! As the richest country the world has yet known, we cannot allow ourselves to slide into financial decline!"

Patriotic support spread enthusiastically through the colonies. The need to salvage Spain's lost treasures became the shout and cry of the newly developing world, especially those of the soldiers-of-fortune whose primary purpose in being there in the first place was to oversee the transport of Spain's treasure. Now was the hour to go treasure hunting. Everyone who could swim, dig or strain their gut underwater, and suffer the consequences was recruited. Every seaman worth his salt was signing on. Volunteering for a chance to attain notoriety among the salvage heroes of the day also provided a once-in-a-lifetime opportunity to achieve personal wealth and recognition beyond imagination.

Past stories of galleon salvage passed around the seafaring circuit for more than a century. To many the rewards far outweighed the risks. The chance of finding lost treasure was a chance worth taking.

The salvage flotilla of the first diving expedition, six small frigates, sailed from Cartagena in company with the fleet of Marcus del Puerto. The largest salvage vessel was the 80-ton *Nuestra Señora del Rosario y San Juan Bautista*, owned by Captain Juan de la Peña. A weathered, small frigate, it was the "lead ship" of Captain Juan de Somovilla Tejada and Gaspar de los Reyes. Other assorted salvage rigs included two longboats for running errands and dispatches.

After leaving Matanzas, Cuba, the salvage fleet encountered a strong southeasterly blow. The ships became temporarily scattered. Most of them soon regrouped, proceeding northward through the Bahama Channel, eagerly headed for the sandbank known as *Los Mimbres*. En route, they stopped at Grand Bahama to try to hire more divers. Offering large potential rewards, they signed on four men.

Approaching the latitude of the shipwreck site, the salvors stopped at a rock and placed a cross at its highest point. Hoping the gesture might favor them with success, they anchored in three fathoms. They remained there for two days, fishing and lobstering in the crystal blue waters. Measuring the altitude of the sun, they found themselves located slightly under 27° (north latitude). This location acquired the name "Black Stone" over the years because of its low-lying rock or coral mass, capable of sinking a sailing ship.[69]

From here, the six salvage vessels sailed wing-on-wing with the boats spread apart equidistantly. They crisscrossed along the edge of the line of reefs and shoals separating the pale green shallows of the Little Bahama Bank from the great blue water depths of the Bahamas Channel. The galleon seekers continued sailing and searching on a north-northeast course, in an attempt to find the sunken hull of the lost *almiranta*. At latitude 27¼° (27°15′), Gaspar de los Reyes knew they were in the vicinity.

On the afternoon of June 17, a shadow was sighted on the bottom. Divers went overboard. One returned to the surface with a piece of brazilwood, another with a piece of hide. Soon after, a silver plate was retrieved. Their exuberance was evident. They had found the *almiranta*. "When we finally discovered the wreck site, everyone was jubilant. The water was so clear that the artillery was visible from the surface. Our divers will try to recover it all."

"The galleon appeared so destroyed, only after putting your nose to it did you recognize it for what it was," Juan de Somovilla Tejada stated. "Main deck planking was caved in on the hull, now settled into heavy sand. There was a huge jumbled pile of rib timbers, frames and *barraganetes*.[70] A large portion of the deck and hull of the *almiranta* had been cast away.[71] It is impossible to determine the direction the chests, boxes, crates and other containers stored above decks floated.

"We worked without delay to recover everything reachable now scattered between the timbers, ballast and artillery. We retrieved much silver and some leather."[72]

In an effort to assist the divers, Somovilla positioned himself in the *chinchorro*. He pulled the lines as the divers tied them to the seventy-pound silver bars. Many of the divers hired in Key Vaca and Matacumbe, Florida were unable to free dive in the eight *brazas*,[73] frustrating Somovilla. Some, able to reach the bottom, could not remain long enough to accomplish anything before having to shoot back to the surface for air. "Monstrous" sharks constantly circling the area were a further hindrance to salvage efforts. It appeared to the divers that the sharks were maintaining a jealous guard of the sunken hull. Even the ocean refused to cooperate, as the better divers had difficulty staying in position on the bottom because of the strong current.

Four of the men were free Indians, hired at Grand Bahama. They were the most proficient underwater divers, and were responsible for salvaging most of the treasure. They were paid ½ of 1 percent of the treasure they recovered in silver.

The salvors took altitudes of the sun while they were anchored over the shipwreck. They described the particulars of the region, including the nearby cays, rocks, breakers, water depths and sea bottom configurations.

The chief pilot, Pedro Gonzalez Montanes was a skilled navigator, nearly a perfectionist. He took a noon sun sight every day, and stated unequivocally they were positioned at 27⅕° (27° 12'N).

The salvage team anchored over the ship for thirteen days. They raised more than 300 silver bars and many chests of pieces-of-eight *reales*. One report stated the amount was 100,000 *pesos de ocho*. It was all stored aboard Somovilla's ship, the *Rosario*. There was so much silver in the small frigate they were forced to jettison their ballast rocks.

Gobernador Marcus del Puerto waited in Havana for word from the salvors. Captain Somovilla drafted a letter to him on June 22. The correspondence described the great success the divers were enjoying. It also recommended a rendezvous so the treasure could be transported back to Spain aboard the fleet under command of del Puerto. The letter was never received.

On July 1, a severe storm blew out of the southeast. They attempted to ride out the heavy weather for two days. Because there was much more silver remaining on the ocean floor, they didn't want to abandon their anchorage over the site. The gale intensified, and three of the salvage ships lost their anchors. The others quickly cut their cables, permitting the wind to scatter them recklessly out and into the frothing Bahama Channel.[74]

It was impossible for them to reach the previously agreed-upon meeting place at Puerto de la Florida (St. Augustine). After four days of being blown blindly northwestward, the entire flotilla thought they would be dashed upon the east Florida coast, the fate of many ships in the past. Some of these vessels lost their masts, while others purposely cut theirs in an attempt to slow their movement. The low-lying Florida shore loomed off to port.

Near the last possible moment the wind shifted and began blowing from the land (southwesterly). Somovilla was alone, none of the other salvage vessels visible on the horizon. Finally able to secure a sun sight, he found their position was 36°. The wind and stream had shoved him more than 500 miles! Realizing he could not make Puerto de la Florida, he set a course for Puerto Rico. At approximately 28° he encountered two large ships. The next day he sighted three more. Despite his attempt to flag their attention, they either didn't see him, or they ignored him.

Somovilla arrived off San Juan de Puerto Rico on August 3, without an anchor or small boat and fired a cannon to announce his arrival. The Governor, Francisco de Novoa, issued a launch to investigate. The Puerto Ricans were amazed to find Somovilla's vessel totally ballasted with silver. There was no news as to the whereabouts of the rest of his salvage fleet.

The amount of salvaged silver inventoried at Puerto Rico totaled 477,146 pesos, the equivalent of 13.5 metric tons. Several other reports confirmed three hundred silver bars and 100,000 pesos in *reales* and gold.

Somovilla told His Majesty's officials who inspected the salvaged silver at Puerto Rico, "This quantity of treasure has been recovered without touching the main strong room, as it remained locked and was inaccessible."

Their scrutiny of the ship and the weighing and counting of the silver took twelve days. Later documents revealed the inspectors were kindly requested to avoid inspection of the areas behind the ship's firewood stack and under the cannon balls in the shot room amidships. Apparently a considerable quantity of silver, gold coin and jewelry was stored in these areas. The exact amount of hidden treasure was never determined, as authorities were paid handsomely for the oversight.

Several weeks later two of the other salvage frigates limped into Puerto Rico. They carried one of the brass guns from the *Maravillas*. They told how another ship from their group was lost on the coast of Santo Domingo. Another salvage frigate arrived in Cartagena on August 3. It was the *Nuestra Señora de la Concepción San Antonio y San Diego*, captained by Manuel de Ribeiro and piloted by Diego Diaz Caravallo. There was no news of the *almirantilla* (*little admiral*), the second primary salvage ship.

The Governor of Puerto Rico called a meeting with the ministers of His Majesty. It was decided to send the silver to Santa Cruz de Tenerife in the Canary Islands. The treasure was to be held in the fort there until it was safe enough to transport it to Spain. The Puerto Rican Governor withheld 20,000 pesos of the shipment, supposedly for repairing the ramparts of El Morro. He was later accused of allocating a major portion of these funds for his own needs.

A Portuguese ship, the *Madama do Brasil*, was in the harbor preparing to sail home. The treasure was loaded on this vessel, under the charge of Captains Somovilla and Reyes. Somovilla took 6,264 pesos to cover payroll expenses for his crew. Another 563 pesos from the recovered treasure went for his "administrative overhead." The vessel left Puerto Rico on November 8, 1656, and arrived at Santa Cruz on December 27.

Shortly afterward, Gaspar de los Reyes boarded a small Dutch ship sailing for Spain. Captain Somovilla prepared a detailed report to the king, describing the diving and salvage efforts at the *Mimbres*. Gaspar was instructed to deliver the report personally. He reached Seville late January 1657, delivered the treasure register, then was interrogated by officers of the *Casa de la Contratación*.

Gaspar was not a newcomer to the court. They recognized him as an experienced pilot and sea captain. His background included twenty-four years in the *Armada de la Carrera de Tierra Firme*, and in the *Plata Flotas de Nueva España*. As the assistant pilot of the *Maravillas*, his salary was fifteen escudos per month. The Marqués de Montealegre reported, "De los Reyes always presented a good account of himself."

Gaspar was looking forward to the privileged appearance before the king and his courtiers. He spent his time waiting for his audience contemplating how to "present another good account of himself."

He told them in eye-opening detail of the nightmarish sinking of the *Maravillas* and of his rescue. He thrilled them with his narrative of discovering the sunken *almiranta* six months later in the uncharted *Mimbres*. He excited them with his account of the treasure lying on the magnificent white sand sea floor. He enthralled the Court with his story of the thirteen days of salvage and his wild odyssey after the storm hit. "We sailed four days under bare poles, having to cut the main mast, flying only the foresail for another ten days, finally reaching safe harbor at Puerto Rico loaded with silver, after a desperate thirty days at sea!"

King Philip questioned the details of the *almiranta*'s location. Gaspar responded, "The site is at the sandbank of the *Mimbres*. The treasure lies in the sunken hull in six *brazas* (thirty-three feet). The sea bottom is fine sand. It is at the deeper section of the north end of the *Mimbre*, at 27¼° (27° 15′ N)."

When asked how much silver was salvageable from the sunken hull, Gaspar responded that he did not know the quantity, but "according to my judgment, there will be more silver under one hatch cover of the lower deck. The treasure can only be recovered during the summer months. The area is open to bad weather, and the strong currents are continuous."

The king congratulated Gaspar, ordering him back to Tenerife to sail again with Juan de Somovilla Tejada. They were instructed to go to Margarita Island to obtain more divers.[75] From there they were to proceed to Havana for provisions, then return to the *Mimbres* to continue the salvage operation.

A March 5 royal warrant to the President and magistrates of the *Casa de la Contratación* in Seville contained the following:

"I am informed by Don Alonso de Avila y Guzmán, my Governor and Captain General of the Canary Islands, that Juan de Somovilla Tejada, in the *Madama do Brasil*, has delivered treasure from the lost *almiranta*. According to the official register in Puerto Rico, the amount is 465,146 pesos in bars, *piñas* and pieces of silver, along with 405 *castellanos* in gold to be assayed.[76] After the governor visited the ship, nineteen uncounted silver bars and seventeen silver cones were discovered. Combined, they weighed 3,449 *marcos*. He declared them forfeited and confiscated. All the treasure was placed in the safety of the castle at the harbor.

"My orders instruct *Madama do Brasil* be readied to return under the leadership of Somovilla and de los Reyes. They are to command the expedition to recover the remaining silver from the *almiranta*." This was the directive from the king himself.

In recognition of his service to the Crown, Gaspar de los Reyes was awarded a lifetime pension of fifty *escudos* a month, paid in the *presidio* of Cádiz. In the case of his death, twenty-five *escudos* a month would be paid to his wife, Mariana Vásquez, as long as she lived. He was also given 1,000 pesos to help cover his expenses.

Captain Juan de Somovilla Tejada was knighted and awarded forty *escudos* a month, in addition to his normal pay. He was also presented with a bonus of 1,000 pesos to help defray his overhead and expenses. Juan and Gaspar were both exuberant over their newly designated positions and recognition. The king realized he truly did have a few good men. For the several months following, their only purpose was to follow his orders to return to *Los Mimbres* and salvage what was left of the treasure of the sunken *almiranta*.

Unbeknown to the Spaniards, the missing *almirantilla* of the salvage fleet was discovered in distress near Bermuda by an Englishman, Justinian Martin. It was dismasted and shoved by the same heavy winds and seas that forced Somovilla northward. The battered frigate and its famished Spanish crew, including a former pilot from the *Jesus, Maria y Josef* were towed into St. George's Harbour. The men were treated well by the Bermudians who, being people of the sea, always assisted their seafaring brethren.

Bermudian hospitality was such that the Spanish sailors became trusting enough to relate the entire story of the lost treasure galleon to their hosts. They even drew a map showing the location of *Los Mimbres*, indicating where the treasure ship came to grief. The Spaniards enjoyed several weeks of good food and dark, heavy Bermuda rum.

It wasn't long before the Governor of Bermuda commissioned Captain Richard Lockyer to "goe forth for the recovery of the described treasure. The Spaniards, eight in number, will be detained here on shore, except that the Spanish pilot shall saile forth with the said Captain Lockyer."[77]

In September, Lockyer entered into an agreement with William Coxen to take charge of the Bermudian diving operation. Coxen was to be paid ten pieces-of-eight of every 1,000 pieces recovered, and a similar share of any other valuables found. They sailed from Bermuda in early October on board the specially equipped[78] salvage ship *Discovery*.

On January 31, 1657, Pedro de Zapata, the Governor of Cartagena, decided a second expedition to salvage the *Maravillas* was necessary. Even though an approximate figure of 500,000 pesos was already recovered, he stated, "There is absolutely no doubt the amount of silver embarked for His Majesty and for private accounts is much more than this."

Captain Don Juan de Ochoa y Campo was placed in charge of the second attempt. Following him in command was Captain Josef de Yriarte, a Basque trader and shipbuilder who was long active in the *Carrera de las Indias*. Captain at Sea and War Juan Bautista de Verde was assisted by Julian Mallesa. Chief of the divers was Francisco de Corpas. He was assisted by Pedro de Pro.

Nuestra Señora de Balbaneda y Santo Cristo de Burgos, referred to as the *capitana*, was the lead ship of this expedition. There was also an *almiranta*, sailed by Josef de Yriarte, and a *gobierno*, the *Nuestra Señora de Begoña y San Antonio*. The designated controller and supervisor, reporting directly to the governor, as well as the general accountant for His Majesty, was Don Pedro de Viellar Vittola.

Governor Zapata issued orders to concentrate on successful salvage, and to avoid contact with the enemy. "No time is to be lost on any account. If other Spanish divers are found with a warrant of His Majesty, they are to fully cooperate," he directed.

The flotilla sailed from Cartagena in April. They arrived at Havana in May. Josef Yriarte was sent to the Florida Keys to try to hire more divers. Ochoa sailed for the *Mimbres*.

Captain Ochoa reached the general area of the wreck site by June 17. He immediately began searching on the Little Bahama Bank. Captain Lucas Diaz, the chief pilot, noticed a dark spot on the sea bed. When they investigated beneath the surface, they saw the sunken hull. The second diving expedition began on June 18. It was exactly one year after the first one.

It was exceptionally arduous for the divers to effectively salvage the wreck. Water depth was eight *brazas* at high tide, and seven at low tide. Ochoa reported this meant free-diving attempts were in approximately forty-four feet of ocean depth, with strong currents ever present.

It was extremely difficult to reach the silver in the forward strong room. The large starboard hatch cover was lying on top of it. "Also atop it are many ballast stones and other jagged timbers, and artillery. There is little space to crawl in or to reach down," Captain Ochoa logged. Stretching as much as possible, two divers were able to get only half of their bodies into the wreckage. They did not have the strength to pull out the silver bars buried in the sand and wood debris. "Working at this depth and against the swift current they tire easily. There are broken jars, exposed iron spikes and nails causing numerous wounds. Some cannot dive for two or three days."

Following several days of underwater toil, Captain Ochoa attempted to move the hatch cover by hooking a grapnel into it. The main winch was then used to move it. They struggled all afternoon, but could not get the hatch cover to budge.

A slave diver, Pedro, was sent down to rearrange the grapnel. A loose cannon shifted and he was suddenly trapped under the hatch cover. His dive mate worked frantically to pull him free. Finally, his lungs about to burst, the rescue diver literally tore the trapped body from the wreckage and raced to the surface with him. Pedro's bleeding was profuse. They managed to pull him into the dinghy as he coughed blood. He died a few moments later. A short prayer was said, then his body was dumped overboard. Diving was suspended for three days.

The captain ordered the chief gunner to prepare some underwater bombs so they could try blasting their way into the buried strong room. Black powder was packed into a wooden cylinder. Arquebus gun barrels were crudely welded together in a futile attempt to waterproof them and were then filled with priming powder. The result was one gigantic fuse they could fire from the surface. When the makeshift bomb was completed, the entire apparatus was charged on a longboat. Divers descended to try to place the device at the forward strong room. Swirling currents caused a joint of the firing tube to separate, allowing sea water to saturate the powder. The bomb would not detonate.

The following day they tried again. This time they structurally reinforced the long fuse with attached oars. However, the barrel bomb became damaged when the divers tried to place it at the narrow entrance to the strong room. It too refused to explode.

They shifted their efforts to what remained of the stern section of the hull and began moving ballast. After two hours divers reached a few silver bars and plates. These were raised to the surface.

"The ballast was very heavy, making it difficult to move," stated Captain Ochoa. "It is very hard work. It requires divers of great physical strength. We can see a pile of silver bars, but in order to reach them, all the ballast must be shifted to one side. The forward storeroom, containing most of the leather, also holds many silver bars. It is locked tightly and will be difficult to get into."

A large bronze cannon sat in the midst of the hole they were digging. The big gun was loose and unstable, causing concern among the divers. They feared it would fall and trap them, and they would suffer the same fate as Pedro.

A line was secured around the cannon. Just as they began working the winch a sudden squall struck them from the southeast. They were forced to stop diving. The salvage vessel had to weigh anchor and run before the weather back to Cartagena. A short time into their return voyage, another diver died. An Indian, Diego de Maria, suffered severe chest pain. His lungs were badly damaged from days of laborious diving.

No artillery was raised because of insufficient lifting equipment. The entire salvage effort resulted in only a little silver, in various sized bars, silver sheets and plates, and a few candelabra.

When they arrived in Cartagena, a levy of 5,000 pesos was placed on the recovered treasure to say 1,000 masses for the many souls of those who died in the shipwreck of the *Maravillas*.

In his debriefing interview, Captain Juan de Ochoa y Campo reported that his divers counted forty-one cannon on the bottom. "The hull of the *almiranta* appears to be intact, except at the bow. The stern section is completely closed in. The forward, amidships and aft strong rooms are tightly locked," he told authorities at Cartagena.

The captain and controller both signed off on the salvaged inventory with plans to return with better equipment and underwater bombs.

A total value of 20,650 pesos was placed on the salvaged silver, contained in two chests.

Enthusiastically armed with a royal license to return to treasure salvaging, Juan de Somovilla arrived at the Island of Margarita in May. He planned to entice a large number of famous pearl divers of the area to embark on his salvage vessel, *Madama do Brasil*.⁷⁹ Somovilla signed on thirty-five divers and purchased five Negroes. Most of the divers were Indians from Goajira or Goaquira.⁸⁰

The salvage team sailed from *Isla de Margarita* to Puerto Rico, arriving in late June. Preparations were hurriedly undertaken to gather supplies and equipment for the second expedition. Knowing they must scramble to utilize the good weather months before the hurricanes came, they sailed for the *Mimbres* on July 24.

According to Manuel Perea, pilot of the *Madama do Brasil*, there were several other ships in the second Somovilla diving expedition. Included were two small frigates, *El Panito* and *San Antonio* and the *El Dragón*, owned by Captain Maldenado. Captains Somovilla and Reyes were on the lead ship, the *Madama do Brasil*.

By this time Captain Josef de Yriarte was back at the *Mimbres* with divers hired at Key Vaca. He had waited in Cuba for two weeks, not realizing Ochoa had sailed to the Little Bahama Bank earlier, without him.

Yriarte immediately spotted the buoys left on the site by Ochoa. Within an hour divers were overboard and silver bars were being wrestled to the surface. The heavy weather, earlier chasing Ochoa away, had moved on. *Los Mimbres* was a millpond as divers gloried in their successful finds. Buckets, lowered to the ocean floor for treasure, surfaced with thousands of pieces-of-eight packed in them. Dozens of seventy-pound silver bars were tied with lengths of line and lifted from the bottom. Yriarte was no doubt picking up the treasure Ochoa reported seeing, but was unable to reach. The amount of treasure salvaged each day seemed to exceed what was retrieved the previous day.

Salvage operations continued non-stop for two weeks. Yriarte sent his tender to Grand Bahama to pick up fresh water and firewood. While on the mission, the tender was intercepted by Captain Juan de Somovilla. He, with Captain Gaspar de los Reyes, had just arrived in the area.

Upon learning of the tender's mission, Somovilla ordered it to return to the *Mimbres*. "Report back to Captain Yriarte," he instructed. "I will bring the wood and water within two days. Kindly advise your captain that my orders from the king are to recover the treasure of the *almiranta*. His Majesty requests all divers to work together for everyone's best interests."

Somovilla sent his controller along in the small boat with instructions to begin tallying the salvaged silver. "Make certain you do not overlook a single *real*," he ordered.

However, as the tender returned to the *Maravillas* site, a most unusual and extremely interesting event occurred. As soon as Somovilla's message was relayed to Captain Yriarte, he immediately weighed anchor and sailed away.

"May you rot in hell," screamed the controller as he was callously forced back aboard his tender, along with some divers "who had not performed."

Somovilla arrived the following day. He was shocked at the predicament he witnessed. Cursing openly, he demanded to be told what happened. His controller replied, "Captain, I can only say the salvor, Yriarte, was most unfriendly. He acted weird and irresponsible. No sooner did I arrive with your orders when the captain weighed anchor and hastily sailed away. They left no message whatever for you, Sir."

While Yriarte's actions were bizarre, he indeed sailed all the way to Spain with an immense amount of recovered treasure.

In a letter dated September 22, Captain Josef de Yriarte advised His Majesty that he was one of the officers aboard the salvage ships of Don Juan de Ochoa, engaged in the diving on the *almiranta* at *Los Mimbres*. "I wish to inform Your Majesty I am now destined for Cartagena with 1,500,000 pesos, recovered at great risk from the sunken *almiranta*. Another vessel is bringing 120,000 pesos more, in large and small bars of silver and gold," he continued. "Salvaging the Crown's treasure was a risk worth taking, even though it is a small amount."

Compared to the total treasure cargo known to have been aboard the *Maravillas*, it was a small amount. He also retrieved twenty-four pieces of artillery, each of "900 weight."[81]

This is not the last we will hear about Captain Yriarte. When his vessel arrived in San Sebastián de Cádiz in October,[82] a considerable amount of its cargo was reportedly taken to nearby Guetaria, and placed directly in the home of "none other than Don Josef de Yriarte." Inquiries and proceedings against him began as early as November 1657. He was accused of embezzling much gold and jewels not belonging to him.

Somovilla spent little time worrying about Yriarte's fast disappearance. He promptly anchored over the *Maravillas* and began work. It was mid-August. He realized the seasonal storms would soon be a hindrance to the salvage operation. For the time being though, the weather was magnificent. Every man on board was motivated. The divers loved the calm, clear water, making visibility on the bottom perfect. At slack tide the current was even submissive.

"I cannot describe to you how beautiful it is down there," reported Alvaro, one of the more disciplined and enthusiastic divers. "I wish I was able to remain longer on the bottom than the few seconds I'm able to work. The little fishes are so friendly. Each day they seem to look forward to seeing us. They know we will stir up some morsels for them to feed."

Within fifteen days the controller recorded the recovery of about 100 large silver bars, 150 small and medium bars, and 30,000 *reales de a ocho*. There was also a great quantity of silver plate, including dishes, water and wine goblets, and a variety of other pieces.

The treasure was stashed aboard the *Madama do Brasil* under the careful scrutiny of Captains Somovilla and Reyes. The ship was beginning to ride low in the water.

Every evening as the sun was setting, the dive boats returned to the *Madama do Brasil*. The exhausted divers were cut and bruised, thirsty and hungry. Dinner was hastily offered, before sleep quickly overcame them.

The captains covetously peered over the shoulders of the accountants as they tallied the day's recovery. It was sometimes the wee hours of the morning before the total number of pesos and valuation was known.

As each day dawned, the divers were hustled back into the small *chinchorros* to descend once again to the treasure-laden sea floor. In the early morning the sea water was refreshing. Later, as the sun rose and the divers waited in the launches for their next descent, the hot sunlight beat down on their salt-infested bodies, burning their wounds and searing their already dark skin. They accepted their toil, recognizing their injuries, possibly even death, as part of their daily chore. Even after two weary weeks of hard diving and long hours, Somovilla and Reyes continued to drive the divers to near depletion.

As of August 18, diving operations proceeded smoothly, continuing to produce daily results. Both captains worked hard to try and beat the hurricanes. On one occasion the ship's chaplain, Don Francisco Deca, loudly objected to the cruel and rigorous demands on the divers. Gaspar de los Reyes, responding to the priest, cursed him continuously. The clergyman later testified that he struck him across the face with a cutlass, wounding him.

Immediately and ironically, a squall from the southwest hit the salvage fleet. It came upon them instantaneously, frightening all of the men.

All salvage vessels attempted to hang on to their anchors. The wind violently shifted to the northwest quadrant. As the storm intensified, both captains realized the imminent danger they were in. The chaplain later stated, "The gale began to blow fiercely, raging until we were lost on Gorda Cay."

The *Madama* and the frigate *El Panito* ran for shelter in the lee of Grand Bahama. The *San Antonio* and the *Dragon* tried to hold at the salvage site. During the night, the *San Antonio* lost its anchors and was broken upon the reefs near the head of the *Mimbres*. At daylight the *Dragon* attempted to reach safety at Grand Bahama, but didn't succeed. The ship struck reefs off what is today Freeport, "breaking into pieces."

By the following day the gale was somewhat diminished. The skippers of the *Madama* and *Panito* decided to head for Havana. That night the wind again veered to the southwest. Without warning they were in the midst of heavy seas and winds. The frigates became scattered and their crews disoriented.

El Panito was the first to encounter breakers and rocks. The ship was dashed ashore in the vicinity of the southeasterly tip of Grand Bahama.

Aboard the *Madama*, Captains Somovilla and Reyes fought for their lives. Silver bars and chests thrown by the seas crashed into any thing or person in their way. Desks, chairs and benches, all supposedly secured, broke loose and flew like missiles. Making repairs was impossible with the seas in such a rage. What little sail had been up was quickly reduced to ribbons. They tried to anchor but could not find bottom. They cut down the main mast to try to slow the wildly rolling and pitching ship. "We were being blown unmercifully to only God knows where," logged Captain Somovilla.

They drifted helplessly throughout the dark night. The overloaded frigate seemed to purposefully put her bow down and plough under and through the monstrous seas instead of rising high above the crest of each trough, causing huge amounts of green water to overwhelm the decks, washing away anything and everything in its wake. It was as if the vessel was overpowered by carrying too much sail, but there was no canvas at all aloft.

The rigging clattered, the wind howled and shrieked like all the devils of hell. The 400-ton frigate trembled and shook like a dying person with a last gasp death-rattle. All aboard were silent, their senses focused solely on the sounds of the storm. Hearts stood still as the ship struggled under the mountainous weight of tons of ocean submerging the decks and inundating the forecastle. One moment the ship gave a great heave and appeared headed for a certain knockdown. But somehow, in the bottomless black of night, the *Madama do Brasil* managed to right herself and come to a standstill. An uncertain shudder, a vibrating lurch, a convulsive jerk, and the entire ear-piercing and head-splitting process began all over again as she penetrated and breached the breaking seas.

Early the next morning, on August 22, they struck a submerged object, breaking the rudder. Shortly after dawn, the vessel now totally uncontrollable, they were thrown against some rocks. Everyone scrambled to struggle through the shallows to reach dry ground. Some of the crew crawled ashore naked. Others swam through breakers without shoes and shirts. Seven men drowned.

"With the constant pounding of the waves breaking against us, the ship opened her seams. It was only a short while before she went to pieces. Most of the treasure slid from the cracked and splintered hull into the crevices of the reef," related Captain Somovilla, years later.

After the storm subsided, the survivors attended to the immediate task of making camp. A pathetic, makeshift shelter was established on a small bight off a brilliantly white sand beach. They collected everything retrievable from the wreckage, including one hatchet and a few knives. They obtained nails and spikes from broken timbers. From the torn sails they gathered cordage and canvas. Fortunately, the frigate's small boat was recovered from the rocks. Although it was slightly stove in, they were able to repair its bottom.

Gaspar de los Reyes, an accomplished navigator, took several sun sights. He determined the small island they were stranded on was Cayo de las Gordas.[83]

The only drinking water they found came from shallow, salty wells, dug out with their hands and knives. The only food they found was coarse, stringy grass or seaweed and small snails, dug from beneath the roots of the mangroves. Occasionally, they caught a sea turtle.

Several Indian divers who survived assisted Somovilla as they slowly and meticulously began salvaging the now twice-sunken treasure.

By the end of the first week, 130 large silver bars had been brought up and carried to the beach. About 150 *barretones* (small and medium bars), miscellaneous silverware and *piñas* were also salvaged.

The fifteen chests and boxes holding the majority of the 30,000 pesos were smashed when the ship broke up. The specie, mostly pieces-of-eight *reales*, were scattered on the bottom, soon to settle among the rocks and under the soft sand. Only 500 to 600 pieces-of-eight were reported to be recovered.[84]

After another week of diving and picking through wreckage, Somovilla decided to suspend the diving efforts. All recovered treasure was stacked under a makeshift lean-to above the beach. He ordered his young lieutenant, Cristóbal de Mundarayain, to take the ship's small boat, and six other men, and try to reach Havana, about 350 miles distant.

"If God permits you to safely reach Havana, hurry to advise the governor of our desperate predicament. Bring us a ship with food and water as fast as possible, before we all die on this miserable isle."

About a week after the *Madama do Brasil's* wreck, near the end of August, word was received by the English Governor of Eleuthera:

"Some wrack was spotted on one of the beaches of the Isle of Neque (Arawak for Abaco). Captain Richard Richardson has been advised."

Sensing an opportunity to seize Spanish loot, local "wrackers" Richard Richardson, John Williams and Asa Eyley sailed on September 12 in two small shallops headed for Gorda Cay. These men were counted among the original, self-sufficient Eleutheran adventurers who settled nearby after being shipwrecked in 1648.

As they approached Gorda, they fired several musket shots at the shipwrecked Spaniards. Not having firearms in their possession, the men on shore were forced to retreat from the wreck area. However, two of the Indian divers swam out to the shallops and offered to show the English where more silver was located on the sea floor, if they agreed to save them. "We have not eaten anything but eel grass for many days," they pleaded with the Eleutherans.

Delighted, the Eleutherans took them aboard. With the help of the Indians, who acquired fast knowledge of the deserted territory, they set up a temporary camp at what today is the settlement of Sandy Point, about ten miles from Gorda Cay. Each day for ten days the Eleutherans returned to the site of the wrecked *Madama do Brasil*, accompanied by the two Indian divers. Their daily ritual of firing several muskets kept the Spaniards out of range. At the end of the third week of September, the "wrackers" returned to St. George's Cay (Spanish Wells) about fifty nautical miles distant toward the southeast. They carried 2,600 pounds sterling in silver with them. After some boisterous wrangling, the booty was divided.

In the interim, the Spanish sailors, who remained with Somovilla and Reyes on the beach, set about building another small boat of about ten feet. Using the hatchet and knives, the only tools available, it took them three weeks to finish the boat. By then they were beginning to collapse from hunger and thirst. One man was already dead.

After sixty days Somovilla was in total despair. His plight appeared hopeless. His men were in agony. Their skin was scorched from the sun and raw from the many insect bites. Their blistered and sore-festered skin burned when they bathed in the sea water. The "glass grass," their primary diet, cut their tongues and lips. Hardly a day passed that another crew member wasn't buried. They wondered and worried about their fate, as well as what might have happened to Lieutenant Mundarayain. Had he reached Havana? Would he bring help to them in time?

Somovilla realized the Indian divers, traitors because of their hunger, had probably told the English about the large pile of treasure stored in their camp on Gorda Cay. He suspected the English were simply waiting for most of the Spaniards to die off before they returned to capture the salvaged loot so neatly stacked under the lean-to. While he was unsure how much the English recovered from the underwater wreck, he guessed it wouldn't be long before they returned, as their appetite for treasure was so easily whetted. He was correct.

Early one October morning, the Spaniards were startled awake by the sound of gun fire. The two English shallops had returned and were firing their muskets. They were hoping the Spaniards might surrender, or at least be willing to part with some of the treasure, in exchange for food. Without weapons of their own, the Spanish wanted no part of them.

The English again began diving on the shipwreck of the *Madama do Brasil*. They remained for five days before returning to Spanish Wells, Eleuthera. Again, the booty was divided with the usual argumentation and haggling. Each man was awarded "eighty pounds per share." The two leaders divided a mass of silver valued at "1,400 pieces-of-eight."

Somovilla continued worrying over how much longer they could survive. An exhausting eighty days had passed since the shipwreck. Already seventy of his men were dead from hunger and hardship on Cayo de la Gorda.

Of course, he wasn't aware that his loyal aide, Cristóbal de Mundarayain, had arrived safely at Havana on September 15. Mundarayain made his urgent report to the governor, who ordered an immediate rescue flotilla underway for Gorda Cay.

The ships of the rescue flotilla consisted of the *Nuestra Señora del Carmen*, *La Garapina*, *El Santo Cristo de San Roman*, and two captured vessels now in the service of His Majesty.

The rescue flotilla sailed on September 30 for Gorda Cay. However, shortly after leaving Havana they encountered several small pirate vessels cruising along the coast for scavenging.

Despite the admonitions and pleas of Mundarayain, the skipper of the flotilla gave chase and captured the pirates in shallow water. "My companions are dying at Gorda Cay," he shouted. "If we don't get to them immediately, their deaths will be on your hands. The English will steal the treasure we've worked so hard to recover."

By October 30, the survivors at Gorda Cay dwindled to a small group. They had lost hope of being rescued. They slowly began to visualize the horrible likelihood of Mundarayain being lost at sea and never reaching Havana.

After many days of conferring with Juan de Somovilla, and weighing their best course of action, Gaspar de los Reyes volunteered to take the small, crudely fashioned dinghy, and attempt to reach Havana. His two brothers accompanied him. The three men set out in the small, crowded skiff. They were armed with nothing, and provisioned with only a handful of mussels and some eel grass.

Two days passed before they sighted the rescue flotilla on its approach to the Gorda Cay region. They were taken on board, openly expressing their thankfulness. They wasted no time in returning to the survivor camp and transferring the walking skeletons and treasure trove to the primary rescue vessel, *Nuestra Señora del Carmen*. The *Carmen* promptly set sail for Havana. By mid-November, the flotilla sighted the Cuban coastline and its mountains in the background. Somovilla made "arrangements" with the captain of the *Carmen* to put into a small village known as Los Rocques, where a partial disembarkment of the treasure was apparently undertaken.

While ashore, he found survivors of two of his salvage ships lost on Grand Bahama. They managed to sail to Cuba from the place of their shipwreck in the ship's small boat. However, they were attacked by the English, who pillaged their meager supplies and stole the boat as well. They were left on an island without food or clothing and were lucky to have reached Cuba in an Indian canoe.

Somovilla took them aboard the *Carmen* and continued toward Havana. He received a grand welcome and a week's rest and recreation. Cuban authorities were mesmerized by his fantastic story.

In early December he and Gaspar de los Reyes loaded their treasure aboard the *Nuestra Señora de la Encarnación y Señor San José*, a vessel they jointly purchased. They planned to sail to Spain with the fleet of the Captain General Marqués de Villanueva, whose vessels were in the harbor making preparations to depart.

They were later accused of having left the fleet near Bermuda, under suspicious circumstances, in order to arrange for the "spiriting away of the silver and gold they were bringing unregistered," according to testimony against them.

As they arrived off the coast of Spain, a gale forced them to enter Ayamonte, a small harbor near the boundary of Spain and Portugal. They claimed they were unable to steer for Cádiz, where the king's controllers were waiting.

11

Treasure Is Trouble

He has paid out more than 24,000 pesos in 'hush money' because the amount he truly recovered exceeded 1,000,000 pesos, including a chest of diamonds, many gold bars, and an immense amount of jewelry.
Lorenzo de Soto.

AFTER UNLOADING THE TREASURE from their second diving expedition in Spain, the two adventurers, Captains Somovilla and Reyes, did not waste time in setting forth on the third one. In early March, they sailed from Spain back to Puerto Rico. They wanted to get the long Atlantic crossing behind them and be able to focus on the *Mimbres* during the short season for good diving.

They had received word from friends that complaints were filed against them. They did not want to be cornered by the king's auditors and forced to certify under oath as to the accuracy of their treasure register. Consequently, they felt considerably more secure at sea.

On June 3, 1658, they sailed from San Juan for the Little Bahama Bank aboard their special salvage vessel, nicknamed *El Champeton*.

They stopped at Gorda Cay en route to take care of unfinished business, namely the uncovering of a cache of treasure they buried earlier "for fear it would be stolen by the English." They also raised some bronze guns from what was left of the wreck of the *Madama do Brasil*.

June 14 found them diving at the *Mimbres*, apparently having had little difficulty locating the site of the shipwreck. They remained anchored over the *Maravillas* until July 3, when they left to return to Puerto Rico. By July 24 they arrived back at San Juan, "having recovered everything they could, the rest now being buried deeply in the sand."

Their registered report of salvage listed twelve bronze guns and 53,000 pesos. They surrendered all to the authorities.

For the three successive diving expeditions of Juan de Somovilla

Tejada and Gaspar de los Reyes from 1656 to 1658, they "reported" finding the following amount of treasure:

First diving expedition,	477,000 pesos
Second diving expedition,	170,000 pesos
Third diving expedition,	53,000 pesos
Total	700,000 pesos

In the meantime, the political enemies of Governor Pedro Zapata of Cartagena brought formal complaints against him, charging that "he committed frauds and embezzlements to an enormous degree."

Zapata was accused of being in cahoots with Juan de Somovilla, who was his "great friend and close partner." Juan de Ochoa also was claimed to be the governor's crony.[85]

Don Tomás de Vega, Secretary of the Inquisition, wrote to the Marqués de Montealegre from Cartagena, advising him that Governor Zapata had taken incredible liberties with the king's money. "He hid, and removed from registry, much of what was recovered by the salvage expeditions. He even reopened the Royal Mint in order to begin producing for his own account silver coins from the bullion registered to His Majesty."[86]

Fray Bernardo de Aquilli, of the Order of San Juan de Dios, wrote that Don Pedro Zapata was the first to profit from the salvage operations.

"I have seen what appeared to be two mountains of silver bars in a warehouse, but the governor has delivered no more than 160,000 pesos."

There was little reported salvage activity after 1658, primarily because the key salvors were either confined to prison, or busy defending lawsuits intended to put them behind bars. Also, the remains of the *Maravillas* were either settled in the deep sand, or became covered with marine vegetation.

Two of the more proficient Indian divers brought from Margarita Island by Somovilla filed an official claim against him in 1659. The declaration stated the divers were to be paid five pesos for every silver bar they recovered, and fifty pesos for each cannon. They swore under oath they salvaged between them thirty silver bars and twelve cannon, but were paid only sixty-five pesos each. In their testimony they also stated they brought up in their own hands a chest full of gold. However, neither the chest nor its contents ever made the salvaged inventory.

More accusations appeared, clearly putting Somovilla and Reyes on the hot seat. Their former purser, Lorenzo de Soto, swore Somovilla bribed everyone in Puerto Rico, from the governor down.

"He has paid out more than 24,000 pesos in 'hush-money' because the amount he truly recovered (on his first diving expedition) exceeded 1,000,000 pesos, including a chest of diamonds, many gold bars and an immense amount of jewelry."[87]

If Lorenzo de Soto was acting out of vengeance was not known, but he certainly was not the only one who stepped forward to present both official and unofficial complaints.

So many accusations poured forth that both Juan de Somovilla and Gaspar de los Reyes were placed on probationary house arrest while they defended themselves against the indictments. They ultimately were imprisoned.

One of the more interesting charges declared that Somovilla hid some treasure beneath the powder kegs and, upon approaching the Cuban coast, he pretended seeing some sails on the horizon and went to the powder room to "make preparations," in case the sails represented enemy ships. When he returned to the quarterdeck, he admitted he perhaps was mistaken about seeing the sails at all, and called off the alert.

He also was charged for collaborating with not only the warden of the Castle at Havana, Joseph de Aguirre, but with Governor Juan de Salamanca, to insure that those officials inspecting his vessels were casual in their duties. (In the trial held the following year, both men testified they did not notice anything wrong or unusual when the returning ship, *El Champeton*, was inspected.)

In the case of fraud surrounding Somovilla's second diving expedition, his defense attorney was able to prove most of the silver reported missing was some that was lost when the *Madama do Brasil* went down at Gorda Cay, and simply was not recoverable. The defense gained considerable support from those witnesses who substantiated the earlier testimony of Captains Somovilla and Reyes. They specifically stated that most of the *barretones* and *barretonillos*, and almost all the *reales* on board the *Madama* when shipwrecked, could not possibly have been recovered after the vessel was lost on the reefs of Gorda Cay. The difference between what was registered as having been salvaged at the *Mimbres*, and what was documented as missing when the salvaged treasure was inventoried at Havana, represented the net loss at Gorda Cay, determined unsalvageable.

"Therefore nothing was embezzled," the defense counsel reasoned.

Despite this, the official controller of Somovilla's various expeditions provided some very damaging testimony. The Council of the Indies recommended both Juan de Somovilla and Gaspar de los Reyes be jailed and held until they were otherwise proven innocent.

The two captains were placed in the prison of the *Casa de la Contratación*, along with a black diver named Francisco. All were accused of having fraudulently disembarked treasure at Ayamonte, "where they purposely went in order to avoid the visit and the subsequent audit in Cádiz. This they would have been required to do, if they remained with the fleet of the Count of Villanueva."

The charge further stated some of Somovilla's Ayamonte treasure was seized, but absolutely none of it was registered. Consequently, their assets were frozen and personal belongings confiscated. Even their wives were interrogated to try and determine the individual net worth of each captain, and to learn where the large portions of the treasure might be hidden. Mariana Vásquez, wife of Gaspar de los Reyes, was particularly incensed about such harsh and inconsiderate treatment of her renowned husband. She expressed herself in the most acrimonious terms to the authorities.

"Treasure? What treasure?" she inquired. "I have seen no treasure! Nor has my husband shared any of the 'illusory' gold and jewels with me. Release the man! He is an honest sea captain!"

The controller, Felipe de la Mata Linates, told the Court how they came to be shipwrecked on Gorda Cay, how he suffered a crippling injury trying to save himself to get off the rocks and out of the water (even though he could not swim), how he lost all his personal gold and clothing, and the official papers of His Majesty "at the deserted Gorda Cay. For these miserable agonies suffered, I blame totally Captain Juan de Somovilla. Captain de los Reyes warned Somovilla earlier that the weather was going to worsen."

The controller continued, accusing the captains of numerous embezzlements, as well as the bribing of officials at both Puerto Rico and Havana:

"Everyone was stealing as much as they could get away with, but I was ordered time and again to mind my own business."

In a final, moving plea, the mistreated controller requested His Majesty award him the salary he was never paid, and to kindly make him a royal judge, "because of all this, I am poor and lame, and my enemies are rich and powerful."

Interrogations continued to be held on both sides of the Atlantic. They would ultimately determine the fate of the Spanish treasure salvors.

On May 5, 1659, the infantry lieutenant of Gaspar de los Reyes, Cristóbal de Mundarayain, gave deposition at Cádiz. When asked if the Governor of Havana was corrupted and if he accepted a 6,000-peso bribe from Somovilla to turn a blind eye, he responded;

"I don't know. I don't understand what you mean. Captain Somovilla has always been fair with everyone."

When asked how many silver bars were recovered, he answered, "About 132 *barras*, as well as some *barretones*."

Had he seen any gold salvaged?

"I have seen none. It would have been stored in chests, and I have seen no chest."

When Somovilla's key Sergeant, Pedro Gallegos, was questioned about the amount of treasure recovered during the second diving expedition, he answered, "About 130 bars of silver, some 2,500 pesos, and silver plate valued at about 800 pesos. Everything was stored on the *Madama do Brasil*, but most was recovered after the salvage vessel was shipwrecked."

When asked if there had been evidence of complicity on the part of the Havana authorities when the treasure was unloaded there, he answered, "To the contrary, the governor sent soldiers aboard to stand guard."

Manuel Perea, pilot of the *Madama do Brasil*, who survived the shipwreck, later told investigating authorities in Spain, "Somovilla retrieved 142 or 144 large bars of silver from the wreck of the *Maravillas*, plus some 31,000 *pesos de ocho*, and some silver plate." He stated that 132 silver bars had again been recovered at the Gorda Cay wreck site, as well as some *piñas* and *barretones*.

Pedro Palacios and Cristóbal de Palacios, both brothers of Gaspar de los Reyes, were interrogated in June 1659. They told virtually the same story as the others who were questioned about the amount of salvaged silver. However, Pedro was most emphatic when he stated, "No gold of any kind was found. No bars, no rings, no jewelry, no gold coin; nothing of gold."

It all appeared to be perfectly orchestrated, even suspiciously well arranged and designed to clear the salvors, who they claimed were framed.

Still, in April 1660, the Council of the Indies wrote to the Governor of Havana to reopen the case against Somovilla and Reyes, and "to interrogate *all* participants."

In 1661 the Governor of Havana stated he was continuing the inquiries. (However, he was also finding that "treasure is trouble." He was charged the same year with the unwise decision of storing some of the salvaged silver in his own home.)

The sea captains remained incarcerated in 1662 and 1663. Lawsuits continued to be heard. Stacks of legal documents were piling up in Seville and Cádiz, as well as in Havana and San Juan. In San Juan, testimony revealed that, when the salvage ship was being inspected in that port, Somovilla had hidden treasure in a strong room under the powder. He reportedly also hid some under the mattress of his berth. A sick sailor happened to occupy it at the time of the inspection!

The *Casa de la Contratación* played every possible card to try and convict the treasure salvors, who after all this time and publicity became heroes to many. Bureau of Trade attorneys even brought some of the Indian divers all the way from Margarita Island to Spain in order to have them testify against the salvors. This tactic did catch Somovilla off guard since his defense was based on no one being around to contradict him, as most of his crew died at Gorda Cay.

One Indian diver, Antonio Gonzalez, testified before the prosecuting attorney, Don Juan Antonio Fernandez de Saldivar, that he personally recovered a chest containing twenty small bars of gold and some doubloons. He said he did not know what happened to them because as soon as they were brought up, they were delivered to Captain Somovilla, and stored aboard the *Madama do Brasil*.

A second diver from Margarita, Jorge de Salzar, told a similar story about their adventures aboard the frigate of Somovilla. While he did not mention any gold having been recovered from the second diving expedition, he did provide considerable detail of what was brought off Los Mimbres during the two weeks the *El Champeton* anchored there and worked the wreck during the third diving expedition:

"We recovered thirty-three large silver bars, each valued at 1,200 to 1,500 pesos. Also, eight *barretones*, smaller than the thickness of one finger, some silver cones and some small gold doubloons of one and two *escudos*. Also recovered were five bronze cannon from the *Mimbres* and seven cannon from the wreckage of the *Madama* at Gorda Cay—all of this was embarked on *El Champeton*. The Indian divers each were paid twenty pesos when they signed on at Margarita. They were paid twenty-five pesos more at Havana, and received an additional twenty at Puerto Rico, but nothing more, although they were promised one-half of one percent of everything recovered. This is why we have come to Seville in order to see justice prevail!"[88]

Documents in Santo Domingo 106 (*Archivo General de Indias*, Seville) offer interesting examples of the difficulty in establishing true facts with the assorted testimony being offered from so many different people in various regions. As far as the salvors were concerned, they had provided inventoried records, signed by auditors of the king. These registers supposedly reflected everything that was salvaged and accounted for. Why did they continue to be questioned?

On the opposing side were the exaggerated accusations by their enemies who, for the most part, were divers who felt they were gypped, corrupt officials who felt shortchanged, and other high level authorities who missed the boat the first time around, and now wanted part of the action—or at lease some form of political upgrade.

Even men of the cloth were involved. For instance, the chaplain who was aboard the Somovilla salvage vessel during all three diving expeditions on Little Bahama Bank later turned against Captains Somovilla and Reyes. He testified under oath that both captains, as well as their brothers and friends, bullied him, pestered him, ridiculed him and constantly cursed and swore at him. They did anything they could to stop him from saying mass.

In a written statement, Chaplain Don Francisco Deca contradicted the official salvage report as follows:

Somovilla Versus the Chaplain

Salvaged by Somovilla (according to the chaplain)		Salvaged by Somovilla per the official inventory list of salvaged treasure:	
Gold doubloons	12,500		
Large silver bars	487	Large silver bars	392
Small gold bars	72	"Virtually no gold was found."	
Silver *piñas*	100	Silver *piñas*	12.5
Silver coins	15,000	Silver coins	6,100 pesos
Small silver bars "There were so many recovered that it was not possible to count them."		Small silver bars	24
A number of gold jewels and precious stones, including seven (7) *veneras* of gold enhanced with emeralds and other precious stones.		Gold jewels	Nothing
A large quantity of silverware, some of which was disembarked in Havana in large shoulder bags.		A small quantity of *plata labrada*	

In studying the contradictory testimony, it is apparent the chaplain developed some serious grievances with both captains. Most likely he was pushed around, and probably mistreated by some of the rough and tumble salvors who did not want to stop diving in order to pray when the priest desired the time for worship, so long as the seas were calm and there was good daylight. Other than these considerations, there is not visible evidence in the ancient documents as to why the chaplain felt such an obvious need to avenge himself. It is left for us to wonder if he was making a strong point about the salvaged treasure, misappropriated by the same hands who badgered and mistreated him.

On June 6, 1663, it was positively argued by the prosecution that a chest filled with gold coins and precious stones had disappeared. Gaspar de los Reyes finally acknowledged a chest was found, but he identified it as his own. He claimed it was his personal property, and described the contents in detail prior to the chest being opened.

"It is regretful this may never be proven as truth. Those who could have confirmed my story perished in the shipwreck or from hunger after we were stranded on Gorda Cay."

Although some actions against Somovilla and Reyes continued, by 1664 the Court could not find enough hard evidence to hold them longer. Besides, the high personal status and prestige of each man had considerable influence on the case. Somovilla was, only a few years earlier, knighted by the king. Gaspar de los Reyes had become one of the most famous seafarers and treasure salvors in all of Spain.

Finally, after seven long and frustrating years, on October 8, 1665, a royal decree confirmed the official pardon of the two salvors. Juan de Somovilla was required to pay 4,000 pesos to the Royal Treasury in exchange for his pardon. Gaspar de los Reyes was levied a 2,500-peso fine for the same purpose. Gaspar refused to pay the pardoning fee, stating he was insolvent, having paid everything he had to his lawyers.

After a lengthy round of arguments on the subject, the Court, with some urging from King Philip IV, released the embargo on Gaspar's personal assets. This became official in December 1666, ten years after the loss of the *Maravillas*.

It appears also that Gaspar was quite a salesman. In lieu of paying the 2,500-peso assessment, he struck a deal with His Majesty, who entered into a new agreement with him, authorizing the eminent shipwreck salvor to set out on a new treasure hunt. Gaspar would have the right to load his two 300-ton ships with trade goods exempt from taxes. By bartering or selling these goods upon his arrival in Puerto Rico, he would have an opportunity to offset or recoup his expedition expenses, whether he found treasure or not. This time, the expedition was heading for "Silver Shoals" to seek the lost treasure of the *Concepción*. Gaspar was named captain general, and he received one-third of everything found.[89]

King Philip also awarded both sea captains their years of back pay, withheld while they stood trial.

Gaspar de los Reyes sailed from Spain in 1667 with the fleet of the Prince of Montesarcho. As they approached the Antilles, he left the fleet to head for the north coast of Hispaniola (now the Dominican Republic). After several attempts, he was unable to locate the wreckage of the *Nuestra Señora de la Concepción*, because of continuous rough weather and several accidents.

A handful of isolated official documents exist, providing a further glimpse into the career of Don Gaspar. It is interesting to note that, on May 30, 1673, the *Casa de la Contratación* recommended to the king that this famous embezzler of recovered treasure be named admiral of the galleons "because he recovered the silver from the *almiranta* lost in 1656, and by doing so has served Your Majesty in a very special and notable way."

In 1688, Admiral Gaspar, now fifty-five, was treasure hunting again, this time on the reefs of the Serranilla Bank. One team of his divers searched underwater, while another group dug holes all over the sandy islet. They hoped to locate some of the lost loot of the 1605 fleet of Don Luis de Córdoba. From the islets of Serranilla, Gaspar then went to Isla Misteriosa, where he continued to search in vain for buried and sunken treasure.

In a letter to the Count of Calzada dated September 15, 1688, following his return to Puerto de Santa Maria, Gaspar explained he was unable to find anything "because it is learned the treasure was removed earlier. A pilot, Antonio Rodriguez from San Lúcar, is responsible for the thievery that took place in 1675. He later disappeared at sea. He paid for his crime with his life, as well as the lives of all the men with him."[90]

During the six years of his trial, Juan de Somovilla continued drawing plans for new forts scheduled to be built in the Philippines, as well as in Spain.

In 1667, Juan de Somovilla was named warden of the Castle San Felipe at Portobelo, Panama where, years earlier, he worked as an engineer improving and extending the fortifications. He later was named as head military engineer in the Indies, prior to his death in November 1670.

JOSEF DE YRIARTE

If prosecuting attorneys were unable to ultimately convict Captains Somovilla and Reyes, they were gaining much more satisfaction in their proceedings against Captain Josef de Yriarte.

Master Caulker Hernando Martin from Cádiz testified how Captain Yriarte quickly abandoned the wreck site of the *Maravillas* as soon as he learned another salvor with a royal warrant would be arriving soon. He also told the Court that upon arriving in Spain, Yriarte took to his home "a large quantity of silver and two chests of gold."

Manuel Perea, the pilot of Yriarte's salvage ship, *Nuestra Señora de Atocha* (named after the great galleon lost in 1622 and for the Madrid devotion and image of Our Lady of Atocha), swore under oath that Captain Yriarte recovered in two days enough silver "to fill four or five launches—plus a chest of doubloons of gold."

Antonio Gonzales, one of the Indian divers from Margarita Island who testified against Juan de Somovilla, also declared under oath he knew that about one million in silver and gold was on the Yriarte salvage ship. The gold had been stored in two very large and strongly built boxes. Gonzales' testimony stated his information came from talking with other divers[91] aboard Captain Yriarte's salvage boat.

Another serious charge against Yriarte was brought by his controller who accused him of attempted assassination. "I was left abandoned on a nearby cay without food or water, when I should have been on board the salvage vessel counting the treasure—which the captain did not want me to see."

The same man claimed that Captain Yriarte apparently recovered the greatest amount of treasure of any single salvage attempt during the first several years after the shipwreck of the *Maravillas*. He authoritatively asserted that a major portion of Yriarte's salvaged goods was not registered in the inventory log after having been lifted to the surface and placed on the salvage ship.

As an example; "I personally saw the large chest belonging to Miguel de Olacaran, supplier of His Majesty. It contained doubloons and large and small bars of gold, and many precious stones. None of this was reported when the salvage ship reached San Sebastian de Cádiz."

For nearly thirty years, Josef de Yriarte was involved in the *Carrera de las Indias*, either for his own entrepreneurial account or in military service of the king. In 1633 he was in the battle to retake the island of San Martin. In 1636 he was involved in the capture of a French merchantman off San Lúcar. In 1638 he fought gallantly with Don Carlos de Ibarra against Cornelius Joll off the north coast of Cuba. In 1640 he was in the midst of the battle between the galleons of Don Gomez de Sandoval and the French and Dutch squadrons in the Caribbean.

In 1652 he entered into a contract to build four ships in the harbor of Cartagena, plus two more at Cantabria near his home. When the agreement was signed by the king, Yriarte took advantage of the occasion to request a knighthood, which the king flatly refused. For many reasons, mainly lack of funding, he had difficulty getting started on these projects. He had been deeply involved in a number of merchant shipments between his native Guipúzcoa and *Tierra Firme*. Funds due him were slow in being received, and the overall profitability of some of his ventures was questionable.

While Yriarte was considered a man of moderate personal wealth through his assorted business enterprises, he also appeared to spend his money as quickly as he made it, all the while carrying the burden of considerable debt.

Consequently, when the first salvage ship successfully returned to Cartagena with a hull full of treasure, Yriarte was among the very first to petition Governor Pedro Zapata to send out another expedition to the Little Bahama Bank, with him personally involved.

The governor was aware of Josef de Yriarte's many personal attributes. He was equally aware of his excesses. He put Juan de Ochoa in charge, with Yriarte second in command. He hoped the highly competitive personal characteristics of the two men would balance and offset one another. This position, as one of the leaders of such an important salvage expedition, was undoubtedly the turning point in Yriarte's career.

While he was perfectly capable of handling this particular searfaring assignment, once Yriarte began staring at a pile of gold and silver on the deck of a ship under his command, far removed from land, things changed. His long-time dream of financial security might suddenly be realized.

He must have thought that certainly there could be no great harm in taking just a little. There was plenty left for the king. Besides, had not Captain Ochoa left the salvage site without waiting for him? Where was Ochoa, anyway? Had *he* run off with the treasure *he* found?

The sudden glint of gold generates varied effects on even the most conservative treasure hunters. Some people go berserk, semi-crazy, and all-out neurotic after a large treasure find. Their personality and lifestyles change. They lose their sense of value. A strange metamorphosis takes place. Could this have happened to Captain Josef de Yriarte?

By 1663 the heat truly was on him. Still, Yriarte behaved as if it was "business as usual," continuing with his wheeling and dealing in the *Carrera* trade.

The payment of his many outstanding debts, both in Cartagena as well as Guipúzcoa, suddenly took place. When he proposed to his fiancee, Doña Mariana de Echazarreta, he presented her with a magnificent ruban decorated with gold and jewels (as was at the time, worn on the dress of the wealthy). Many of their friends around Cádiz wondered about the source of these fine jewels.

One of the controllers on his salvage ship sided with him, declaring some gold, much silver and some bronze artillery had been recovered, but no serious accounting was maintained because no precise scales were on board to monitor these items.

Other witnesses declared there were, in fact, several pairs of scales available, even those used every day to measure rations of food.

One of the men taking part in the salvage expedition told the Court, according to the ship's guardian, the gold brought on board was weighed with the scales used to weigh food portions and the actual weight proved to be "four *arrobas* and four *libras*" (104 pounds).[92]

After all the testimony and hearings, Josef de Yriarte was declared guilty of having embezzled much gold and silver, and of making himself the unlawful owner of many precious stones and other valuables which did not belong to him.

For this he was given the death penalty and sentenced to be hanged. When the judgment was served, he vehemently appealed the decision, perhaps greasing the palms of a few of the important authorities. After considerable haggling and plea bargaining, his sentence of death was commuted in return for a 10,000-peso fine. The matter thereafter disappeared from the records forever.

Of all the salvors who worked the wreck of the *Nuestra Señora de las Maravillas*, Josef de Yriarte probably made the single most successful salvage and lived financially secure ever after.

Somovilla and Reyes hauled in the most total accumulated wealth for themselves, but it took them three expeditions to do so.

MARCOS DE LUZIO

In January 1667 Marcos de Luzio, the military engineer of New Spain, personally applied for and received a salvage contract. By February he had sailed from Vera Cruz to Havana to organize a salvage expedition. His objective was to search for the treasure remaining in the sunken hull of the *Nuestra Señora de las Maravillas.*

By March of the same year, he had obtained a ship and some divers and headed for Little Bahama Bank. The name of his salvage vessel was the *Nuestra Señora de Aransasu y las Animas.* Aboard the ship were the official controllers, Don José Santa Maria Nazare and Don Antonio de Vallador Velasco.

It took him some time to locate the wreck site, but within four days of doing so, he recovered 190 *marcos* of silver and one bronze cannon in thirty-two to thirty-three feet of water.[93] His report refers to how many silver bars had worked their way down into the soft sand, even settling beneath the ballast.

Realizing he needed better lifting equipment and more supplies, he sailed from the *Mimbres* in April for *San Agostin* (St. Augustine) where he met with the Governor of Florida. There he obtained some booms, heavy line and other gear and provisions.

The bronze gun was off-loaded and left with the artillery officer at this first established Florida port. Although Don Marcos returned a second time to St. Augustine for gear and provisions, there was no additional report of treasure other than the 190 *marcos*, representing a value in silver of some 1,560 pesos.

A later report indicates Luzio had a problem with his divers. They apparently went on strike, refusing to dive because of harsh treatment. Luzio admitted to his irritation with the divers as being his reason for returning to port. "May lightning strike them," was his wording in one report.

One of Luzio's lieutenants, Captain Primo de Rivera, applied for salvage rights the following year. He claimed the instruments and equipment brought to the wreck site by Luzio were useless. He also said:

"The divers refused to perform because Luzio treated them like dogs. This applicant begs for the opportunity to go forth at his own expense in a vessel of 70 to 80 tons to recover the silver. Half of all treasure salvaged will be His Majesty's, and half for myself. His Majesty will also be named executor of my will."[94]

MARTIN DE MELGAR

Don Manuel de Melgar of Guipúzcoa spent much of 1674 seeking permission from the Council of the Indies to salvage the silver and artillery possibly still remaining in the great *almiranta*, which sank eighteen years earlier.

On May 8, 1675, a contract was approved under the "now standard" conditions. Melgar would assume all costs and risks in return for a fifty-fifty share. All cannon recovered must be turned over to the king. A bond of 20,000 pesos was required to be posted in Havana. On February 2, 1676, as he was preparing his salvage ships for the anticipated expedition, Manual de Melgar had a seizure and died.

His brother, Don Martin de Melgar, who was the scheduled salvage operations chief, assumed responsibility for the royal agreement. He paid the 20,000-peso bond, received the official title of *Capitán de Mar y Guerra*, and was loaned two Cuban divers from Morro Castle. He sailed for Little Bahama Bank on March 25 with the *Santo Cristo de Potosí* and the *Nuestra Señora del Rosario*.

Besides the two Cuban divers, there were a number of divers aboard the two salvage ships. To keep a watchful eye on the activities of the salvor, Don Francisco de Mella y Frias was appointed overseer of the salvage operation. It was his responsiblity "to keep the accounts of the ship, take inventories of what was recovered, make certain that the governor or royal officials of Havana (or any other Spanish harbor where the salvor might arrive) are diligent in their inspection of the salvage, and that His Majesty receives his one-half share."

Foul weather greeted their arrival at *Los Mimbres*. The salvage ships and their crews spend a good part of their time anchored in the lee of Cayo de Rosario (today Sandy Cay).

Although they were occasionally bothered by pirates thought to be Bermudian "wrackers," they finally had a few calm weather days and were able to recover some silver bars and silverware. Francisco de Mella y Frias would report[95] that, "Five cannon have been spotted, but not brought up. They should be worth more than 25,000 pesos, since a small one Marcos de Luzio recovered was sold in Florida for 5,000 pesos. There is much silver remaining in the sunken hull, and since all the silver bars we found were piled in a group, it is my feeling there remains a strong room in this area. The remaining bars should also be found well grouped together."

Martin de Melgar later stated that only eight of the divers were useful. The others were virtually unable to reach the depth of eight *brazas* (forty-four feet), "where the bottom and ballast of the *almiranta* now lies."

There are hundreds of documents relating to the Melgar salvage years, and much of the information is repetitious. However, one document mentions "we found the hull," not *fragments* of the hull. This would be important for future salvors.

Even as June approached, fair weather came infrequently. The salvors were able to dive only five days: June 7, and from June 14 to 17. When bad weather was encountered, they took shelter in an anchorage near Grand Bahama. They attempted to return to the wreck on four separate occasions, but could not stay because of the storms.

Since neither salvage vessel was satisfactorily equipped with heavy lifting gear, and provisions were running low, the expedition departed *Los Mimbres* in late June. By July 13 they were back in Havana.

On August 17, Francisco de Mella y Frias submitted his report to officials of the Royal Treasury. Listed were "3,718 *marcos* of silver and 3 ounces" (30,208 pesos) recovered by the Melgar group. This consisted mainly of twenty-four large bars, ten small bars (flat pieces of silver), 93 small silver plates, a large cluster of coral-encrusted silver coins, and some damaged silverware, including a section of a sword hilt. The total was valued at 21,911 silver ducats.

The controller reflected some criticism of Martin de Melgar when he stated in his report that in his opinion the salvor's percentage should not be paid because "Melgar selected ships that were too small. He was not sufficiently armed to protect the treasure of His Majesty, and he was insufficiently equipped to lift the heavy bronze artillery lying on the sea bottom and clearly visible from the surface." This strong statement by Don Francisco de Mella y Frias regarding not paying the salvor his fifty percent share apparently carried some weight in Havana. Martin de Melgar had considerable difficulty receiving his half portion of the 30,208-peso recovery. Even this amount would not cover the previous bond he posted, let alone his salvage expenses.

The authorities in Havana displayed an amazing degree of bad faith, claiming that there was no contract at all with him, even though Melgar assumed the responsibility of his dead brother's position, paid the bond, performed the dangerous work, and surrendered every peso. He resolutely claimed he was legally entitled to that portion his brother would have received. He had divers and salvage personnel to pay, and he needed to return to the shipwreck site as soon as possible to bring back even more silver.

"My chief pilot, Pedro de Ojeda, knows exactly where the *almi-*

ranta lies, and we can find the wreck again. We can salvage much silver if we hurry," he said. After vigorously pursuing the royal officials, and dramatically emphasizing there was much more silver, as well as guns to be brought up, he finally received his money.

1677

The following summer, on May 4, 1677, the frigate *La Machanga* sailed from Havana with Captain Martin de Melgar. They stopped at Cayo de Hueso (Bone Key, today Key West, named by the Spaniards who first explored the island and discovered a number of sun-bleached skeletons). They dove on a Dutch wreck, *The White Lamb*, lost some eight or nine months earlier. They recovered two iron guns, one a three-pounder, and 300 cannon balls.

Before crossing the Bahama Channel they hired some Indian divers[96] from Key Vaca, then headed for the *Tumbado*. From there they sailed for the *Mimbres*, where they anchored on June 15, after finding the remains of the sunken hull almost immediately, thanks to good navigating by Pedro de Ojeda. Longboats and *cayucos* were placed directly over the wreck and buoys dropped fore and aft on the coral-cloaked hull. The weather still did not cooperate. They had only three days good enough for diving. However, in those few days, they successfully brought up the following treasure:

> Inventory of Salvaged Silver—1677
> 68 large ingots of silver
> 4 medium ingots of silver
> 20 small ingots of silver
> 10½ clusters of silver pieces-of-eight
> 15 small silver plates, corroded
> 1,254½ silver pieces-of-eight
> 2 large silver candlesticks
> 1 small silver candlestick
> 3 large silver plates
> 2 silver jugs, very worn and corroded
> 6 wedges of silver
> 1 silver tray stand

Francisco de Mella y Frias continued to urge Captain Martin de Melgar to try and save the bronze guns, along with the silver they were finding. Melgar was primarily interested in silver since the cannon would have to be turned over to the Crown. It took much badgering, but he finally agreed to try and recover the guns.

Using the heaviest piece of hemp rope, a diver secured a noose around the muzzle of one of the large guns, then doubled up around the trunnions. With the help of a hawser, the cannon was lifted. About halfway to the surface however, the line parted. The gun fell heavily to the bottom, nearly crushing one of the divers. Captain Melgar reported, "It is mandatory to utilize a salvage vessel large enough to lift the heavy guns, but with shallow enough draft to permit clearance of the numerous reefs existing nearby on all sides. The bottom near the hull is very hard, and the anchors do not hold well in it."

Melgar's divers found the sea in the vicinity of the sunken ship unusually tranquil, and the water beautifully clean and clear. Everything recovered was found in the area where the cannon lay. "The sand bottom is of good consistency," he reported. "Since the poop castle has broken off and many of the deck timbers have rotted away, we hope the Lord will help us reach the inner ballast and save the treasure remaining. There are magnificent marine growths of many colors now decorating the grave of Don Matías de Orellana, and coral covers what is left of his *almiranta*."

Apparently, the force of the current running through the reef had caused part of the wreck to shift. The divers found a small cave, formed by coral and sea growths around the wreckage, tunneled out by the action of the currents. Inside the cave they discovered a number of small silver plates lying perfectly exposed, together with several clumps of silver coins. The largest discoveries were made within the area of the "little cave." There was also a small octopus credited with making this natural depression its home.

On their return to Havana, they reached the *Tumbado* after a half day's sail from the wreck site, and from there, Cayo de Rosario after one day of sailing. Being concerned about pirates and afraid of the often violent thunderstorms kicking up almost every afternoon, the salvors did not remain long at the *Los Mimbres* anchorage.

Melgar arrived in Havana on July 11, 1677. He was quick to report salvaged treasure amounting to 6,143 *marcos*, "of which half has been delivered." It is apparent that on this second trip the captain wisely paid himself first by withholding his half-share of the recovery—no doubt having learned his lesson. He also reported 1,254.5

"worn pesos" had been awarded to the Indian divers "as motivation and encouragement, and to secure their valuable services in the future, since they are the main instrument of our success."

The ever-diligent controller Francisco de Mella y Frias continued to pursue his responsibilities as chief watchdog of the expedition. A 1677 letter to the Governor of Havana offers further evidence of his job dedication:

"It seemed to me that some of the divers who came aboard had some silver *reales* hidden in their pants. While I was in the poop of the frigate, they moved the launch close to the bow, suggesting the captain go in the other boat to look at something very valuable beneath the sea. When the men climbed up to the frigate to rest, some silver pieces fell out on the deck. I quickly put these with the rest of the treasure."

1678

On the afternoon of March 24, 1678, our salty salvor Martin de Melgar again sailed out of Havana harbor to salvage the silver of the *almiranta* of galleons lost in *Los Mimbres*.

As had been his custom, he first stopped at the lower keys to take various "trade goods" to the Indian chiefs to encourage them to loan him some of their better divers. Melgar then headed for the Little Bahama Bank. The salvage vessel for this operation was the *Nuestra Señora de Candalaria y las Animas*.

On April 30, Pilot Ojeda had located the wreck and ordered the ship anchored. The longboat, towed astern of the salvage frigate, was brought alongside. Nine divers and a few boys boarded it. Other divers jumped into two *cayucos*.

"We all began diving and working very hard to retrieve as much silver as possible while the water was calm," de Melgar logged.

The weather cooperated. They were able to work for five days, putting in six hours of diving each day. On May 4 the seas kicked up, so they buoyed the wreck and sailed to Cayo de Fabrica (today, Great Sale Cay), where they anchored for a few days, catching fish and lobsters.

Upon returning to *Los Mimbres*, and just as they spotted their buoy, tied to a bronze artillery piece, the winds increased with tremendous gusts. They were again chased to a safe haven, this time taking refuge at Cayo de Rosario.

Melgar had been warned to be on the lookout for enemies and to take no chances of losing their treasure. Because they enjoyed such good success in a short period of time, they decided not to press their luck and sailed for home.

As they approached Key Vaca they were confronted with another series of storms.

Melgar sent his lieutenant, Simon de Noroña, with the longboat to notify Havana authorities of their position. He was also to report the amount of recovered treasure they carried, valued at 7,572 *marcos*.

List of Salvaged Treasure—1678
46 silver bars, one of middle size
3 small bars
8 small bars in 9 pieces
Cone-sized silver balls
11 large and small cones
2 pieces of cones
150 small bars of silver
6 long bars
1 small silver plank
Broken silver plate: 30 small plates, 1 basin, 2 eagles with wings, all embossed and worn
Other pieces of candlesticks, little pans, ewers, bowls, spoons, candle-holders, candlestick-pans and chocolate-cup bases
In a letter dated June 17, 1678, de Mella reminds the authorities that, during these three expeditions, 17,471 *marcos* (about 143,000 pesos) of silver were recovered.

1679

On his fourth successive diving expedition, Martin de Melgar sailed from Havana on April 13, 1679. That year he had two ships: a 45-foot frigate carrying twenty-five guns[97] and an especially built salvage barge. Accompanying him were sixty men and twenty-five divers. Their reliable pilot brought them safely to *Los Mimbres* and positioned the salvage barge over the hull of the *almiranta*.[98] The small, armed vessel was anchored nearby "to protect them from the menace of pirates."

Shortly after they started diving, a French ship sailed onto the scene, threatening salvage activity. With the armed frigate providing a source of security, Melgar began firing at the Frenchman, who turned to run. The confident Spaniards gave chase in their small frigate, with both vessels firing at each other. Suddenly, one of the guns on the Spanish frigate exploded, causing a nearby box of powder to detonate. This freak accident created a disastrous turn of events.

Captain Martin de Melgar was killed instantly, along with thirty-six of his men.

Seeing the Spanish ship in trouble, the chased French pirate quickly became the pursuer, attacking and capturing the frigate, then taking control of the salvage barge, using the Indians hired by the Spaniards.

Francisco de Mella, who was burned on the face and hands from the explosion, was marooned on Sandy Cay, along with others in Melgar's crew who were not divers. The controller later told Spanish officials: "We were left on a deserted isle for two months with hardly any water and very little to eat. Most of us had little or no clothes. With constant exposure to the sun during the day, we felt we would surely die. Some nights were so cold, many of us became sick."

The French pirate drove the divers unmercifully, threatening them with death. The more treasure they brought up, the more he desired. He sent them down time and again, until the evening's darkness precluded visibility.

The Indians staggered back aboard the barge, tended to their wounds, cuts and bruises, then fell into exhausted sleep. They were awakened at sunrise each morning to again begin their diving.

Occasionally, Pilot Ojeda and a few other Spaniards on the barge were permitted to take a little food and water to those who were sick and dying on the cay, some thirty miles distant. Finally, as his ship rode low in the water with quite a few tons of silver, the Frenchman wrote a receipt for the treasure he loaded into his ship, and graciously thanked those Spaniards who remained alive saying, "I am most pleased with the results of our joint salvage activity. We Spanish and French must team up and cooperate more frequently."

De Mella and the other survivors sailed their vessels to Santo Domingo where they made their sad report.

Although he was still suffering from his burns and the privations of his marooning, de Mella immediately suggested that a new expedition be organized before the pirate decided to return. This new diving expedition would not get underway until the following year.

According to de Mella and other Spanish seamen who survived to tell their story, some 200,000 pesos of large and small bars, and many pieces-of-eight were taken aboard the French ship. If this amount is a correct inventory, it is significant in that 200,000 pesos were many times more than the average annual amount of salvage reported during recent years. Could this offer additional evidence that much more really was salvaged by Spanish salvors than was reported?

A letter[99] dated 2 November 1679, from Jean-Baptiste Patoulet, a French envoy, confirms that.

"The privateers from Saint Domingue[100] have taken the Spanish salvage ship by surprise, with all salvage equipment. They have successfully utilized it to enable them to return to Saint Domingue with 140 silver bars worth 200,000. I believe Monsieur de Pouançay[101] has sent them back to attempt additional salvage."

The French report further confirms what other Spanish and English accounts state—there were numerous attempts to pilfer the wreck site if the location could be found.

1680

The expedition of the year 1680 was headed by Captain Esteban de Veroa. Francisco de Mella y Frias was still the designated controller.

Unlike the Melgar contract, which was at the risk and expense of the salvor, the entire cost of the 1680 diving expedition was personally funded by the Governor of Havana. The salvage party set out from Morro Castle on July 16.

The governor completely ignored the request of the widow of Martin de Melgar, Doña Maria Josefa Hidalgo, to be refunded at least half of her husband's performance bond.

In September, Esteban de Veroa returned to Havana with 3,370.5 *marcos de plata*, four *castellanos de oro*, and two bronze guns. (The gold was a little jewel in the form of a rose.)

The armada of Don Enriquez de Guzmán returned to Spain with 33,767 pesos, representing His Majesty's share of that year's treasure recovery. It is presumed the governor received the remainder.

After having been slighted by the Governor of Havana, the widow of Captain Melgar was determined to have her day in court. A 310-page lawsuit demanded she be justly compensated for what was rightfully hers.

On July 6, 1682, the Council of the Indies finally settled the dispute, acknowledging that the governor acted irresponsibly and illegally. Doña Maria was awarded 10,000 pesos as settlement, plus court costs.[102]

1681

In 1681, the Governor of Havana wrote to the King of Spain about the continuous attacks by the English. "A group of these English have set up a permanent camp on the island of Grand Bahama in order to have a convenient base of operations. From here, they go to fish on the *almiranta*, lost on the *Mimbres*."

One Spanish group attempted to work the wreck, but was chased away by some English salvors from New Providence (Nassau).

The Governor of Jamaica, Sir Thomas Lynch, wrote to Captain General Robert Clarke, Governor of New Providence.

"Pillaging Spanish wrecks is a national pastime for the Bermudians, who either kidnap Indian divers in Florida, or entrap them, in order to work the wrecks."

It does appear that Bermudian "wrackers," working with their crude diving bell referred to as the "Bermuda tub," recovered ten to twelve pounds of silver per man, totaling some forty to fifty pounds (at the time, enough to buy two slaves in Jamaica).

These divers also utilized the age-old, glass-bottomed-bucket to view the sea floor from the surface.

Apparently, the Spanish got a piece of the action in 1681, because the returning fleet of New Spain of General Gaspar de Velasco brought back 41,300 pesos from the salvage of the *almiranta* in the canal de Bahama.

There is no question that English salvors from Bermuda and New Providence also reaped a harvest of silver from the now twenty-five-year-old galleon wreck on Little Bahama Bank. How much total treasure they recovered is anybody's guess.

1682 - 1683

In 1682, a report reached Spanish officials in Havana. Several salvage boats from New Providence and Bermuda had been working on the wreck site of the *Maravillas*. There is no record referencing how much treasure might have been found.

In 1683, "six ships of Englishmen with eighty divers between them" were said to be over the wreck. One of the vessels was under the command of Captain Peres Savage, who had been six months at the site. When he returned to Boston in November, he declared to a naval agent that there was not much left.

Apparently, Captain Savage's haul averaged only seven and a half pounds of silver plate per man. He moved debris and rotting timbers by dredging throughout the wreck area.

"Ten paths were made by dragging from stern to stern athwart her, and found but thirty sowes of silver in all. I believe there is very little left in her, for I took as much time as a man possibly could, bringing up several pieces of her keelson and some of her hooks."

Another Englishman, Captain Welch, was not very optimistic either. He worked the wreck for ten months, recovering very little.

Among the English who anchored at the *Maravillas* wreck site that year was Captain William Phipps. Phipps, along with Captain Warren, was aboard a former Royal Navy ship, the *Rose of Algaree*, chartered to them specifically for salvage work. Also in their party was Captain Charles Salmon, who later drew two very good charts of the Little Bahama Bank, showing the locations of the *Maravillas*, the *Genovese* wreck, and what was called the Copper wreck.

Phipps and company stayed at the site for a fortnight. They had with them only three good divers, all sick with smallpox. Consequently, Phipps teamed with another English ship, *Good Intent*. Despite the numerous divers on board, they reportedly recovered only one bar of silver.

Four years later, in 1687, Captain Phipps proceeded to fame and fortune with his discovery and successful salvage of the 1641 galleon, *Nuestra Señora de la Concepción*, wrecked on reefs north of Hispaniola, known today as Silver Bank.

The dredging and dragging around the sunken hull of the *Maravillas* probably further dispersed and destroyed some treasure and artifacts covered with soft sand.

While numerous contracts later were entered by prospective salvors, there is no indication in Spanish archives that anyone found, or salvaged, the historic shipwreck after this period. In 1688 a contract good for eight years was signed between the Council of the Indies and Josef de Acevedo, a resident of London. It allowed him to "go and fish for silver on Spanish wrecks that might have been lost off the coasts of Spain and in the Americas."

This was just one of many contracts issued to an assortment of adventurers in England, the Netherlands, France and Spain, as a result of the craze for treasure hunting following the publicity of the astounding success of William Phipps in 1687 on the *Concepción*.

There is no indication that Josef de Acevedo ever went to the *Mimbres*. What local Bahamians, the English from Bermuda or New England, or other hopeful salvors might have accomplished after this period is unknown.

The remains of the *Nuestra Señora de las Maravillas* would lie dormant for some 300 years.

REGISTER AND SALVAGE SUMMARY

A List of the Treasure Cargo of the *Maravillas* and a Summary of the Amount of Salvage from 1656 to 1683

Although the original cargo manifest of the *Maravillas* was lost with the ship, the register was recreated from copies upon His Majesty's order on December 15, 1657 because of the continuing investigation and inquiries. These registers can be found in *Contratación* 2382 and *Contaduria* 3 at the General Archive of the Indies in Seville, Spain.

Contratación 2382

The Portobelo register, relating to the cargo brought on board at Panama, consists of 326 pages, with 50 pages missing. (It bears the note that it was received in the accounting department of the *Casa de la Contratación* in Seville on December 7, 1659.) This document lists:

    421 silver bars
    43,958 pesos
    368 *marcos* of silverware and old silver
    (There was also a small *cruzada*, a tax supposedly for the maintenance of Holy places, going to the Church of Spain.)

The Cartagena register (62 pages) is a certified copy made in 1658 from one original copy of the offical register of 1655. It lists as follows:

    85 silver bars
    28,927 pieces-of-eight
    328 *marcos* of worked silver

The Portobelo and Cartagena combined registers amount to:

    506 silver bars
    72,885 pieces-of-eight
    696 *marcos* of worked silver and silverware

(There was also one chest containing official mail for His Majesty which was shipped from Cartagena.)

The pieces-of-eight generally were packed 2,500 to the chest. Most of the listed items belonged to private owners, with the exception of one (1) silver bar that was consigned to the Convent of San Francisco in Seville and 23 silver bars that had been salvaged from the 1654 *capitana* off Chanduy, Ecuador. (Since those 23 bars had not been registered, they were promptly confiscated for His Majesty.) There was also a large silver bell of 35 *marcos*, and a silver lamp not included in the total.

Contaduria 3

This copy of the *Maravillas* register was certified by Don Fernando de Villagas, Chief Accountant for Life of His Majesty, at the *Casa de la Contratación*, on February 24, 1660. It was produced to facilitate the distribution of that treasure salvaged to all legal owners. The Council of the Indies also wanted to precisely evaluate what the percent of tax should be on the goods and treasure transported by the fleet of the Marqués of Montealegre. The original document bears the signature of Don Diego de Yuste, silvermaster.

From Portobelo:

    412 silver bars plus 7 *barretones*
    53,193 pieces-of-eight
    110 *marcos* of silverware
    8 chests full of silverware
    1 silver oil lamp

From Cartagena:

    94 silver bars, plus 1 *barreton*
    29,027 pieces-of-eight
    328 *marcos* of silverware

While the silver bar totals in each of these registers match, the pieces-of-eight and worked silver totals probably can be reconciled somewhere in the breakdown of the chests of silver and *marcos* of silver. All silver bars are carefully described by weight, fineness, number and owner's marks, if any. A typical entry reads:

"In the city of Cartegena of the Indies, on the 22 of this month of May of 1655, in front of me, the subsigned witness, Don Diego de Yuste, Silvermaster of the Galleon *Nuestra Señora de las Maravillas*, vice-flagship of the royal fleet under the orders of the General Marqués de Montealegre which has come from the Kingdom of Spain to fetch the Royal Treasure and property of private owners, by the voice and in the name of Don Esteban de Valdez y Godoy and in virtue of the proxy he has delivered to me in the City of Portobelo in front of Juan de Ysassu, a citizen (of the said city), on April 30 past of this present year 1655, and in the name of the above named, I do register in the said galleon vice-flagship, 34 silver bars from Peru and one chest of silverware of 128 *marcos* which I undertake to keep in his behalf as the silvermaster of this ship, and I declare that the said silver bars are the ones with the following numbers, fineness, weight and value:

Bar number 2765; Fineness 2376; Weight 127 *marcos* and 11 ounces; Value 301,237 *maravedises*, etc."

What is particularly interesting is the fact that nowhere in either of these lengthy documents is there any mention of the registration of gold, jewels or trade goods.

The only official indication that there was a likelihood of considerable jewelry being on board this galleon came from the silvermaster, Captain Diego de Yuste, when he swore under oath in Cartagena attesting to his certification of the cargo:

"I beg Your Graces to acknowledge that I have been officially licensed to manifest the gold, silver, the coinage, the jewels, the small pearls, the indigo and cochineal which the shippers might wish to register in the said galleon."[103]

As it turned out, none of the shippers apparently wished to register their gold, jewels, coinage, small pearls, indigo or cochineal. There was no doubt the magnificent articles of gold and jewelry found on the wreck site were either personal possessions of passengers—or were being smuggled! Admiral Matías de Orellana had 32,508 pesos registered in his name in Portobelo. Diego Portichuelo de Rivadeneira had registered 20,836 pesos in Cartagena. These were not his funds. He was simply transporting them under the direction of the bishop of the Lima cathedral.

No registers appear to exist from Vera Cruz or from Havana. It seems hard to believe that no cargo was brought aboard at either of these major ports. (While the armada was not scheduled to stop at Vera Cruz, they put in there for thirty-five days to avoid the large English fleet patrolling between Jamaica and Cuba.)

After the Marqués of Montealegre returned safely to Spain, and before there was any official word of the *Maravillas* being lost, the *Casa de la Contratación* asked the marqués if he recalled what the register of the *Maravillas* contained.

"Although I do not have the original manifests, I do remember that the *almiranta*'s register showed 464 large silver bars, 13 chests of worked silver, and 81,629 pesos in restamped[104] *reales*, counted at 2,500 pesos in each chest. This would equate to about 470,360 pesos."

The marqués also recalled that on the *Jesus, Maria y Josef* of Juan de Hoyos there were registered 85 large silver bars, 4 small bars, one chest of worked silver, and 66,063 restamped pesos.

This reference comes from Contratación 3120 and 2381, and also reflects that the total value of registered treasure brought by the entire fleet of the marqués, including some of the salvaged treasure from Chanduy (the reason for the long delay of the fleet in *Tierra Firme*), amounted to 19,062,417 pieces-of-eight. From this gross total amount there were deducted 873,297 pesos for expenses, and 189,120 pesos for maintenance of the fleet. This left a net balance of 18,000,000 pesos which were registered among all the vessels of the fleet. The *capitana* of the marqués carried 1,035,218 pesos under register. This was broken down as follows:

    57,304 *pesos* in large silver bars

    177,381 pieces-of-eight

    5,501 *pesos* of 7 and 3 (devalued)

    99,379 *marcos* (795,032 pesos) of worked silver

Contratación 5122 values the cargo at 431,000,000 *maravedis*, or 1,585,000 pesos.

As the first diving expedition was under preparation during March of 1656 there was an estimate given of 5,000,000 pesos having been aboard the *Maravillas*.[105]

In a 1661 lawsuit it was stated as being common knowledge that more than 5,000,000 pesos were on the *Maravillas*.[106]

The diary of Diego Portichuelo records there was 5,000,000 in gold and silver on the *almiranta*.

e two ships, *Maravillas* and *Jesus, Maria y Josef,* carried more than 12 million
veen them." Barrionuevo

)M PORTOBELO AND CARTAGENA

JRCE		SILVER		GOLD		VALUE
	Large Bars	Small Bars	Worked Silver in Marcos	Pieces-of-Eight		
tra. 2832	411		369	80,892	None	507,000
tra. 5122						1,585,000
tra. 3118	463	24	81,629		None	560,000
. 3	506	9	446	82,220	None	608,000
tra. 3120	412	24	13	81,629	None	470,360

erenced Treasure Aboard the *Maravillas*

lichuelo de Rivadeneira	5 million in gold and silver
taduria 1435	5 million
taduria 1432	3 million for His Majesty Only
ibania 103 B	More than 5 million (estimated in a law suit during 1661-1662)
nimo de Barrionuevo	More than 6 million

Summary of the Salvage

A List of the Treasure Cargo Recovered from the Shipwreck of the *Nuestra Señora de las Maravillas*

1656 through 1683

YEAR	SALVORS	TREASURE DESCRIPTION	OTHER SALVAGE/ COMMENTS	VALUE	
				Marcos	Pesos
1656	Survivors	1 large bar 30 small bars 2 *piñas*	1 silver snail (all items placed in rescue launch)[107]	275	2,260
1656	Juan de Somovilla Tejada and Gaspar de Reyes (1st diving expedition)	300 large bars 17 *piñas* 100,000 pieces-of-eight 405 *castellanos* of gold	1 bronze cannon 1 chest of worked silver		477,146[1]
1656	Controller Juan de Posadas Vergara	Miscellaneous worked silver found on Cayo de Rosario			210[1]
1656	Capt Lockyer from Bermuda	unknown			
1657	Juan de Ochoa y Campo	Assorted silver bars and worked silver which filled two chests			20,650[1]
1657	Josef de Yriarte	Many hundreds of large and small bars of silver and gold	24 cannon		1,500,000
1657	Juan de Somovilla Tejada and Gaspar de los Reyes (2nd diving expedition)	160 large bars 105 small bars 60 *piñas* much worked silver 50,000 pieces-of-eight	1 cannon		170,000

Year					
1658	Juan de Somovilla Tejada and Gaspar de los Reyes (3rd diving expedition)	38 large, 27 small bars 12 piñas much worked silver	5 cannon	6,000	53,000
1667	Marcos de Luzio	some small bars and worked silver	1 bronze cannon	190	1,600
1668	The Dutchman from St. Augustine	unknown amount			
1676	Martin de Melgar	24 large bars and 10 small bars 2 piñas much worked silver, including 93 silver plates		3,718 (21,911 silver ducats)	30,500
1677	Martin de Melgar	68 large bars, 25 medium/ small bars 8.5 piñas, much worked silver 1254.5 "worn" pieces-of-eight		6,143	55,000
1678	Martin de Melgar	46 large bars, 178 medium/ small bars considerable worked silver and corroded coins		7,572	68,000
1679	Martin de Melgar	Melgar was killed	the Spanish lost their treasure to French privateers		200,000[113]
1679	French Pirates	amount unknown[114]			
1680	Captain Esteban de Veroa	considerable silver and four castellanos of gold		6,370.5	67,534[115]

1681	Bermuda "wrackers"	unknown amount	Approximately 50 pounds	1,000
1681	Spanish expedition from Havana	various silver bars and plate		82,600[116]
1682	English salvors from Nassau and Bermuda	30 silver bars and miscellaneous worked silver and corroded coins		50,000[117]
1683	New England sea captains	1 bar considerable worked silver	60 pounds	100,000

Total Treasure Salvage Recap 1656 – 1683

Large silver bars	1,068
Small/medium bars	362
Piñas	112
Worked silver	many tons
Pieces-of-eight	151,254
Cannon	34
Total value in pesos[118]	2,909,500

This reconciliation of ancient salvage reflects a total of 1,068 large silver bars which were known to have been recovered, compared to a combined Portobelo and Cartagena registered number of 506. There were many more recovered which we will never know about. The recap also shows 151,254 pieces-of-eight were known to have been recovered from 1656-1683, against a registered amount of 72,885. Certainly, many more thousands of unreported pieces-of-eight were taken off the wreck.

When one considers the gold and silver coin and bullion, the emeralds and other jewels, the highly crafted rosaries and crosses, and the many tons of hand-fashioned, worked silver which was recovered but never reported, it is easy to see why the *Nuestra Señora de las Maravillas* is today, and always has been, one of the world's great lost treasure ships.

The *Maravillas* Sketch

No shipbuilder plans or drawings, no painting, no woodprint, or any other official piece of art of the *Maravillas* has been found, or is known to have ever existed.

This ancient sketch (partially enhanced by a modern artist) is believed to be of the galleon *Nuestra Señora de las Maravillas*. It was discovered on the damaged vellum cover of the *Registro de Plata* of a sister galleon, *Bendición de Dios*. Perhaps it was the silvermaster himself, Esteban de Piñalos, who was the artist. If this assumption is correct, we can thank Señor de Piñalos for enabling us to perceive today what our 1656 *almiranta* may have looked like. With her three decks, three masts, and the lovely oil painting of Our Lady of Marvels so vividly decorating her sterncastle, she is truly resplendent (although not exactly to scale.)

12

Destruction at Santa Cruz de Tenerife

Our foremast fell by the board. We no sooner cleared ourselves of it by cutting it away, but down falls our mainmast. We cut it away presently, then down falls our mizzenmast. We had only our bowsprit to friend.
Squadron Commander Richard Stayner

Madrid, May 28, 1657

Madrid is in shock over the catastrophic news of Spanish losses suffered again at the hands of the English at Santa Cruz de Tenerife. Our entire fleet returning from the Indies has been destroyed.

Don Diego de Egues y Beaumont was named captain general of the squadron of New Spain in 1652, his most prestigious and responsible assignment to date. He made one successful voyage across the Atlantic to Vera Cruz, then to Havana, and back to Spain. His most eventful trip did not begin until March 10, 1656, when the New Spain fleet sailed for Mexico. As they departed Spain the fleet consisted of his *capitana*, the *almiranta*, one *patache*, two galleons belonging to the king and four merchant vessels.

The fleet left Vera Cruz for Havana on August 21, 1656, and finally departed Havana for Spain on December 2. Spread between the *capitana* and the *almiranta* were 672,228 pesos in gold, silver bars and *reales*. The entire amount was sent from the Royal Treasury of Mexico, Guatemala and Campeche, and was registered for the account of His Majesty. Other products and merchandise included leather and hides, indigo, Brazil wood, Campeche wood, cocoa, chocolate, various drugs, copal resin and balsam bar.

The original register of the *capitana* of New Spain reflects the name of the silvermaster as Captain Gaspar Gutierrez, who apparently died during the voyage. His assistant, Matías de Iraurigui, assumed his responsibilities.

The following summary shows the allocation of treasure for His Majesty, for the *cruzada* (royal revenue decree), for the *donativo* (crown forced donation), and for individuals (private citizens and merchants):

	HIS MAJESTY	CRUZADA	DONATIVO	INDIVIDUALS
capitana	16,137,488	22,800,944	3,066,902	88,129,394 *mis*[119]
almiranta	15,145,232	22,800,944	3,066,902	85,113,118 *mis*
Total	31,282,720	45,601,888	6,133,804	173,242,512 *mis*

The Spanish fleet arrived at Santa Cruz around mid-February 1657. After learning the distressing news about the disaster off Cádiz the previous September, and of the very strong English presence within Spanish territorial waters, they decided to remain until they felt assured the area was clear. Don Diego in no way wanted to lose his valuable cargo to the enemy, as had happened the previous year.

The English general-at-sea, Robert Blake, already had learned of the impending return of a large fleet from the Spanish officers aboard the galleon of Don Juan de Hoyos, who had been captured. In late February he again received fresh news of the Spanish treasure fleet holed up at Tenerife.

Captain David Young of the *Catherine*, an English merchantman returning from Barbados and bound for Genoa, spotted some two dozen galleons of the eastbound treasure fleet a short distance west of the Canaries. When this news reached Blake, a Council of War was convened with great enthusiasm. He held a number of meetings with his captains as he weighed the pros and cons of going after the Spanish at Santa Cruz.

It was decided to send a squadron southward in anticipation of intercepting the Spaniards in case they attempted a direct approach to Cádiz. After several weeks no galleons were sighted, so the frigates returned to their dull blockade duty patrolling off Cádiz.

Two months later an English privateer delivered updated news to Blake. The entire Spanish treasure fleet was at anchor in the harbor of Santa Cruz. Blake again called for a Council of War. He and his officers discussed the situation for an entire day. His captains, recalling Stayner's conquest the previous fall, encouraged immediate action. They already knew how they would spend their prize money.

Vessels of the *Egues y Beaumont* 1656 *Plata Flota*

The *capitana*	*Jesus Maria*
General	Don Diego de Egues y Beaumont
Captain	Don José Marqués
Silvermaster	Gaspar Gutierrez Arias
The *almiranta*	*Nuestra Señora de la Concepción y San Luis*
Admiral	Don José Centeño
Captain	Don Juan de Bobadilla
Silvermaster	Pedro de Aranguirvel
The galleon	*Nuestra Señora de los Reyes*
Governor (Infantry)	Count of Bornos
Captain	Roque Galindo
The galleon	*Nuestra Señora de la Soledad y San Francisco*
Captain	Francisco de Ortueta
The *nao*	*San Juan Colorado de Honduras*
Captain	Sebastian Martinez
The *nao*	*San Cristo de Buen Viaje*
Captain	Pedro de Arana
The *nao*	*Campechano Grande*
Captain	Pedro de Urquia
The *nao*	*Campechano Chico*
Captain	Miguel de Elizondo
The *nao*	*Vizcaiño*
Captain	Cristóbal de Aquilar
The *nao*	*Santisimo Sacramento*
Captain	Francisco de Villegas
The *nao*	*Patache*
Captain	Pedro de Orihuela
The *nao*	*Nuestra Señora del Rosario y San Francisco Solana*
Captain	Fernando de Ybara
The *nao*	*Nuestra Señora de Guadalupe y San Antonio*
Captain	Antonio de Alcala
The *nao*	*San Cosme y San Damien*
Captain	Antonio Vega
The *nao*	*Nuestra Señora del Rosario y San Juan de Puerto R*
Captain	Pedro Figueroa

A decision was made to take the fleet to the Canary Islands. Several vessels were left behind to keep an eye on the Spanish coast.

Blake put his flag on the *HMS George*. The fleet, consisting of thirty-three men-of-war, sailed on April 24. Landfall at Tenerife was made on Saturday evening, but Blake spent most of Sunday April 29 contemplating various strategies.[120]

On April 25 at Santa Cruz, Don Diego de Egues learned of the death of his brother-in-law, Don Pedro de Ursua y Arizmendi, Knight of Santiago, Count of Gerena and Captain General of the galleons. A memorial service was held for him the evening of April 29 aboard the *capitana* at Santa Cruz. A short while after the service an aviso arrived from Las Palmas with the ominous news of the approaching enemy fleet.

Besides the New Spain fleet of Don Diego de Egues, several other ships arrived in the Canaries. Included were two ships from Honduras, one from Havana, one from Campeche (the *Jesus, Maria y Josef*, with Francisco de Chavez as captain), a ship from Santo Domingo (the *Nuestra Señora del Rosario* with Fernando Yzcurra as captain), and from Maracaibo, *La Bendición de Dios y San Juan Bautista*, with Captain Juan Gonzales de Araup. According to the Spanish records, there were about twenty ships in the harbor.

On the morning of April 30, Blake designated twelve frigates for the primary attack squadron. They included the *Newberry, Centurion, Worchester, Plymouth, Winceby, Foresight, Newcastle, Lyme, Maidstone, Longport, Bridgewater* and the *Speaker*.

Rear Admiral Richard Stayner, the hero of the engagement off Cádiz the previous September, was named to lead the attack. A second squadron was to follow and take positions just beyond the harbor. Blake held the *George* just offshore. Four other English vessels waited in reserve.

"The commanders spoke to the general asking that I command them. The general relayed the request to me. I told him, with all my heart," Stayner later wrote in his narrative on the battle of Santa Cruz. "I gave them a verbal order to follow me in a line. Wheresoever I saw the greatest danger I would go. They were to fire not a gun until they were at anchor three or four cables' length from the shore."

The harbor at Santa Cruz was partially protected by a quay constructed at a northerly angle about two thousand yards from the curving shoreline of the town. It provided good anchorage in all weather.

To the north was the primary fortress of San Felipe, equipped with sixty cannon. There were additional batteries beyond it. Also smaller bunkers and entrenchments filled in toward the castle of San Juan to the south. These included musketry mounds and barriers, three deep in some places.

Stayner approached the town at approximately eight o'clock in the morning. He counted the Spanish ships in the harbor. Several deep-drafted men-of-war were moored along the quay. The *capitana* and *almiranta* were outboard, broadside to the sea. The smallest vessels (300-500 tons) were lined side by side, stern to the shore.

With an onshore breeze from the east, Stayner made a direct approach for Santa Cruz. The rising sun was rapidly burning off Santa Cruz's early morning mist. Fort San Felipe, substantially embedded in the hillside, stood out like a silent sentinel. Stayner could see the sharp features of the gun parapets, their hardware gleaming in the ever brightening day.

There was much activity on the roads and foot paths above the harbor. People were scurrying. Dogs were barking. Carts piled high with boxes and chests from the last galleons to be offloaded were pulled by oxen in the direction of both forts.

As he led his attack straight for the harbor entrance, Stayner could sense the incoming tide flowing with him. He watched a flight of shore birds sweeping across the *Speaker*'s bow. He took a deep breath, filling his lungs with the clean, cool, fresh air. It was going to be an exhilarating day.

There was little humidity, and the crispness of the morning was both calming and invigorating to the nerves and senses of the English crews. A pale blue canopy of sky above them was interspersed with wisps and puffs of cumulus. The light easterly sea breeze filled the English sails just enough to provide steerage and maneuverability of the warships.

Beyond the Santa Cruz harbor entrance the shoreline was uneven and rocky, evidenced by breaking seas. The possibility of anchoring or landing there was imprudent. Stayner realized their success would be dependent on an expeditious harbor entry, creating as much destruction as quickly as possible. Unsure how much depth of water the harbor carried, he took note of the larger galleons moored on the outboard side of the breakwater. For now at least, the tide and the wind were with him. He expected to be fired at from shore at any minute, but it did not happen. Perhaps he would be fortunate enough to extend the first broadside. Standing on the forecastle of the *Speaker* in order to better determine water depth and position, he signaled the other eleven frigates of his squadron to follow him.

They boldly sailed directly into the harbor between the royal galleons on the outside, and the line of merchant ships inside the quay. The English captains were ordered not to fire until they were certain they could make good their broadsides.

"We went as near as possible, still insuring safety. We were within pistol shot of the admiral and vice-admiral, and a little more of the rear. They were all great ships riding near the castle, 1,000 and 1,200 tons apiece. Seven or eight were 650 to 800 tons. Four more made the rest. The whole number was seventeen sail," Stayner recalled.

There was sporadic shot and shell from shore. The English wondered why it was not heavier. The fact was that the Spaniards at the forts dared not fire through their own ships to get at the enemy just beyond them. The Spanish ships in the harbor served as a screen for the English warships. To fire a cannon from Fort San Felipe, the Spaniards would have to shoot through their own merchantmen and warships. The situation, and the problem, was the same at Fort San Juan.

Although it was Stayner's intention to be the first to fire an English gun, the *Plymouth* beat him to it before all the frigates had positioned themselves for adequate broadsides. Whether this was a misunderstanding of Stayner's orders, or nervous anticipation was never determined. Regardless, by nine o'clock the primary attack group was at anchor inside the harbor, and the English began unleashing a merciless bombardment. With their close range and superlative fire power, English gunners jumped on their adversaries and gained the advantage. Not only was the *Speaker* in the midst of action, but the *Lyme* and the *Bristol* were scoring major hits. Spanish sailors abandoned their ships. Fortress gunners ran from the hillside in panic.

By eleven o'clock, most of the Spanish merchant vessels were on fire near shore. The English now concentrated on the *capitana* and *almiranta*. Fort San Felipe, directly in front of the action, sat silent for half-an-hour. From land positions small arms fire continued, but very few large caliber cannon shots were being fired. However, within the smoke and flame at the jetty, the warships of Castile were not to be easily outdone.

Both royal galleons fought valiantly until a group of the second English squadron moved in for closer range. The Spanish men-of-war began receiving heavy shelling from both sides. Stayner's ships were on the inside, and the second squadron was on their opposite beam. English guns were simply overpowering.

The *almiranta* was blown to pieces first. Shortly afterward the *capitana* exploded.

Thomas Lurting, boatswain's mate in charge of two hundred men on the English frigate, *Bristol*, told it this way:[121]

"The captain called to me to get a hawser out of the gun room and clap a spring on the cable. When done, we veered our cable and lay just across the hawser, about half a musket shot from the Spanish vice-admiral (the *almiranta*). Then we ran all the guns we could on the side toward him. In number, this was twenty-eight or thirty. All hands went to it in earnest."

The *Bristol* was well inside the harbor "half a cable length" (about 300 feet) from the *almiranta*, a galleon of over 1,000 tons, with fifty guns and 300 men. The 1,200-ton Spanish flagship *capitana*, carrying sixty cannon and 400 men, was another 100 yards distant. Both war galleons were fighting doggedly. Their cannon shots were not nearly as numerous as the volleys they received, nor were their gunners as efficient. However, their extreme nearness to the English warships caused damage when an occasional shot landed true. The close range fighting was creating casualties on both sides, but it was clear from the first shots fired who would prevail in the struggle.

The dramatically bold offensive maneuver by the English placed them in a dominant position. With twelve warships occupying premier space in the harbor, and a back-up force positioned immediately outside, they were able to fire aggressively from all sides at close range. The Spanish were totally intimidated.

The daring English assault also created unbelievable good luck for them. A shot from a broadside of the *Bristol* fell into the powder room of the *almiranta*. She blew up. No person below deck escaped. There was fire, extreme heat and much screaming. The main deck was swarming with men trying to get overboard.

When the *almiranta* exploded, there was a huge burst of flame followed by a meteoric shower of sparks hissing and spewing into the harbor. For those witnessing nearby, it was not the explosion, but the immense fireworks display that was remembered. The momentary

Battle at Santa Cruz

The English warships made a direct approach for Santa Cruz. They boldly sailed directly into the harbor, between the royal galleons on the outside and the line of merchant ships inside the quay. The problem for the Spaniards was that the forts did not dare fire through their own ships to get at the enemy. The Spanish ships in the harbor actually served as a screen for the English men-of-war who soon began unleashing a merciless bombardment.

spectacle, brilliant and mesmerizing, was extinguished as quickly as it began when the burning debris hit the sea water.

Boatswain Lurting watched the incendiary exhibition in awe. A boundless cheering resounded from the English ships throughout the harbor. Though his nostrils burned from the acrid black powder, he could smell the unmistakable stench of freshly seared human skin. He watched as Spanish sailors, their clothes ablaze, jumped into the water. Others dove in head first, hoping to dodge an English musket ball.

The Spanish captain general, now fighting alone, brought as much force to bear as he could against the heavy English bombardment. The few guns he was able to levy roared forth on both his port and starboard sides. There was devastation and death, but the English kept coming. Close range artillery was deafening. Heat from the burning ships was scorching. Smoke and flame and burnt powder filled noses, throats and bronchial tubes.

A deafening broadside from the *Bristol* was the finale. As the English scrambled to reload, the Spanish *capitana* exploded, revealing a bright orange glow distinguished in the midst of black smoke. Many of her sailors were seen on the burning deck and in the water.

The usually serene and placid harbor was now a junkyard of charred remnants, mutilated bodies, smoking sail and cordage, and shipboard odds and ends. Through this maze of floating embers and residuum those who could not swim dog paddled and floated any way they could manage to the safety of shallow water. A few heroes endeavored to assist other less fortunates. Cowards and those in shock struck out on their own.

With the entire Spanish fleet in devastation, renewed cannon and musketry fire resumed from the forts and breastworks. All of the anchored English ships were easily within cannon range, and those closest to shore were taking some serious musket fire.

"They could not bring upon us but two or three guns," reported Stayner. "We were so completely into the harbor."

It was now about two p.m. English firepower was directed at the forts ashore. The tide was ebbing and the wind continued to blow in the direction of the harbor. Soon there was only small arms fire coming from shore, the cannon having been silenced. Some of the English busied themselves finishing off the few merchant ships that had not been totally sunk.

"We made them weary of it," Lurting stated. He took the *Bristol*'s pinnace and boarded one Spanish ship heeled over in the shallow water. As the English sailors clambered over one side, the few Spanish crew remaining exited over the other. The vessel was set on fire. Similar procedure was repeated on other nearby ships.

Lurting later would acknowledge, "Some silver was found on board." (There is no record as to what happened to this silver, but we can certainly guess.)

The smaller *naos* moored along the shore were burned. Most of their treasure cargo had been carried at great haste to the castle on the hill. Not all of it made the safety of the vaults, nor was it recorded in English ship's logs. Such is the way of sailors during the heat of battle.

Boatswain Lurting's script vividly relates his close calls with death during the historic battle of Santa Cruz. There were four occasions when he easily could have been killed. "Having full sight of us, the breastworks opened fire. They discharged a volley of fifty or sixty small shot. Two of our men were killed, a third was shot in the back. I received no harm, although a shot cut the bolt-rope a little above my head. This was my fourth deliverance, and all in six hours time, never to be forgotten by me."

Several of the English ships captured prizes (small ships) and were trying to get them out of the harbor. This was contradictory to Blake's standing orders. He signaled for his men to drop the prizes and set them on fire. However, the English skippers were not about to relinquish their trophies easily. These included the *Maidstone*, *Plymouth* and *Bridgewater*. Renewed cannonade from the Fort was aimed at those English ships with prizes. Musket shots rained down on Stayner aboard the *Speaker*.

Blake communicated his orders once again. "Fire the prizes!"

By mid-afternoon the shellacking was complete. Santa Cruz Harbor was choked with sunken and smoldering wrecks. The wind direction was still easterly. It was blowing directly into the burning bay. Exiting the harbor was going to be difficult for the English. They were faced with sailing against the wind and through the smoke and flames of the burning Spanish fleet.

Seeing the English attempting to steal the few Spanish vessels left afloat kindled a renewed vigor among the gunners on shore. They fired away relentlessly as the English attempted to withdraw.

The *Winchester*, sitting close to the shore batteries, took several heavy hits as it tried to kedge and warp out of the harbor. Another large frigate, upon weighing anchor and attempting to tack against the wind, was blown into a shallow area. It became temporarily stranded.

Recognizing the difficulties of withdrawing, the English captains finally obeyed Blake's orders to release the prizes. They were set on fire and adrift.

The *Speaker* was the last English vessel out of Santa Cruz Harbor. She was barely afloat. The Spaniards focused their fire on Stayner's besieged ship. The *Speaker* took a continuous volley until she warped her way out of range. It was approximately seven p.m.

"We had holes between wind and water, four- or five-foot long and three- or four-foot broad. By nailing hides over holes and staves along the sides of the hides, we managed to keep her afloat," Stayner stated. "For we had eight or nine feet of water in the ship."

As the sun set in the west, the wind began to blow offshore. This probably saved the *Speaker* as she limped out of the harbor.

"They paid us extremely," Stayner added in his report. "I struggled to get the ship underway. We had not one whole rope overhead, but we set those pieces of sail[122] we had and cut away her anchors."

Just as Stayner's frigate passed by the great castle, a magnificent explosion took place at the hillside bastion. "After this, they never fired one gun more at us," he reported, wondering whether the detonation was caused by his shot, or some accident ashore. Then all hell broke loose on his ship.

"Our foremast fell by the board. We no sooner cleared ourselves of it by cutting it away, but down falls our mainmast. We cut it away presently, then down falls our mizzenmast. We had only our bowsprit to friend."

The *Plymouth* came to the aid of the *Speaker* and took her in tow. Even after temporary repairs were made, the *Speaker* never regained fighting trim.

"The commanders of other ships said we should never save her. Still, through mercy we did. She was almost full of water. We spoiled all our dry provisions, and all things else in the hold," Stayner recorded.

As darkness fell on Tenerife, all Spanish ships at Santa Cruz were destroyed. Not a single English vessel was lost. There were many casualties on both sides, though the English reported only sixty killed. Thirty were wounded and fifteen killed aboard the *Speaker* alone.

"It was, without question, the boldest undertaking of its kind ever performed. The Spaniards, romantic enough in their own conduct, were so much astonished at his (Blake's) aggressive and surprising approach, they quite lost their spirits. Thenceforward, they never thought themselves safe, either from numbers or fortifications."[123]

With reluctance, but duty-bound humility, Don Diego de Egues y Beaumont reported to King Philip:

"On Monday at two o'clock a.m., I was advised of the arrival, three leagues from here, of thirty-three English ships. I immediately warned Admiral Don Jose Centeño, as well as the captains of other ships. I also sent word ashore to Don Alonso Davilla so everyone should ready themselves."[124]

Before dawn the Spanish assembled to take fighting posts. Even some passengers who didn't have fighting posts took positions. At daybreak they nervously watched the enemy approach from a distance of two leagues. The east wind was favorable for the English. "Soon we were attacked by twenty-eight ships, formed in two squadrons," reported General Egues. "The other five ships kept out to sea, as a rearguard.

"The first squadron led by their *gobierno* initiated the attack." (The rear-admiral referred to here was Stayner aboard the *Speaker*.) "Steering with only their topsails, the English maneuvered with amazing perfection, right into us. Others anchored a musket shot away, along and in front of our ships. I was able only to use the bow chasers of the *capitana*, and the two or three first guns near the bow to respond to the enemy fire."

The Spanish were truly unprepared for such a battle. Their artillery was light, their men obviously not seriously trained. Many of their people lacked the determination to hold at all costs. Still, from the initial shot their posts were all manned. The merchant vessels, surprisingly enough, fought with more resolve than might have been expected. As shells began to burst and fires began to burn, the hot tide of the fight began to turn.

When a few of the captains were killed or wounded, many of the crew jumped into the water to swim to the safety of the shore. The English frigates kept coming. As a result they boarded five or six of the galleons, setting fire to everything. The fate of the *almiranta* was the worst because she was closer to the enemy and was unable to avoid their firepower. The admiral tried twice to set her on fire, but each time it died out. Most of his crew already had jumped ship and were swimming toward shore. The admiral personally went below a third time to put the ship on fire. An incendiary device he carried exploded in his hands. He was severely burned. Finally the *almiranta* was ablaze.

Once the *almiranta* was lost, the English frigates moved in for the kill on the *capitana*. This was now the primary target as every English vessel fired at the big galleon. Flames from the burning *almiranta* made matters worse. The ships were moored right next to each other and the blazing fire from the *almiranta* was now beginning to lick the side of the *capitana*. The flames already reached its standing rigging.

Don Diego de Egues fought for another hour. Finally the heat from the fire of his burning sister ship became too hot. The cables were slipped to further avoid the flames. It was then his stern came too close to the edge of the shore where the *capitana* grounded.

"My chief gunner and four trusted men went below to set the *capitana* on fire. Some of my men then bodily threw me in the water so I might risk drowning instead of being killed by the fire or flying bullets. Just as I reached shore the incendiary device blew up the *capitana*. It was one p.m., after four hours of fighting.

"In the afternoon the wind came around to southwest. Even though some of the English captains tried to take as prizes those Spanish vessels not burned, they were prevented from doing so. Consequently, they abandoned the idea and set them all on fire.

"Throughout the afternoon the English exchanged fire with the shore batteries.

"More than five thousand cannon balls were shot at us. Our land based artillery was not very efficient. Only the rear admiral (Stayner) lost his main topsail and his mizzen. The loss of treasure and merchandise was not great because the unloading of the vessels was already nearly completed.[125] May Our Lord guard the Catholic Royal Person of Your Majesty for the many years Christianity needs it."

Diego de Egues y Beaumont, General, Puerto de Santa Cruz, May 8, 1657

After a few days of reflecting on this most unhappy report, the king responded to Don Diego.

"I have received your various reports where you inform me of the disastrous battle against twenty-eight English warships on April 30. Your summary reports you fought with valor until such time you and Don Josef Centeño put fire to the *capitana* and *almiranta*. I consider I have been well served by you and am satisfied with your services and behavior."

Duro notes that General Egues was later presented with a group of Indian slaves valued at 2,000 ducats, in appreciation for his bravery against the English. Admiral Centeño also received a similar award, his valued at 1,500 ducats.

Don Diego appeared at the king's court a few months later. His Majesty named him a member of the Council of the Treasury.

A number of well-known Spaniards were killed, including the chief pilot of the *capitana*, Lazaro Beato. Also killed in the battle was Captain Miguel de Elizondo of the ship *Campechano Chico*, Don Pedro de Argos, Don Pedro de Medina and Don Pedro de Navarrete. Admiral Don José Centeño was badly burned.

Fernando Duro, noted Spanish historian, thought it worthy to not overlook the fact that in addition to the human fatalities, "Father Andres Valdecebeo, the naturalist who was on board, was much saddened by the loss of a very rare species of four *colibris*, or hummingbirds, he was bringing from the Indies."

Following the battle of Tenerife, and in view of their tremendous loss of sea power, even the Spanish acknowledged the English were now "lords of the sea." They possessed the ability to keep large fleets cruising simultaneously in the eastern Atlantic, as well as the Caribbean. The few ships remaining in King Philip's fleet were forced to stay in port. The English succeeded in breaking the confidence of many Spanish sea captains and sailors.

Barrionuevo's summary in Madrid on June 2, 1657 stated; "They say here, this loss is huge. More than one thousand times worse than the one of Juan de Hoyos. There will be no way for most of the merchants of Seville to avoid bankruptcy. This coming year we shall have no armada to go to the Indies. Nor will anyone dare risk his capital in such a risky business. Nor will anyone attempt to organize or finance such an enterprise. On the day of the Corpus, His Majesty marched with the procession. His eyes sunken and deep in shadows, his sadness was clearly evident."

Also stated in Duro's *Armada Española*, "The organization and artillery of the [English] Navy was known to be superior to our ships. We remained locked in Cádiz because of the large number of warships on station permanently off the coasts of Andalusia. The exploits of Robert Blake truly did merit admiration and praise since he was merely a student from Oxford. An accidental military man, he was an improvised admiral with no other secret than his force of will and character. He transformed, or better said, created the real English Navy. Later it became famous because its operational efficiency was supported by an inexorable discipline from the highest level to the lowest, fostering the principles of duty and the understood obligation of service."

The "discipline" referred to by Fernando Duro can be well illustrated by an example set by General Blake following the battle of Santa Cruz. The incident involved his brother, Captain Benjamin Blake, along with Captain Stayner and several other of the more ambitious commanders. They unnecessarily endangered themselves and the lives of their crews by remaining within the harbor in an attempt to pillage the abandoned vessels as they burned, the very actions the general gave direct orders against. As a result of their misbehavior, General Blake removed his brother as captain of his ship and gave the command to another officer.

"To say the truth, discipline is the soul of service. Men are apt to measure the consequences of things by the rewards and punishments attending them. An officer such as Blake, who will do justice upon his own brother, will be generally feared and highly admired. Yet he will be sincerely beloved. His sailors will be ready to undertake anything at his command."[126]

In recognition of Blake's astonishing success at Santa Cruz, Parliament ordered a day set aside for thanksgiving. A diamond ring valued at 500 pounds sterling was to be presented to General Blake. An award of 100 pounds was presented to the captain who brought the news. Thanks were extended to all officers and soldiers concerned in the action. But the general never received his ring.

After destroying the Spanish fleet at Santa Cruz, the English returned again to patrol off Cádiz. Soon after, General Blake's health began to fade. Continuous poor diet and three years at sea produced a severe case of scurvy. It was coupled with a worsening edema, leaving him bloated and without energy. Sensing his time was short, he headed for England. General Blake died as his flagship entered Plymouth Sound on August 17, 1657. He was fifty-nine.

"He was a man deserving praise, even from his enemies. Being advanced to command at sea, he subdued the Scilly Islands, near home. Having attained the office and title of admiral, he performed things worthy of immortal memory abroad. He humbled the pride of France. He reduced Portugal to reason. He broke the naval force of Holland, driving them to the shelter of their ports. He suppressed the rovers of Barbary, and twice he triumphed over Spain."[127]

Blake's body was transported to London where it lay in state. It was finally, with great pomp and ceremony, interred on September 4 in the chapel of Henry VII at Westminster Abbey. In 1661 it was removed from the Abbey and buried in the churchyard.

When Richard Stayner returned to England he was knighted by Lord Cromwell for his deeds both off Cádiz and at Santa Cruz. His wife died a year later and he returned to sea. In the summer of 1659 he was named rear admiral of the fleet, along with Admiral Mountagu. He was again knighted by the King of England on September 24, 1660, his earlier knighthood not having been recognized by the Royalists.

He continued to serve as vice-admiral of the fleet, first under Mountagu, the Earl of Sandwich, and later under Sir John Lawson. On July 2, 1662, it was reported Stayner was desperately ill in Lisbon. He died in October.

The Spanish Crown was not in a position to even arm a special fleet to fetch the treasure in Tenerife, especially with the likelihood of again facing the English squadrons. Consequently, the king decided the official termination point of that year's New Spain fleet would be Santa Cruz. He ordered his trusted Don Diego de Egues to settle and close the registers then and there. Don Diego capably and independently carried out the orders to His Majesty's satisfaction.

After carefully auditing and receiving all registers, Don Diego realized that his own fleet was not exempt from the rampant fraud and smuggling known to be routine among the *Carrera de Indias*. After his audit, he subsequently reported to the king: "The treasury probably will receive more in royal tariffs that merchants will have to pay on their recently discovered unregistered goods, than what was lost in the disaster."

The guns from the burnt and sunken vessels were awarded to the citizens of Santa Cruz by the king. A portion of the cargo was also bestowed to them so they might rebuild their city and fortress. This included eighty *quintales* of gun powder, fifty of musket shot and thirty pieces of artillery.

His Majesty then began discussions with some of the more powerful merchants and noblemen in Spain and Europe to buy and lease ships. Spain actually acquired thirty ships from Prince Rupert of the ex-Stuart Navy. Privateering was organized and encouraged. Foreign merchant vessels, especially Danish ones, were subsidized to bolster trade with Spain.

The final assemblage of treasure resulting from the liquidation at Santa Cruz was embarked in several small coastal vessels arriving at Puerto de Santa Maria in March 1658. It is interesting to note that among the few ships carrying treasure from Santa Cruz to Spain, one of the smaller ones, the *Fama Volante (Flying Fame)* took off without authorization from Don Diego de Egues. If he merely didn't follow proper protocol, or if he had other intentions with the loot is not known. However, via several memorandums, Don Diego made it clear he was upset over the situation. When the *Flying Fame* had the Spanish coast in sight, she was spotted by several English vessels on patrol. The chase began.

The *Flying Fame* succeeded in outrunning the English pursuers, but was forced to enter the Bay of Huelva where the little ship purposely was beached on the bar. The crew proceeded to jettison all the silver bars and chests overboard, then they headed for shore, "some in the longboat with their most precious valuables and some swimming," quoted one Spanish report.

The English appeared on the scene, refloated the ship and took her away. No diving was undertaken by them. There is, however, considerable documentation about successful Spanish diving operations. Considerable work was carried out afterwards on the bar of Huelva for the purpose of recovering the jettisoned cargo of treasure. There is also a long account about a diver who disappeared after having recovered part of the treasure. He was chased all over Andalusia.

Don Diego entered His Majesty's service in 1624 as a page to young King Philip. He faithfully served his king and his country for the next forty-one years. There was virtually no administrative field or military position in the army or navy he did not occupy as a highly ranked civil servant. He also served in Peru as *Corregidor de Cochabamba*, participated in the campaign of the *Salses* as a captain of infantry, took part in the battle of the *Escuadra de Indias* against the

Dutch at Havana in the late 1630's, fought against the French in 1641 off Cádiz, and was involved in the next battle off Cabo San Vicente. While in Havana in 1643, he was badly wounded when he entered into a duel one night with Don Bartolomé de Osuna, Governor of Santiago de Cuba. In 1650 he was supervisor of the galleys.

Don Diego de Egues y Beaumont went on to serve as one of the eminent members of the Council of the Treasury. He was a Knight of Santiago and Mayor for fourteen lifetimes, including his heirs, of the Imperial House and Irrigation System of the Council of Tudela de Navarra. He was actively involved in the management of his family estate and in rebuilding the chapel in the church of Tudela when administrative problems developed in 1661 in the new Kingdom of Granada (today's Colombia). He was asked to assume the Presidency of the *Audiencia de Santa Fe de Bogota*, and reinforce the management of the Marqués de Santiago, captain general of the newly designated territory. This was with the understanding he would retain his Treasury Council status and be next in line to govern New Granada upon the death of the incumbent marqués.

Egues y Beaumont assumed his post in 1662. He was credited with much good work in establishing missions among the wild Indian tribes, and building roads and bridges within the province. He served loyally for almost three years, until his death on Christmas Day, 1664.

13

The Enigma of Padre Diego

While I may have committed grave excesses, let me remind you; I am a virtuous and exemplary priest with a good reputation. Therefore, I ask, please do not judge me too harshly.

Madrid, New Year's Day, 1658

The year 1657 was an especially busy period. I received permission to relate my experiences at appearances before the Court of King Philip. There were also numerous official hearings, as well as meetings necessary to the success of my mission for the church. Heavy focus on the writing of my memoirs, finally published late in the year by Don Garcia Morras in Madrid, added to the business demanding my attention.

To my delight, on March 23 the following year, a royal warrant was signed through the most noble efforts of my sponsor and other references of merit. This confirmed for me an official half salary prebend at the Metropolitan Cathedral of Lima. The promotion necessitated a request for an extension of my visa, as I was not yet finished with my church activities. I was permitted to delay my departure from Spain to Peru.

The *Contaduria* arranged for my forthcoming voyage and the accompaniment of one servant. I was to be permitted to embark on any ship of my choice in the fleet to *Tierra Firme*, along with my books and personal belongings.

My return voyage to Cartagena, the subsequent transit to Portobelo then across to Panama, and the ensuing southerly trip to Callao, were a pleasure compared to the nightmare trip I experienced two years earlier. On October 15, 1658, I assumed my post as the oldest chaplain of Lima's most holy cathedral.

During the next several years I pursued my religious responsibilities with fervent Christian dedication. I was instrumental in founding a school of Christ Our Lord in each parish, similar to the School of the Hospital of the Italians in Madrid, founded by Don Mario Rupo de Toledo. Over one thousand people attended the Bible study held between the hours of six to eight every evening. A similar school for women of the Hospital of Charity in Lima was also initiated, with classes offered on Friday afternoons.

On February 20, 1660, the Council of the Indies notified the king of the need to fill a vacancy for a full *ración* at the Lima Cathedral. While I was one of the three recommended, His Majesty chose to name Juan Francisco de Valladolid.

My performance over the past few years had received considerable praise from my peers. This most negative news of once more being passed over for promotion was a bitter pill to swallow. I became melancholy and extremely dispirited. What depressed me most was not so much missing out on the monthly prebend of 177 pieces-of-eight, but that Juan Francisco de Valladolid was made to travel all the way from Rome to fill the vacancy. My presence in Lima would have saved the Crown the huge amount of lost time and the heavy expense in their transfer of clergy. Nevertheless, I endeavored to continue with a positive mental attitude.

Another vacancy occurred three years later. In all its wisdom, the Chapter procrastinated and did nothing.

Over the past several years I have been in contact with another chaplain. Now residing in Madrid, Padre Francisco Deca served as chaplain on many seagoing vessels and suffered the agony of shipwreck, as did I. He has kindly kept me informed on the news in Spain. More recently, he shared word regarding the treasure salvaging activities of Gaspar de los Reyes and Juan de Somovilla. They have been working on the shipwreck site of Admiral Orellana's *Nuestra Señora de las Maravillas*. Because so many of my friends were drowned in the awful calamity, and will forever rest in the ocean graveyard, I have followed the salvage results with strong interest. It is amazing to my simple mind to find that some men possess such ingenious and creative faculties enabling them to retrieve hundreds of silver bars and other lost valuables from the deep sea waters. If only I could swim perhaps I would better understand how such inspiring feats might be accomplished. Such courageous exploits are beyond my ability to even imagine, much less comprehend.

Having recovered lost treasure worth hundreds of thousands of pesos, the salvors' underwater heroics, though dangerous, have certainly proved to have been worthwhile, for the divers as well as for the Spanish Crown.

In his most recent letter, my friend mentioned the ever present human weaknesses of gluttony and greed. Both have apparently overtaken the noble seafarers, Somovilla and Reyes. He says these two heroes of Spain have been indicted and are under house arrest for stealing treasure from His Majesty.

One would think with so much money being recovered from the bottom of the sea, there is certainly enough treasure so all the parties might sufficiently share, without some of them having to resort to thievery.[128]

Even with the excitement of sunken treasure on my mind, some having been my own, with some 20,000 pesos registered on the *Maravillas'* silvermaster's books, I continue to pursue my daily duties with steadfast perseverance.

The viceroy wrote to King Philip in November 1664 advising him that there were now two vacant full *raciónes* in the Lima Cathedral. I felt it was the first time in many years something positive was happening in my behalf.

Learning about the viceroy's report was enough in itself to brighten my hopes.

"The number one candidate should be Don Diego Portichuelo de Rivadeneira[129] who has been a *medio racionero* since 1657. In this capacity he has displayed a fine example of all the Christian virtues. He has been well received as a preacher in the pulpit. He has enjoyed the best possible contacts with both governmental and secular officials. He has founded the *Santa Escuela de Cristo Nuestro Señor*, and has done much work in our hospitals."

In recognition of my diligent educational efforts the archbishop also proffered a praiseworthy recommendation for me to fill the vacant post. The promotion finally became effective on July 25, 1665.

While it may not be characteristically proper and fitting for a priest to be concerned about monetary compensation, a certain degree of financial well-being has been a matter of increasing concern as my years have advanced. Here I was, fifty-one years old and finally with an income level of 2,000 pesos annually! One of my first priorities is to arrange for a gift as a token of appreciation to my sponsor for so many years of financial support.

In the meantime, a strange bureaucratic metamorphosis took place within the confines of the Cathedral Chapter. Considerable organizational changes within the administration became effective. For all practical purposes, this left me without any meaningful mission or job description. It was obvious I was being squeezed out of the church's administration.

Worrying about my sudden lack of ecclesiastic responsibilities made me sick. Certainly I was not as agile and alert as I once was. I recognized my age might be a factor, but I badly wanted to make the golden years of my life a productive final phase. Why was I being shunned? Did I not serve loyally over the years? Had my trials and tribulations of shipwreck, capture and torture by a pagan enemy not earned for me appropriate recognition and a rightful place within the church? Why had the Lima Chapter closed the door on me? I cannot take this isolation any longer! Perhaps in Spain they will still remember me. I must seek out higher authority who will listen with compassion to my needs.

In an inexplicably sudden and mysteriously dramatic move, apparently calculated for some time, Padre Diego clandestinely boarded a *patache* sailing from Callao to Panama in late September 1666. Insuring his departure would be in secret, he forewarned no one. As a result, he did not possess a valid travel license. Furthermore, this strange action was sure to sour his already shaky relationship with the Lima Cathedral Chapter, most likely for the remainder of his life.

As a guilt-ridden afterthought to his hasty exit, and in an attempt to obtain an approved visa, he wrote letters to the archbishop and the viceroy in Lima. These were dispatched from the first ports of call. In the letters he endeavored to inform them of his poor health, stating he suffered from hypochondria.

"Only the good air of Spain can cure me. It is a matter of life and death. Since it would have taken two years to have officially obtained a travel visa, I probably would have died before it arrived. I therefore humbly and respectfully request I be given a mission in Spain."

On November 9, 1666, the *Real Audiencia*[130] in Lima wrote to the Queen-Governor in Spain.

"Madam,[131] we have received in these royal offices, a letter dated September 30, sent to this city by the doctor Don Diego Portichuelo de Rivadeneira, full *racionero* of our saintly church. In his letter he refers to all he has done in this ministry over and beyond the call of duty. He explains he has become the victim of the very serious illness of hypochondria, a mental state of permanent melancholy and imagined illnesses. According to his physician, there is no remedy other than the benefits of the clean air of Spain. In order to go there, he decided to embark secretly. Indeed, it appears this is what he has done as no one here could provide him with a visa without having received the order of Your Majesty.

"In his letter he requests we inform you of his good behavior. However seriously we may have to judge the grave excesses he has committed, he is a virtuous and exemplary priest with a good reputation. He asks you not judge him too harshly."

However, the Archbishop of the Lima Cathedral, Don Pedro de Villagomez, recommended not to honor Padre Diego's request for a visa and a mission. It was his opinion that the chaplain should renounce his prebend before departing. On March 12, 1668, he wrote to the Queen:

"I have already reported to Your Majesty the manner in which Don Diego Portichuelo de Rivadeneira, being in possession of a full *ración* awarded to him by His Majesty, departed without telling anyone or giving any forwarding address. Nor did he obtain any travel license. He left secretly for Spain in a *patache* sailing at the time. He has written to me twice from various harbors along the way requesting a visa. I do not wish to give him one because the provincial council has denied it. Also, a prebendary is required to renounce his prebend before leaving his position.

"I beg Your Majesty decide what you wish to do about this full *ración* position, now vacant. I shall be in favor of whatever decision you make." (Lima 304.)

Church accountants were instructed to pay Padre Diego for only the period of time he actually worked in residence as *racionero*, and to cancel his prebend.

When he reached the Andalusian shores, Padre Diego traveled directly to the home of his sponsor, protector and long-time friend, Don Juan Gonzalez de Uzqueta y Valdes. Valdes was an extremely influential member of the Council of the Indies as well as a good listener to the woes of the insubordinate priest. In time, Don Juan made certain the Council remembered the heroics and devoutness of Diego Portichuelo de Rivadeneira. This resulted in a royal pardon and the issuance of a round-trip visa, enabling Diego's honorable return to Peru. This voyage was undertaken in the Spring of 1669 and ended in January, 1670.

By a royal warrant[132] dated April 20, 1669, the Queen directed the judge and officers of the *Casa de la Contratación* in Seville to arrange for the return to Peru of Padre Diego. He was requested to present his official *racionero* nomination certificate to authorities of the *Casa*, in order to obtain his travel visa.

While Padre Diego may have been reinstated on the payroll of the church, the cathedral officials, all members of the Chapter who still smarted over the reinstatement of the priest, made sure that his duties constituted little more than those of an errand person.

In June 1671, he was again chosen to travel to Spain to represent the cathedral. In 1673 he repeated the arduous voyage all the way back to Peru, arriving in 1674.

Apparently the purpose of this final trip, though undertaken "on business of the Cathedral Chapter," was actually to promote his nomination as a canon. Padre Diego had now served more than a decade as the official long-distance courier of the Santa Iglesia Cathedral. The Chapter believed it to be not only a responsible assignment for the padre, but few of the other priests were in any way anxious to undertake the long, arduous and dangerous journey.

Padre Diego was politically well connected in Spain. Other trips to the motherland proved this beyond doubt. He previously and successfully pleaded his cause before the Council of the Indies for a full *ración*. Now, perhaps with a little luck and the help of well-placed friends, he might achieve his wish to be elevated to the status of canon. In fact, an endorsement for him to be thus named was written by the Lima *Real Audiencia* on May 26, 1673. Padre Diego, however, would never receive the nomination from the Crown.

Upon his belated return to Lima, he learned of a serious disagreement again taking place over the payment, or rather nonpayment, of his prebend while he was away. He despondently resigned his position as *racionero*. On May 30, 1675, he entered the order of the Augustinian friars as a novice, and a little over a year later took his monastic vows. This religious order was officially established as a congregation in 1256 by Pope Alexander VI. The shift from an independent salaried priest of the world to an Augustinian mendicant friar, now vowing to renounce all ownership of property and independence, is bewildering indeed.

Archives of the Indies, dated July 2, 1676, record the Padre taking his vows in the Order of San Augustin. It was a vow of poverty. Still, all the while he was behind the walls of the monastery, he continued to write the Cathedral Chapter in Lima demanding the back pay of his prebend.

On November 23, 1677, the Lima *provisor*, Don Diego de Salazar, recommended to the Chapter the account of Diego Portichuelo be closed once and for all. The Chapter agreed. In August 1678, the Archbishop of Peru, in his usual timely manner, reported a full *ración* was available because Diego Portichuelo left the church (three years earlier).

Padre Diego's written memoirs stopped toward the end of 1656, after the disastrous battle with the English off Cádiz. His text was published in Madrid in late 1657. Extensive research enabled us to know a little about the last twenty years of his life that followed publication of his book.

It is obvious he was distraught with the politics of the Lima Cathedral. Our padre refused to participate in this ecclesiastical and political clique, whose top echelon appeared to have as much to say about the business of running the viceroyalty as did the viceroy.

The question of why he was out of favor with the Lima Chapter still remains. The answer can only be speculative.

Perhaps the cathedral hierarchy was jealous of Diego's personal accomplishments beyond his clerical duties. Maybe they were envious of the publication of his remarkable, true-adventure diary, or of his high-level connections in Spain. Maybe they were unable to understand his willingness to undertake the long-distance courier voyages back and forth to Spain without concern as to the dangers to his life in the process. They no doubt wondered if he volunteered himself for the overseas assignments to honor God, Country and Church, or to further his own personal recognition.

To Padre Diego's way of thinking, the Cathedral Chapter was an age-old example of an entrenched management with little empathy for underlings who didn't fit their mold. He found it all disheartening.

Few young clerics of his generation seemed better equipped than Diego Portichuelo de Rivadeneira to mount the glittering staircase of advancement in the early 17th-century Spanish church in the New World. With advanced degrees from Salamanca, Spain's premier university, important family connections leading into the highest governing circles, and financial backing of a wealthy grand patron, Padre Diego had everything going his way.

What was in his mind as he departed sunny Seville on that zestful spring day in 1641? What thoughts occupied his brain as he stood on the crowded deck of his galleon en route to Lima to take up a new career as a chaplain in the metropolitan cathedral? Ambitious, somewhat vain, conscious of his superior intellect and personality, he was no doubt attempting to balance his worldly learnings with his sworn dedication as a man of the church. He faithfully recorded the events and reflections of each day, stating his goal of bringing "blessings to the infidels of the vast New World."

Shortly after his arrival in the Peruvian capital, Diego was appointed by the archbishop vice-director and regent of the archdiocesan seminary. The next year the archbishop ordained him to the priesthood. In his diary, the young cleric simply observed, "My work pleased the archbishop."

Over the following ten years, Padre Diego continued to exercise important leadership in every aspect of the cathedral's daily life. However, he had enemies within the cathedral Chapter. One in particular engineered a formal reprimand, charging that he was not properly doing his duty as keeper of the choir. More seriously, twice when his name was mentioned for a benefice and the sizable salary accompanying it, the appointment was denied him. This was despite his name heading the list of candidates. On the second occasion he became irate. Disappointment and resentment occasioned his successful plea to return to Spain to seek justice in person.

The terrible trauma of a double shipwreck and capture by the English was waiting to be piled upon the poor padre, whose mental frame was already shaky as he prepared for the voyage to Spain.

Then came the black Monday night of October 26, 1654, when he witnessed the shipwreck of the *capitana*. Certainly, this man of the cloth felt compassion for those who would suffer the misfortunes of that shipwreck. It would go down in history as the single worst sea disaster of the *Armada del Mar del Sur*.

In less than a year our padre would face the same scenario, on an even more horrible level, off the coast of Florida on the Northwest corner of what is known as Little Bahama Bank. Prepared or not, he and his doomed shipmates trembled in the fateful vortex aboard the almiranta *Nuestra Señora de las Maravillas*. Over 600 people were lost. Padre Diego was one of forty-five survivors.

On the final lap of the two-year trip home, Padre Diego's ship, part of the treasure fleet, went down under the cannonade of English warships within sight of the Spanish city of Cádiz. What an unpredictable destiny for an academic, a quiet man of God, to be hurled into one of the bloodiest seabattles of the century.

Later, Diego could still write of this experience, "The moaning and screaming was like a nightmare breaking our hearts and tearing our spirits. Those of us still alive were worse than the dead."

The English plucked him from the inferno around the sinking ships and kept him brutally captive until ransomed weeks later. Six months of normal living at home in Spain did much to restore his mental and physical well-being. The padre then returned to Lima and tried to reorganize the shreds of his life. However, it was only in November 1664 that he felt, "something positive was happening in my behalf for the first time in many years." The viceroy was again recommending Diego's promotion to a full benefice and a salary of 2,000 pesos annually. The report praised him as an exemplary priest, a popular preacher, a church official enjoying "the best possible contacts with both governmental and secular officials."

Were his troubles over? Not for this man of twisted destiny. Rivadeneira speaks of "a strange bureaucratic metamorphosis taking place within the confines of the cathedral Chapter . . . It was obvious, I was being squeezed out of the church's administration."

His enemies succeeded in isolating him. He had nothing to do. His mind spun, often out of control. He wanted to return to Spain where he would be remembered as a hero and martyr. Without proper civil and church permissions, he booked passage. Even when his powerful friends straightened out his situation and succeeded in having his benefice and salary restored in Lima, the cathedral Chapter excluded him from church activities. His position was ostensibly reduced to a mere Chapter messenger with a route back and forth on the *Carrera de Indias*.

His well-placed friends in Spain were still trying to help him, but their last effort failed. He was endorsed for the clerically noble status of canon, but the nomination was never effected. After much prayer and deliberation, the sixty-one year-old padre surely felt defeated. On May 30, 1675, he entered the novitiate of the order of Augustinian friars where he pronounced his monastic vows just over a year later. He was dead within three years.

Padre Diego did not forsake his belief in God. To the contrary, his sudden switch to the hardships of an Augustinian monk from the previous plush life at the Lima Cathedral was a daring re-confirmation of his faith. The isolation and solitude of the monastery, coupled with the simple shared poverty with his Augustinian brethren, would bring him even closer to God.

He knew his place in life. He did not fear death. After losing two ships from under him, he had seen his share of hell on earth. He was satisfied with his life, except for the higher title he felt was denied him. He helped many throughout his adventures and traumas; his compassion comforted hundreds in their time of need. Despite his own problems and perils, Diego tried to reach out to others. His life was an affirmation of faith and hope and love.

Our good padre is the only person known to have recorded explicit details of the many events on which this book is based. Without his memoirs we would be forever void of the rich historical detail included herein. Padre Diego will be remembered accordingly.

Diego Portichuelo de Rivadeneira died in 1678 at the age of sixty-four. (A.G.I., Lima 253, no. 7.)

14

Epilogue

THE DISCOVERY OF THE 1654 *CAPITANA*

The American dived off his boat, swam five miles to our concession to steal relics, then swam back to his own boat. He claimed the finds were from the capitana.
Rony Almeida to the *New York Times International*, April 14, 1997

THE GUEST SUITE DOOR opened at the Grand Hotel in Miami's fashionable Coconut Grove. Rob McClung stepped forward to shake hands and introduce me to his Ecuadoran business partner. Three hours of intense discussion followed.

The purpose of the meeting that memorable night was to size up one another and determine if we could work together. The reason? "They" had found "our" galleon wreck!

A year earlier my company, Maritime Explorations International, Inc., had teamed up with Herman Moro's SubAmerica Discoveries, Inc., which held an approximate 100 square mile lease off Ecuador's Punta de Chanduy. It was within this area that Moro and I both believed the *capitana* of 1654 rested. In fact, I was so certain we could come within several hundred yards of the shipwreck site that Maritime funded two successive geophysical surveys utilizing our Geometric G886 magnetometer and Fisher P-10 towed metal detector with Moro and personnel from Global Explorations.

Both expeditions revealed highly interesting magnetometer anomalies to the east of a clump of offshore rocks known as El Negro, or more affectionately by the locals as *Los Negritos*. This rock cluster was a key landmark because its position was vividly described in the old archive documents recording the shipwreck scene, as well as in early Spanish salvage reports immediately following the disaster.

Having learned of our intention to bring a large salvage vessel to our lease area in order to further investigate our undersea magnetometer findings, McClung and his Ecuadoran group, who held an

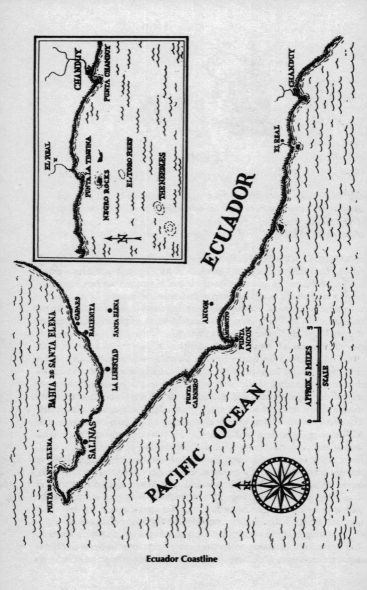

Ecuador Coastline

adjoining lease to the west of El Negro, became concerned that we were close to discovering the shipwreck they had secretly stumbled upon while quietly "inspecting" our lease area several months earlier. Consequently, they were eager to strike a deal.

"You hold the key lease," they emphasized, "but we hold the treasure! Possession is nine-tenths of the law! We should pool our equipment and resources and cooperate together. We already have air compressors, scuba gear and boats available locally."

"The wreck is covered with four or five feet of sand and mud," explained McClung. "Maybe you'll find it, and maybe not. By Ecuadoran law we are entitled to a finder's claim for 25 percent. So, unless we work together, there won't be much left after the government gets its share."

They had a good point. I knew that excavation of the shipwreck would be a major undertaking in a hard-to-reach location such as Chanduy, where diving supplies, spare parts and even water were hard to come by. We had experienced electronic problems with our magnetometer on the site a year earlier, necessitating expensive long distance telephone calls to the lab technicians back in California. The electronic experts walked our survey crew through enough repair steps to temporarily patch it. Still, taking care of the logistical requirements of our dive operation would not be easy.

We would also need dependable operational and communication support systems and a sizable, but yet undetermined, source of funding. I also realized that in order to undertake a high visibility project such as treasure salvage in a remote place like Chanduy, and in a developing country like Ecuador, we would definitely need some good Ecuadoran friends. The prominent Ecuadoran family who had hired McClung to find the long, lost galleon was well connected politically and socially. Gloria de Vinueza, widow of a former Minister of Defense, and granddaughter of a former President of Ecuador, had been looking for the legendary *capitana* for almost two decades. She controlled the minds and pocketbooks of the Ecuadoran group.

After a number of conferences with Herman Moro, my Maritime partners, and Rick Robol, our Maritime attorney, as well as numerous teleconference calls to Ecuador, a Joint Venture Agreement was signed by the various parties.

We had reached a point where the newly formed team felt they could trust one another. On a special occasion when Rob McClung and I were together, he voluntarily recounted his historic discovery for me.

"We found this kid in the nearby village who told us his father had discovered a nice plate of pottery in the ocean, about a mile offshore. When he showed us the handsome piece I knew right away we were hot on the hidden trail, but how could we find it?

"A $5 bill provided the answer. I sent several of our men to get the boat while the youngster and I headed for the beach. Once offshore we dropped several buoys marking the general area. I began diving while the boy was taken home. There were a few pieces of broken pottery, but nothing else.

"Visibility was very poor, hardly anything, and I swam along slowly crisscrossing the ocean floor," McClung paused and looked at me with a glint in his eye. He was enjoying his recreated dramatization of the discovery. "There was a moment when I stopped to rest, and in attempting to balance myself on the bottom in about twenty-five feet of water, I suddenly found my hand on an oval or circular piece of something.

"When I put my head down near the object and brushed the sandy crust away, it took a moment for the current to carry off the sediment. When it did, I couldn't believe my eyes. The article I focused on was most definitely the neck of an amphora that once held wine or olive oil. I certainly hoped this particular one had been on the *capitana*!

"As I was working my arm down into the semi-soft bottom, I brought up a spongy mass of decayed wood. Carefully I dug around the ancient jar. It had been cushioned by the wood and had accumulated buildup of ages of sand and silt. The artifact was slowly loosened from the silent grave where it had rested for almost three and a half centuries."

One of the amazing aspects of this shipwreck is the large amount of wood hull structure which has remained intact over the years. While it is not unusual to find large wooden hull pieces such as the keel, keelson and beams still identifiable on the sea bottom, the fact that large sections of flooring and hull remain in this ancient shipwreck is indeed a rarity. Most certainly the cold Pacific water, along with the mud and silt accumulation, has helped preserve what remains today.

Enthusiasm was running high in the winter of 1996 among members of the newly structured joint venture and salvage team.

However, before we could implement salvage plans, the old adage "Treasure is Trouble" began appearing in the form of other rival groups who began hearing barroom rumors. Grapevine reports soon became the talk of the town. The 1654 *capitana* shipwreck, for which all serious treasure hunters in Ecuador had been searching, finally was found. It was impossible to keep the divers quiet. Whispers became buzzes and the buzzes turned into buzzsaws.

An unbelievable array of accusations, derogatory remarks and false claims were brought against the joint venture group as jealous competitors attempted to jockey into position to file their own claim and have our lease canceled.

One of these adversaries was an Ecuadoran named Rony Almeida. He held a lease ten miles from ours near Ancon. He had raised considerable funds from foreign investors claiming he had found the *capitana*. Almeida began a campaign of writing letters to local news agencies. Through his connections with cultural patrimony insiders he was successful in stirring up a plethora of emotional sentiment against our group.

This negative press was detrimental to our ability to raise funds. Although we had found a few coins, cannon balls and pottery, we desperately needed to get a properly equipped vessel on the site in order to excavate the huge amount of covering sand and mud. This would cost big money. Dates on the coins certainly indicated we had the *capitana* but we needed to clean out the hull and study the remaining primary timbers. Also, identification of registered silver bars would be useful. Most importantly, we didn't want to prematurely notify the government until we knew we could protect the offshore site.

Soon, overzealous news reporters got into the act.

"The wreck of the *Jesus Maria* was found by a group of persons who had a contract with the government to search for shipwrecks. They did not inform the government of their discovery, according to what the law stipulates. Instead, they decided to plunder the treasure, sending their finds outside of Ecuador to be sold. During 1995 approximately 10,000 coins, artifacts, and gold and silver ingots with a value of around 3,000,000,000 *sucres* were recovered from the wreck and sent illegally to the United States," one news article stated.

The accusation named all the companies involved in the joint venture, their officers, attorneys and even the divers. Not only did it claim that coins, artifacts and silver ingots were removed from the shipwreck of the fabled *capitana*, and taken out of the country, but it also named top Ecuadoran officials conspiring with the joint venturers and not enforcing cultural patrimony laws.

"It is known that the National Congress has made inquiries to the appropriate departments, and these have not responded with the urgency the case merits. Some persons of respectable organizations like the Commission of Human Rights and the Municipal Museum of Guayaquil are interceding in favor of these people who are accused of being looters of the national archaeological treasure. The shipwreck, *Jesus Maria*, and the treasure it contains ought to be protected until that underwater site can be properly salvaged under procedures stipulated by law. The treasure that has been smuggled to the United States should be returned to Ecuador."

With a national election approaching, the top admirals and cabinet ministers were under serious public and political pressure. All search and salvage leases were put on hold, and salvors were ordered not to undertake further diving until an investigation could be concluded. The unfortunate timing of this bureaucratic decree exhausted not only our patience, but also the remaining good months of the 1996 diving season. Sensing a long sequence of delays and problems we covered our preliminary excavations and prepared to ride out the storm of criticism.

In the meantime, letters of protest were written with regularity to the Department of Cultural Patrimony. News releases were sent to every conceivable local publication openly condemning our group. First, our competitors accused us of stealing Ecuador's national treasure, "which was sufficient to retire the country's entire federal debt." Then, they announced they had definite evidence the *capitana* lay in their territory. They simply were waiting for the arrival of necessary equipment and good weather to bring up the treasure. The next day they would state we had "salted" our site with relics and coins from other shipwrecks. Theirs was a major campaign of subterfuge designed to confuse the locals and discredit the North Americans.

Having paid off one of our original divers who knew the shipwreck location, the rival group boasted they could direct authorities to the precise coordinates of the galleon wreck where government officials could see for themselves the looting taking place. This absurd degree of braggadocio caught the attention of the Department of Cultural Patrimony whose officials insisted the Ecuadoran Navy investigate.

For two weeks, twenty-four navy divers combed the Chanduy seafloor with metal detectors and side scan sonar, but were unable to find any shipwreck. Our crew watched from the El Real hillside, contemplating our fate.

It was the end of July before Admiral Fernando Donoso Moran declared the accusation against us was without merit and all salvors could resume diving operations. Unfortunately, it was already winter in Ecuador, and unfavorable weather had set in. Maybe 1997 would be our year. Maybe we could now put our funding together.

On one occasion I was returning from a trip to Ecuador and a man boarded the airplane with a diving helmet on which he had printed "*La capitana*, 1654-1996." After clearing customs in Miami, I introduced myself to him in the baggage area. He told me in very positive terms that he had been diving on the *capitana* shipwreck near Anconcito. I told him he was about ten miles away from the real *capitana*, and invited him aboard our salvage boat on his next trip. So effective had been the propaganda of our competitors that he became totally confused. Afterwards, he confided in me that he and others had made major contributions in the form of money and equipment to Rony Almeida for a percentage of interest in his *capitana*.

The most favorable diving months in the sea waters of Ecuador generally are January, February and March. Even during the summer season there are periods of extremely high tides and surf usually occurring a few days before and after a full moon when sea conditions are unsafe. Even with good weather, tidal variances of twelve to thirteen feet cause considerable sediment to be constantly suspended in the highly saline Pacific Ocean water, hindering underwater visibility.

The next few months were spent reviewing my research, double checking the *capitana* cargo manifests, and tallying time and again the totals of early Spanish reported salvage.

On several occasions my knowledgeable researcher Robert Sténuit and I reviewed our calculations on the amount of *capitana* treasure still likely to remain on the Ecuadoran seafloor. We knew the majority of the loot left consisted of silver bar and coin. We then devoted considerable effort reconciling the amounts finally acknowledged to have been on board, after the 17th-century investigations took place. Allowing for the large sums officially and unofficially recovered, reported and otherwise stolen or plundered, we determined the following:

1. From a "records standpoint," there was a minimum of 132 tons to a maximum of 270 tons of silver originally on board the ship, and most of that unrecovered was left in the lower hold on the starboard side, unreachable by the early divers.

2. Because the *capitana* stranded cleanly in twenty-four feet of water at low tide the ship did not break up upon impact. Consequently, everything the vessel carried should remain in that general proximity.

3. The rare Potosí coins and other meaningful artifacts should be in a relatively good state of preservation.

4. But . . . the unanswered questions: How much really was *stolen* after the shipwreck? And, how much early salvage went completely and forever *unreported*?

"Can you visualize a wall of silver about a mile off the Ecuadoran coast?" I asked Robert as we weighed the magnificent possibilities.

His response at first was a faraway stare, but with an interesting twinkle in his eyes, perhaps recalling his own successful treasure recoveries. He answered, "Eighty-pound silver bars don't float very far, Dave. Whether there is an actual wall, I'm unsure. At least there should be a very large pile. And it can be found!"

In the fall of 1996, another development almost capsized the joint venture. Herman Moro notified all the partners he was withdrawing and taking his lease with him if he couldn't have a higher percentage of the deal. He also insisted on being named managing director of the operation. This might not have been an unreasonable request except for the fact he already had been awarded a percentage of investment interest for his lease. The lease itself was only worth so much, and Moro had no other money in the deal. Furthermore, he had no management experience.

Contending with the "Moro factor" was one thing, but the sticky situation also complicated raising funds for the forthcoming season. No investor wants to put money into any operation where there exists dissension within the ranks. To further confound the situation, Moro's attorney was designing a new contractual agreement to bind the group, and it was a beauty!

The delays created by this havoc kept us from signing investors.

There were long, expensive and argumentative deliberations. Our Ecuador discovery consortium strived diligently to get its act together. With five corporations, five attorneys and at least five huge egos in the midst of the negotiations, coming up with a master agreement governing the affairs of the project became an impossibility. If one principal agreed on a business point, another would not. If all the partners agreed, an attorney would change or complicate an already complex matter. With the good weather months fast concluding, it was imperative we get the salvage boat to the wreck site. We knew our Ecuadoran enemies were attempting to file a claim on our general coastal coordinates to argue for a right to some of the treasure. With only partial funding in hand from loans of several principals, the 100-foot research vessel, *Explorer*, sailed for the silver-laden seafloor off the coast of Ecuador.

By late March, the ship's huge blowers were lowered over its five-foot propellers and we started digging.

Aboard the salvage boat were the Honduran captain, Everrett Pastor, chief engineer and diver, Mike Cundiff and his wife, Nancy, who did the important job of cooking as well as other shipboard duties. Rob McClung was in charge of diving operations, his brother, Mike McClung, a key diver, Dan McArthur, assistant engineer and diver and Mick Murray, an extra crew member and diver. Bob Logan also was aboard, and responsible for the care and use of my Ikigama video camera, and the recording and production of what we hoped would be an award-winning documentary.

Once in Ecuador, our locally hired divers consisted of Vicente Parrales and his sons, Plinio, Mauro and Antonio, along with Raul Baquerizo, Pedro Pinagu, Don Schaeffer and Vicente Arcos. Maritime Explorations International staff member Joel Ruth established, with the assistance of the Ecuadoran Navy, a conservation laboratory at a facility in the Naval Base at Salinas. A precise daily log was maintained on everything recovered and tagged. He was supervised by officials from Ecuador's Department of Cultural Patrimony. American archaeologist, John de Bry, along with friend Bob Colombo, made several trips to the site, as did the author.

Teams of four navy divers were constantly in the water with our salvage divers. Ecuadoran marines with automatic weapons took stations aboard the R/V *Explorer*. Whether their primary purpose was to guard us, or the treasure, was never completely determined.

"We felt we were being held prisoner on our own boat," Rob McClung lamented. "We had a gunboat anchored right beside us each day. Every evening armed soldiers collected what we found during the day and took it aboard the gunboat for safekeeping. We barely got a chance to look at what we had recovered."

The Ecuadoran military personnel were a constant source of problems for the salvage team. "These guys were looking over our shoulder and were in our face the minute we came out of the water. They were a daily nuisance," McClung reported. "We had to feed them so our provisions rapidly diminished. They ate everything in sight. Shipboard gear began to disappear, from razors and toothbrushes to radios and cameras. We were stunned to learn later we were even going to have to pay their salaries."

Stringent security procedures were established and maintained by the Ecuadoran Navy during the course of the recovery of the *capitana* treasure and artifacts. Each of our divers was monitored and accompanied underwater by navy divers. Upon returning to the surface and the salvage boat, artifact recoveries were handed over to a team of Ecuadoran archaeologists who had been assigned to the vessel and were working under the direction of the Navy and Department of Cultural Patrimony. Each diver re-entering the salvage boat via *Explorer*'s tall stern ladder was required to remain behind a designed quarantine zone located at the aft end of the vessel. Dive gear and wet suits would be removed and a metal detector check would be run across the diver's body to determine if he was "clean." On one occasion, a silver cob was found concealed between the cheeks of an Ecuadoran diver's butt. Another time, a small slit in a neoprene foot boot contained a treasure coin.

This is not to say that the system of control was impeccable. There was a time when a local notable visited the boat and, upon exiting, managed to carry off a piece-of-eight under a hatband. There was another situation when one of the American divers had accumulated a pile of coins in his underwater ditty-bag. Suddenly he got stomach cramps and the obvious need to evacuate became a problem. Swimming away from the side of the hull where he had been working, the diver carefully placed the coin bag under a piece of coral rock and covered it with sand. He immediately surfaced and ran straight to the *Explorer*'s head, reaching it just in time. Fifteen minutes later, he was back in the water. Returning directly to the underwater rock where he had stashed his loot, he could not find his coin bag. Neither the coins nor the bag that contained them ever showed up again.

All recovered items brought aboard the salvage boat were carefully identified, counted and re-counted, before being bagged, labeled and recorded in an official inventory list, or *Acta*. The sealed bags were then placed into one of several large steel containers, the size of a large freezer chest, and padlocked. The chests were under constant 24-hour guard by a rotating shift of hand-picked Ecuadoran sailors and marines with automatic weapons. The contents were removed periodically from the chests under the supervision of naval officers and transferred to the *Chimborrazo*, the Ecuadoran gunboat which provided security throughout the salvage project. At the time of transfer, each artifact bag, called a *funda*, was matched to the inventory lists prepared by the archaeologists and certified by the naval officers present. The treasure and all artifacts were transported to Salinas where they were unloaded and brought to the conservation lab under heavy guard. The entire re-checking process was repeated, with each bag and artifact again matched to the inventory lists, one at a time, before being brought to the lab.

The lab itself consisted of a one-story, semi-detached, concrete block building, located across the street and north of the Naval College. There was about 1200 square feet of working space among three rooms. The first and largest room contained three long worktables, two of which extended the entire length of the room along opposite walls, about 25 feet. In the center of the room was the third work table with two sinks and faucets. At the far end of the main lab room were two other rooms. One of these, about 12 feet by 7 feet and windowless, became our main storage vault.

Security enforced at the lab was as rigorous as on the salvage boat. The lab entrance was guarded by armed marines round the clock. Guards were rotated every three hours and new faces always were present. Entrance was restricted to those holding a special identification badge. Only our conservator, Joel Ruth, and Herman Moro were issued passes.

There were also two archaeological representatives of the Cultural Patrimony Department along with two students of archaeology who were sent to assist from the University of Guayaquil. All others, i.e. official guests, media representatives, etc. came at pre-arranged times and were always escorted by the base commander with armed marines. The usual metal detector check, emptying of pockets, shaking out clothes, taking off shoes, and physical pat downs were prevalent and usually over-emphasized. Every person going in and out of the lab had to sign a log giving identification, purpose of the visit, and the time of entering and leaving. Several gung-ho marines aimed their weapons at passing vehicles and pedestrians to stress the seriousness of guarding the treasure. Lab workers continuously heard the sharp click of a weapon's trigger being pulled, as the guards passed the time of day. No one was ever caught taking artifacts out of the lab. Anyone doing so would have been subject to immediate arrest.

Several weeks after the start of the conservation work, the first delivery of conserved and identified artifacts was ready to be shipped to the Banco Central in Guayaquil. It was to be held in safekeeping until a division could take place. Under the supervision of a committee consisting of bank, naval and government officials, the material was again inventoried. Coin bags and other *fundas* were re-matched to the original numbers of the original *Acta*. Those present signed and witnessed affidavits. Everything was again checked off as the entire pile of booty, including pieces of ship's timbers and amphorae, was carried out the door under the supervision of the base commander. As a cover to fool potential thieves, the treasure was transported in a military ambulance, crammed full of heavily-armed marines. Upon reaching the bank it was locked inside a high security vault . . . but only after it was again inventoried and the entire count confirmed.

Six weeks into the conservation work, special auditors from the National Patrimony Department conducted an unannounced visit at the Salinas naval base preservation lab. All coin bags and artifacts remaining in the lab's storage room were counted and re-counted during the three-day audit. The result of this surprise check proved that everything was in order. In the few cases where discrepancies existed, overages actually were found! There were eight more bronze cannon balls than originally reported. In a bag showing forty musket balls there were really eighty. One coin bag was short ten coins. Another was over by fifteen.

Due to the high degree of security, the multiple audit checks, and the paper trail of accountability, there was no possibility to manipulate, remove, or other wise cross-contaminate artifacts from the *capitana* salvage boat or conservation lab. This is contrary to rumors spread by our rivals about treasure being smuggled out of the country. The bona fide integrity of both the numismatic assemblage and other artifacts recovered from the *capitana* site was completely maintained afloat and ashore from start to finish. The measures taken by the Ecuadoran military and other associated government interests precluded otherwise.

While the dive team persevered through its daily difficulties, the joint venture's administrative abilities on shore also were being tested. Our hastily established pool of funds was depleting quickly. This, complicated with the lack of local leadership directing how the funds should be spent, was creating a new set of problems. Because the group's Ecuadoran divers were being paid salaries considerably less than the American divers, a management decision was made to continue to pay the locals, but not the Americans. It took about a week for this inequity to be recognized, and it created a furor among the hardworking Americans.

Not only was a shortage of funds affecting our salvage operation offshore, but the conservation effort was being diluted as well.

"I had requested several hundred gallons of distilled water," stated Joel Ruth. "This was needed to mix pure solutions containing a neutralizing electrolyte of soda ash to conduct proper electrolytical cleaning and reduction of the various silver artifacts that were being found. When my supply of soda ash was exhausted, I was told there was no more available from local sources. I also ran out of baking soda because this item was on a restricted purchase basis since it was frequently used by narco-traffickers to process cocaine. Despite promises of the Patrimony officials at the lab to cut red tape, no more soda ash or baking soda was ever made available to me. The commitments by the Patrimony people simply went unfulfilled."

To make matters worse, a water main in Salinas broke and there was no running water on the naval base for two months. The only source of fresh water was from a tanker truck that would periodically fill up individual cisterns at the troop barracks and the military hospital next door.

"I was reduced to carrying a bucket next door to the hospital and ladle my water out of the toilet tank reservoirs in the bathrooms," deplored Joel Ruth. "As a result, it became increasingly difficult to clean coins and artifacts as I was forced to extend the use of all the water I had. This often meant I was using dirty water to rinse the artifacts I was trying to clean."

The intense shortage of funds put unfair pressure on the daily available food supplies as well. Days passed when there was only bread and water. Some of the crew went ashore and brought back a vat of local fish chowder. Everyone had diarrhea for days.

In the meantime, the hoards of reporters who bombarded the Chanduy area after the first coins began coming up forced a new kind of friction and frustration upon us.

The Quito newspaper, *El Comercio*, reported four billion U.S. Dollars to be in the hull of the recently discovered *capitana*, being worked by the American salvage team. Four billions! Wow! What science-fiction writer did they send to cover this story?

Every poor fisherman who could swim, anyone who could beg, borrow or steal a boat or get their hands on face masks and swim fins appeared. It was their duty and obligation to come and dive on what was rightly Ecuadoran, the treasure wreck of the *capitana*. Everyone imaginable swarmed the region.

At night, mysterious, unlighted vessels were seen silhouetted by moonlight as they hovered nearby. During daytime, it was worse.

After the navy began firing overhead warning shots, there were few potential poachers. Still, our adversaries continued to harass us.

"As word filtered out that Mr. McClung had come upon the wreck,[133] a second group of treasure hunters disputed his find. That group, led by an Ecuadoran history buff named Rony Almeida, and a man suspected of bilking investors in the United States, argued that the *capitana* was really some five miles away, where they had a permit to search.

"Mr. Almeida has campaigned to discredit Mr. McClung, saying, 'The American planted false artifacts, or dived off his boat, swam five miles to Mr. Almeida's concession to steal relics, then swam back to his own boat claiming the finds were from the *capitana*,' he said, dismissing Mr. McClung and his team as 'vulgar adventurers.'

"Mr. McClung, for his part, calls Mr. Almeida a 'con artist.' "

The *Palm Beach Post* ran a feature, *The Cutthroat Battle For a Galleon's Booty: Who owns the treasure of La Capitana, a galleon that sank in 1654?* "A West Palm Beach diver claims he's found some of the ship's silver, but a rival salvager, who says he sailed on the galleon in a past life, will do almost anything to claim the riches. Almeida claims McClung's discovery is a scheme to fool investors and mine millions from book, film and merchandising rights."

American archaeologist John de Bry authenticated the shipwreck as being the *capitana*. The Ecuadoran Navy whose divers were in the water with us every day confirmed the discovery as the *capitana*. Other Ecuadoran officials cheered our discovery.

But conflicting reports created questions. Ecuador's Institute of Cultural Patrimony refused to acknowledge the find, "withholding judgment until further testing of the relics takes place, because of the atmosphere of uncertainty."

By the end of April some 5,000 coins, a number of silver bars, bronze cannon balls, silver candlesticks, plates of majolica, as well as personal items, including emerald earrings, a gold cross, silver spoons and snuff boxes, hundreds of pottery shards and other shipboard arti- facts had been recovered and were undergoing preservation at the Naval Station Conservation Site.

Comparing the *capitana*'s register with the list of known passen- gers revealed that some of the galleon's officers did record personal treasure on the ship's official inventory. The fact that most of these were at the end of the registry might indicate that these people stepped forward after the shipwreck to get on the record and to keep their particular items from being confiscated for the king. Captain Bernardo de Campos acknowledged having a chest of 2,500 coins on board with his special mark: ♌

Captain of Infantry Juan Julio de Melo registered a chest of sil- verware weighing 140 *marcos*. Francisco Tello de Guzmán registered 40 silver bars and eight chests of coins with this marking: ⋀

Captain Bartolomé de Chavarria, the ship's scribe, registered one chest of silverware. And Juan Fernandez de Orozco registered 17 chests of coins, one chest of silverware, and 35 silver bars with the fol- lowing marks: ⌞ ⋀ A 70-pound silver bar bearing the mark of Orozco was recovered by Mike Cundiff, one of the R/V *Explorer* divers. This eliminated any further question about the *capitana*'s identification.

In an amazingly short time, some four to five feet of sand and mud were removed from the wreck site. An extremely large section of heavily wooded hull flooring was revealed—the gigantic timbers just as solid as the day they were laid in place. In less than a month the en- tire hull was blown clean. That's when the panic began.

Late one evening the phone call came. "Dave, we're running out of treasure," Rob McClung whispered over the long-distance line from Ecuador. "There's still scatter around the ship, but we've totally cleaned out the existing hull. I don't know what to do. Gloria refuses to believe me. She absolutely cannot accept this bad news. There's no wall of silver, and if there's been a pile, we've gotten it. There's still stuff scattered around the ship, but we've definitely swept out what loot was left within the hull as it sits today. There may be coins under the hull, but the lead sheathing throws off a false reading on the metal detectors."

It took a while for this startling news to sink in. No wall of silver! Not even a pile! After all this expense and trouble!

There were only two answers. Either Bernardo de Campos accomplished a much better job of early salvage without reporting it, or what was left unsalvaged drifted off for an unknown distance as the hull broke apart. There is the slim possibility that someone else may have salvaged the shipwreck in relatively modern times, but the covering alluvium appeared to have been totally undisturbed for centuries. What happened to the millions that supposedly were left? This was the subject of numerous late night discussions.

The shortage of treasure to be recovered brought about instant heartache, headache and stressful evenings, especially for some of the principal investors who didn't want to believe that "the richest treasure ship" of the South Sea fleet had been found, but lacked the valuable cargo it was supposed to be carrying.

There is the likelihood that some treasure may have worked its way beneath the floorboards of the hull. There are also signs of a scatter trail leading off the starboard side of the wreck remains, toward the northeast. Serious examination of this possibility was not pursued by our divers because of lack of funding.

Although the novelty of the shipwreck discovery had worn off for most reporters, the news soon began to leak. The sudden lack of treasure being brought to the surface by our divers reached the ears of our rivals up the coast. They managed to raise considerable funds (much more than we were able) from foreign investors, even with their questionable evidence of a shipwreck existing. They readily seized the opportunity to badmouth us.

"We have found the *capitana* electronically in our own territory," stated their press release. "We expect to bring treasure to the surface any day now. The Americans have found nothing more than the contents of several chests from an overturned small boat, lost in the surf near the early salvors' camp."

The shortage of treasure, coupled with a shortage of funds and persistent bad weather, brought the project to a halt in May. By June, everything had been turned over to the Central Bank in Guayaquil. The R/V *Explorer* sailed away.

The sinking of the 1654 *capitana, Jesus Maria de la Limpia Concepción*, off Ecuador's coast would be written in history as the single worst shipwreck disaster in the 300-year era of the *Armada del Mar del Sur*. At 1,150 tons, this galleon was the largest ship built for the South Sea fleet. Two new vessels of 825 tons each were constructed two years later in order to replace the "Queen of the South Sea."

The shipwreck also caused numerous bankruptcies and business closings in Lima and in Spain. The most significant outcome of the accident was the magnitude of fraud involved with the amount of contraband silver brought on board, but not registered on the books of the silvermaster. This silvermaster, Bernardo de Campos, also happened to be captain of the ship. He would later become the primary salvager, reporting 407,771 pesos having been recovered by his efforts between 1656-1662. Bernardo considered this "a successful effort." As we look back three and a half centuries, we can only speculate on his definition of "success."

On December 14, 1657, the viceroy in Lima wrote the king, "I have appointed Captain Bernardo de Campos, who was second in command of this ship when she was lost, in charge of the next diving expedition."

Bernardo de Campos? Hadn't he been indicted, among others, for being responsible for the loss of the great *capitana*, the huge cargo of treasure, and other valuable merchandise? Had he not been accused of stealing from the passengers? Was he not fined, forced to take a salary cut, and assigned to the garrison of Callao?

In his letter to the king,[134] the viceroy, Count of Alva of Aliste, explains his reasons, "Since there are different opinions concerning how much treasure remains underwater, I asked the merchant *consulado* if they would be interested in contracting for the salvage at their expense, under my control. No one was willing to agree, so I decided to risk some of Your Majesty's money on the effort to determine the truth about what still remains to be salvaged. I have been assured the work would be done with the greatest diligence and care. It is now believed there still might be some silver under the water and some guns."

Whether he was plea bargaining or not, Bernardo de Campos managed to convince the new viceroy that if there was treasure on the bottom he could find it. Of course, he would surely bring it back to the King of Spain, all of it. His only request was to receive necessary funding, have adequate divers at his disposal, and sufficient motivation for each one of them. The viceroy committed to the following incentive, "Since the divers are slaves, I promise them two pesos for each silver bar they find."

The only detail of any salvage noted in official records was a letter dated August 25, 1658, from the viceroy to the king. It reported 26,000 pesos had been recovered from this operation, more than expected, offsetting the cost of the effort.

Did it really? Were the 26,000 pesos truly all that had been found?

A diver later testified, "More holes had been dug in the nearby hillside in which to bury treasure than one would find graves dug during the year of the plague."

More than a year later, September 13, 1659 (Lima 60) the viceroy reported, "Although the merchants thought nothing was left in the shipwreck, there were others who still believed there was. Consequently, it was officially made known to the public that salvage offers would be received."

The contract was awarded to Don Luis de Osores, who was assisted by (here he comes again) Captain Bernardo de Campos. Their percentage was to be two-thirds of what they might recover, considering the undertaking would be totally at their expense, and one-third was to go to His Majesty.

Official records reflect these opportunistic entrepreneurs were successful in salvaging 117,771 pesos and three *reales*, together with 128½ cannon balls.

In looking back over the years, and judging this venture, it is interesting to note how much more successful the salvors were after they invested their own capital in the project, in return for a high percentage of the find. But was this all they *really* found?

Bernardo de Campos was so taken with his newly discovered ability as a salvor after his successful treasure hunting efforts of the past few years that he, along with Don Juan Osores de Sotomayor, again applied for, and received, contract rights to the now famous shipwreck.

During the period 1660-1662, they "reported" recovering 264,000 pesos under a salvage contract issued in Lima by the Count of Alva of Aliste. This was several years after the Spanish government had given up funding the salvage operations, since they were told very little remained. Under the contract terms, the salvors received 176,000 pesos and the king got 88,000 from what was found.

Since charges had been brought against all the high officials involved in the loss of this royal *capitana*, it is interesting to note that Bernardo de Campos, who was indicted in the fiasco because he was second in command of the ship when it struck the reefs (resulting in a 4,000-peso fine, and four years on half salary) was later granted not one, but several contracts to search for the *capitana*'s lost silver, treasure he was responsible for losing in the first place. That he was so successful as a salvor, and was allowed to keep two-thirds of what he found, is even amusing, as we look back on the event several centuries later. As master of the galleon, his salary would have been little more than 50 pesos (400 *reales*) a month. Yet he and his partner split what was left of their 176,000 pesos after expenses—and probably laughed all the way to the bank! Within a few years he became a rich man. But how rich?

We will never know exactly how long Bernardo continued to work the wreck, or how much he truly found. Although his salvage reports stopped at 1662, two heavy rock "Indian anchors" were found just off the starboard side of the hull by our divers. They had been there for centuries. It's likely the site was worked for years, considering what little remained within the confines of the hull today.

There are some who believe the *capitana* was wrecked on purpose. If so, those in command certainly didn't intend to strike the outer reefs, lose their rudder and take on a hull full of water a considerable distance from shore. There is little reality to this premise.

The galleon's treasure register reflected a cargo of 3,000,000 pesos in silver bar and coin. Eight years after the *capitana* had become one of the New World's worst sea disasters, Spanish sailors and Indian divers reported recovering 3,339,751 pesos, "with much more unreachable in the lower section of the starboard side." Auditors of the king later declared that somewhere between nine and ten million pesos was the true amount on board when the ship sank.

LA CAPITANA SALVAGE, 1654—1662
Reported Treasure Recovered

PERIOD	SALVOR	AMOUNT
1656 - 1658	Bernardo de Campos	26,000 pesos
1659	Bernardo de Campos and Luis de Osores	117,771 pesos
1660 - 1662	Bernardo de Campos and Juan Osores de Sotomayor	264,000 pesos
1656 - 1662	Treasure Reported Salvaged	407,771 pesos

SALVAGE RECAP IN PESOS

1654	1,870,525
1655	1,061,455
1656 - 1658	26,000
1659	117,771
1660 - 1662	264,000
Total Treasure Reported Salvaged	3,339,751

The South Sea armadas generally consisted of the *capitana* and *almiranta*, carrying most of the treasure, one or two auxiliary *chinchorros* and one, two, or three merchantmen. These few ships almost always carried more treasure on the northward journey than the larger armadas that sailed across the Atlantic.

The possibility of a great amount of treasure having been transported on just a few ships was a tremendous reality, as Josephe de Mugaburu wrote in his *Diario de Lima*, referring to the armada shipments during this period.

GOLD AND SILVER SHIPPED FROM PERU
FOR CREDIT OF HIS MAJESTY AND OTHERS ACCOUNTS

PERIOD		PESOS
1652	Two years' silver production	12,000,000
1654	Two years' silver production	13,060,000

1664	"More than had ever been sent from the time of discovery"	20,000,000
1669	*Patacones* and bars, including private merchant money on five ships	16,000,000
1677	Three years of Peru's silver production shipped on nine vessels	22,000,000
1681	Money for the king plus that of Portobelo merchants on seven ships	24,000,000
1685	The king's register plus Portobelo Fair merchandise on seven ships	20,000,000

Ecuador today is a relatively small country of seven million inhabitants, bordered in the north by Colombia and in the south by Peru. The country gets its name from the Equator running through the northerly section. In the east, a living rain forest is the source of the headwaters of the Amazon River. At sea level along Ecuador's Pacific coast there are tropical sandy beaches, rugged and rocky bluffs and numerous coral reefs creating danger for any seaward approach to the shoreline. Snow-capped Andean mountains with active volcanoes can be found at a twenty-thousand foot altitude.

Ecuador trades internationally from four major seaports with principal exports of oil, shrimp, bananas, cacao and coffee. The small country also hosts a strong tourist industry, both on the mainland and to the Galápagos Islands, situated 600 miles off the coast.

The sea floor in the Chanduy region is a combination of sand and clay. The sea bottom may have built up somewhat near the shoreline from land erosion over the years, sending more clay into the sea. The ocean bottom also is highly concentrated with volcanic rocks, driving a magnetometer crazy. It is a dangerous area for both small and large boats in a blow.

Local fishermen from nearby villages of El Real and Chanduy have found pottery as it became entangled in their nets about a mile from the shore. Certainly, with the amount of wine the 1654 *capitana* was transporting, there would be a lot of broken pottery on the bottom. Years ago there was a rumor that one lucky fisherman spotted a section of gold chain neatly wrapped around a piece of coral in shallow water. Two gold Inca ceremonial masks reportedly were found near a seawater intake for a nearby shrimp aqua-culture farm. Could they have come from the *capitana*?

On the bluff above the *Playa de El Real* there is evidence of the early Spanish salvors' camp, established out of necessity in 1654, following the shipwreck. The old lime kilns, though nothing more than shallow holes and relatively undefined depressions in the ground, are still there today. They once stored the heavy silver ingots retrieved from the shipwreck. A careful search of the area reveals small pieces of broken pottery, mostly a faded blue or green tinted *majolica*, scattered among the dried scrub-brush and bramble. Looking back today, and recognizing the amazingly successful Spanish salvage efforts in the mid-1650's, we can only marvel and wonder at how they were able to accomplish what they did on this wild and desolate coast. Such positive salvage results have to reflect on the leadership qualities of General Francisco de Sosa, and on the abilities of the Indian divers who were brought in from Panama to help recover and transfer the treasure.

Heavy wooden *pangas* of the local fishermen today are parked above the high water mark on the narrow beach, or anchored just beyond the breakers offshore. To the west is the lookout tower (former light) at Punta la Tintina. At the end of the El Real Beach Road there is a small resting area intended for locals, furnished with a simple bench or two and a sheltered roof to help ward off the high density ultraviolet rays of the relentless tropical sun.

To the east is an abandoned concrete block beach house, last occupied by the Ecuadoran military during the 1994-1995 border dispute with Peru. When Peru was threatening its neighbors to the north, the Ecuadoran Navy expected an invasion to take place at Chanduy along the beach at El Real. Marines occupied this area for a number of months. Most of the windows in the old house are broken, or were stolen. We inspected it, hoping it might provide a base camp house, but it reeked of urine.

Between the towns of El Real and Chanduy are a number of fish processing plants with their unloading platforms located offshore. Major shrimp aqua-culture farms also are situated nearby. The area thrives on seafood.

The adjoining terrain, unmercifully pierced with numerous, now abandoned oil drilling rigs, is still the desert it was in the days of Bernardo de Campos and Francisco de Sosa. An unattractive dull-brown assortment of leafless brush covers the harsh and dry soil along the entire coastal region. For the natives, fresh water must be imported by truck. Although few gardens are visible, some farm for their family's survival. It takes a hardy person to live here, and the men who work the sea for a living are indeed a hardy group. The results of their labor often bring in a mere few hundred dollars annually. Still, in these destitute communities every dollar and every Ecuadoran *sucre* counts. The average family includes six to eight children. Most appear to get enough to eat, and their clothes are clean and adequate, but there is never enough money to cover everyone's necessities.

It took Cirilio Cruz, one of our guardian-guides, three years to become financially able to add another ten-foot room to his small, single-room home at El Real. His wife, six children and two pigs share a common dirt floor. It would be two more years before he could save enough to add a roof of corrugated tin over the new addition. Cruz is one of the more successful of the local natives.

Today Ecuador has very specific shipwreck search and salvage laws. Key ministers in appropriate branches of the government must approve a potential applicant's request for the exploration and exploitation of shipwrecks within Ecuador's territorial waters. The maximum search area is limited to 100 square miles, defined by coordinates of latitude and longitude.

Concessions and contracts are awarded for a period of one year and can be renewed with satisfactory performance. Once a search has located positive signs of a shipwreck trail, artifacts, ship parts and such, the contractor must notify the Minister of Defense so the navy may have the opportunity to place divers on board the salvor's vessel. They also appoint archaeologists or representatives from the Department of Cultural Patrimony to the salvage operation. The navy may also consider necessary measures to protect the salvor and his crew against acts of piracy. The state must approve all personnel who work or visit the salvage vessel, and the boat must be pre-cleared to transit Ecuadoran waters. With unfavorable reports, the law permits authorities to hold the salvage vessel and crew, and to levy certain fines, duties or penalties as the situation might warrant. The Ministry of Finance and Public Credit is responsible for collecting tax on the earnings of the contractor, who may be personally held in port until the tax has been paid.[135] The one obvious thing in the case of significant profits is that the salvor probably would need a good Ecuadoran lawyer.

The salvage contract may not be assigned or subcontracted and the state may cancel the contract at any time and for any reason, with any controversy being resolved according to Ecuadoran laws. No contract may be awarded if the requested area is situated in a strategic security or frontier maritime zone.

The agreement between Ecuador and the salvor calls for a fifty-fifty split of the value of anything recovered. However, valuation consideration in the case of coins or bullion is limited to metallic weight only[136], i.e. up to 50 percent of the value in the weight of the metals, without any consideration of cultural or numismatic values. Furthermore, at the time of distribution, 75 percent of the amount of the salvor's award could be paid in state bonds, and 25 percent in salvaged goods that would not constitute cultural patrimony, if the state so desired.

The salvage award is to be distributed by the Central Bank of Ecuador after having been reviewed by the Director of the National Institute of Cultural Patrimony and the administrator of the contract, the Director of the Merchant Marine of the Seacoast.

Valuations of treasure and artifacts found would be determined by two experts designated by each party. In case they are not in agreement, the state would designate a third expert.

The salvor also must post a bond of 150 million *sucres*, the currency of Ecuador, plus pay for notary and professional experts. This surety bond will be held until it is determined the salvor has performed satisfactorily and no ecological contamination or other damages have been incurred.

Just to make an application, a prospective salvor must file for lease rights through an acceptable Ecuadoran maritime attorney. If approved, he will have to operate out of an Ecuadoran corporate structure, post the required surety bond, hire a crew of at least 50 percent locals, including at least two divers from the navy and two Ecuadoran archaeological graduates or graduate students, supervised by a recognized archaeology expert to oversee professional preservation of all artifacts. All the "additional crew" also must be provided with food, housing and transportation expenses.

The salvor is required to provide a monthly report in writing, describing in detail the fulfillment of his contractual obligations. He must keep an accurate log of his magnetometer and sub-bottom profiling routes listing all anomalies registered. He then must turn over all treasure and artifacts found to the Central Bank. (Items defined as cultural deposits are forbidden to be taken from Ecuador.)

Thus, it appears the days of Bernardo de Campos are gone forever. No more holes to be dug on the hillside above the wreck site to stash cash, no more loose reporting that "virtually nothing was found and nothing remains" to be salvaged, no more two-thirds for the salvor and one-third for the king deals, no more take what you might safely get out of the shipwreck and live happily ever after opportunities. *No mas!*

The *capitana* rests today about a mile offshore between the landing beach at El Real and Punta Chanduy. What's left of her treasure cargo is guarded by the old ghosts of Bernardo de Campos and Francisco de Sosa, along with new generations of sea snakes, sharks and maggot-worms. There is also the Curse of Collasuyu[137] to be reckoned with. It is a definite *gafe traer mala suerte* (jinx to bring bad luck). The hex is purportedly levied by the spirits of thousands of Inca Indians whose short lives were conscripted to hard labor in the deep and treacherous mines of Potosí. There they sweated and slaved to dig the ore in the narrow and noxious tunnels deep within the bowels of the 15,800 foot, rusty-colored core of the barren and bleak mountain of silver. Many thousands more died from toxic exposure to mercury vapors during the crude refining and smelting procedures for the almighty silver.

If this shipwreck is truly voodooed, the Ecuadoran divers will tell you it is because of the greed of the *conquista*, and of the ancient Inca curse. "The *capitana* hit the rocks and foundered under an evil star," they will say. "Those who pursue her will be borne unto trouble."[138]

In September 1998, the Government of Ecuador made good on its contractual obligation to release fifty percent of treasure and artifacts salvaged by our group. This was truly a momentous occasion, and was covered by the local television and press in Guayaquil. This distribution also confirmed the recent statutory revisions of the country's shipwreck salvage laws. Our Ecuadoran partners had been working diligently to modify the existing regulations which were inequitably one-sided in favor of the government. Thanks to the good work and sound reasoning of Santiago Cuesta and Javier Vivas, the Attorney General of Ecuador ruled that silver bullion and coin mined, refined, and minted in Peru (today Bolivia) may not be considered cultural patrimony of Ecuador, even though the shipwreck in which the silver was contained lies within Ecuadoran territorial waters.

This historic distribution also served to officially acknowledge on the part of the government our group's discovery and identification of the 1654 *capitana*. The most supporting evidence was proved by the dates of the Potosí mint coins, 1648-1654. Of the thousands of coins recovered, not a single one was dated later than 1654, the year the great ship foundered. The size of remaining wooden hull parts, especially keel, keelson, ribs and deck planking confirmed that this was no small coastal trader. John de Bry, Director of the Center for Historical Archaeology, inspected the shipwreck shortly after its discovery. "Examination of elements of the hull remains and measurements of various parts such as futtocks and floor timbers suggest a very large sailing vessel. The size of these timbers, as well as distance and space between single and double frames, suggest a ship of between 1,000 and 1,300 tons displacement, with an overall length of 100 to 130 feet," stated de Bry in his archaeological report.

Paul Karon, Spanish colonial coin and mint numismatist, was approved by the Government of Ecuador to represent both parties in the division. Herman Moro of SubAmerica Discoveries, Inc., represented the salvage group. Gathered at the Central Bank and representing Ecuador was the engineer Julio Real, Under Secretary of Finance Dr. Mauricio Oliveros, Legal Advisor to the Minister of Education and Culture, and Commander Edgar Yanez, for the Merchant and Coastal Marine.

Paul Karon spent the better part of September 7 and 8 allocating equal divisions of treasure and artifacts, which were placed in two proportionate lots. The government was allowed to select their share first. They picked "Lot B." This included several very special jewelry items, such as an ornate gold crucifix, gold earring with two pearls, and an encrusted navigational divider, all one-of-a-kind pieces. Each group received the same number of silver coins (2559), silver bars, bronze cannon balls, musket balls, silver plates, silverware, reliquaries, majolica, pottery, and other items of worked silver, such as snuff boxes and candlesticks.

According to John de Bry, "The copper-based cannon balls are remarkable in the sense that copper-based or bronze cannon balls have never been reported in the archaeological or historical context. The intrinsic value of copper during the seventeenth century was very

high. The production of a bronze cannon, for instance, typically cost
seven to eight times more than an iron one. The presence of the
copper-based cannon balls might be explained by the fact that there
was no known source of iron in the New World during that period.
The entire region of Chile, Peru and Ecuador was rich in copper deposits. I surmise that the cannon balls were also considered as bullion.
If not needed for defense during the sailing from Callao to Panama,
they would be traded and/or bartered, and taken back to Spain to be
melted down."

It is believed that this pro-rata distribution between Ecuador and
the salvors is the first of its kind among Latin American countries in
recent years. Certainly, after the recurring frustrations of having to
deal with three different administrations from the time of the *capitana*'s discovery to the date of the distribution, everyone who participated in the salvage effort felt an extreme sense of both relief and
accomplishment.

The day after the division of the booty, another letter was written
to *Treasure Quest* magazine by . . . guess who? Rony Almeida again
was claiming there was not sufficient evidence indicating that the
1654 *capitana* had been properly identified.

"Based on all the cultural material that I have examined, I can
safely state that the ship presently excavated is the *Jesus Maria de la
Limpia Concepción*, also known as *La Capitana*. There is not one single element that could suggest another identity or dating for this particular shipwreck," John de Bry summarized.

"The *capitana* artifacts and especially the Potosí reales are from an
extremely interesting and important period of Spanish history," stated
Paul Karon. "The fine quality of the coins places them among the top
5% of all shipwreck treasure coins I have examined during my lifetime."

NUESTRA SEÑORA DE LAS MARAVILLAS
1972 TO THE PRESENT

Modern navigational charts do not feature a listing of *Los Mimbres*
anywhere along the route sailed by the 1656 *almiranta*, nor does the
modern translation of *Los Mimbres* (translating today to "Willow-
twigs" or "Ripples") offer any meaningful clues to those who might
be interested in the final resting site of the long lost *Maravillas*.

However, if one went back a couple of centuries[139] and researched various charts of this region, a notation might be discovered

on the northwest corner of Little Bahama Bank listed simply as "Maravilla Reef."

Today, modern navigational charts still relate to the location, with a slight misspelling: "Matanilla Shoals." (There is also "Matanilla Reef" twenty miles to the east, but our wreck location is the Shoal, the *Mimbre*.)

Over the more than three centuries since the 1656 shipwreck of the *Nuestra Señora de las Maravillas*, the word "Matanilla" on modern charts is the century-old misspelled derivative of Maravilla. Early cartographers often worked from notes and drawings of any seafarers who would assist them. More often than not the notations of ancient mariners were hardly what we today would consider "scholarly prepared," nor was their handwriting especially neat and legible. Mistakes in spelling were common. Even crucial directional errors such as mislabeling east from west occurred, sometimes with disastrous results for unwary sailors who accepted the mapmaker's directions without local knowledge or normal common sense vigilance. (The Spanish word for east is *este*, and for west *oeste*. The similarities often created directional difficulties.)

In looking at the spelling of the word Maravillas today we can understand how the "r" might have been dropped by one printer, and substituted to "t" by another, and the "v" interchanged with "n" without even a proofreading or second thought.

Thus, cartographers over the years have provided a documented reference, a clue out of the past, introducing us to the location of the long lost *almiranta*.

As for the salvors and speculators who would come, year after year, to the general area to invest their money with hopes of locating the sunken hoard of silver and gold, they would often go away, never to have even located the wreck site. (The approximate latitude had been actively passed around the seafaring circuit.)

Why? They and their diving crews never really understood the difficulties of diving in the open water currents of *Los Mimbres*. They did not understand how the heavily laden hull of a galleon like the *Maravillas* could settle in the soft sand bottom, but still break apart and shift for miles in the open tidal area.

Those early salvors who were first on the scene, and were able to see the silver bars resting on the bottom, waiting to be picked up, were the truly lucky ones.

Years later, others had to hope that storm tides during the winter months would move sand off the sunken hull so an identifiable clue to the *almiranta*'s location might be sighted during the summer diving season.

The problem of strong currents and sudden storms that plagued early salvors continues to be prevalent today. The shifting sands and "monstrous sharks" are still there as well—no doubt protecting and hiding the *almiranta* of Don Matías de Orellana.

Gaspar de los Reyes, Assistant Pilot of the *Maravillas*, knew the latitude (see appendix D) where the *Jesus, Maria y Josef* was anchored, about a quarter of a league[140] from the *almiranta* wreck site. For it was the *Jesus Maria* and Captain Juan de Hoyos who saved the lives of Gaspar and forty-four others who miraculously survived the sinking of the *Maravillas*. He also was aware that the *Maravillas* had settled on the bottom, about "a cannon shot away" from the edge of the channel where the shallows of the Little Bahama Bank drop off into much deeper water. Most importantly, he had great confidence in his sun sights since they were taken on a daily basis while the Hoyos crew was forging a new rudder for their galleon. The galleon of Juan de Hoyos was anchored in the same spot for six days. The seas had calmed, so the pilot should have been able to obtain very accurate observations, as opposed to astrolabe readings that might have to be taken on the unstable deck of a galleon underway in rolling seas. Consequently, he was the most able person to know the precise latitude, depth of water, and bottom conditions and would have the best chance to locate the site of the shipwreck.

In the summer of 1656, after his superb navigation led the salvage flotilla to the location of the wreck, Gaspar reported considerable marine vegetation already growing on what was left of the hull, after only six months of submersion. Those who would later seek the *almiranta*'s grave would have difficulty finding the remains on the bottom because shifting sands would almost completely have hidden the ballast pile, and undersea flora would proceed to camouflage the cannon and decaying wooden frames and timbers.

The most significant fact concerning modern salvage possibilities of this sunken galleon is that the sterncastle broke off and became separated from the hull of the ship. This huge poop section, three decks high, split apart from the hull when the galleon was breaking up. It drifted off and settled somewhere, and was not located by the early Spanish divers who worked only around the ship's submerged hull.

Chests of gold coin and jewelry together with much private treasure would have been most likely stored in this stern section of the galleon where the officers' quarters and the more expensive passenger cabins were located.

Registered bullion for His Majesty and for private accounts was stacked in the *pañol de plata* at the bottom of the hull because of its heavy weight, in order to lower the center of gravity and to ballast the ship. Valuable contraband cargo generally was packed in personal luggage and belongings, or even in private chests and boxes and carried to the owner's quarters, where it was carefully watched.

How far distant this huge stern section might have drifted is unknown. How much was broken up and scattered over the bottom of the sea is anybody's guess. We do know that various boxes and assorted cargoes, being transported on the *Maravillas'* main deck, washed ashore on Cayo de Rosario. The contents were discovered by a search party six months later. Cayo de Rosario, today Sandy Cay, is about twenty-seven nautical miles from the *Maravillas* wreck site.

Robert Marx reported in *The Search for Sunken Treasure* that his Seafinders, Inc. found the wreck site of the *Maravillas* in 1972. They salvaged "more than five tons of silver bars, around fifty thousand silver coins, twelve gold discs weighing eleven pounds (5 kg) each, more than a hundred gold coins, many exquisite pieces of gold jewelry, hundreds of uncut emeralds, a large ivory tusk and about half a ton of other artifacts."

Seafinders, Inc. also reported taking off the wreck two ornately decorated eighteen-pound calibre bronze cannon bearing the coat of arms of King Philip IV, as well as four huge iron anchors.

Was Marx the first in modern times to have located wreckage from the *Maravillas?* During the early 1960's Paul Nixon of Fort Lauderdale brought a boat to the Mantanilla Shoals where he propitiously anchored in a most opportune spot. Donning scuba gear, he went over the side and into the water. He soon discovered a unique formation of a small coral cave. The entire hole, or depression, looked as if it might have once been a part of a ship. Inside the hole he found dozens upon dozens of large silver bars. Returning to Florida, he unloaded nine tons of this cargo of silver on a Miami River dock. The entire lot was sold to a scrap metals dealer. Unfortunately, the silver bars were never identified, nor were their markings recorded.

Nixon claimed the location was within sight of breakers on the northwest end of the Bank. Could this have been part of the stern-castle of the *Maravillas*? Or was it an entirely separate treasure wreck? We know the 1657 salvage vessel *San Antonio* (one of the ships of Juan de Somovilla Tejada and Gaspar de los Reyes) was broken apart on reefs near the head of *Los Mimbres* at the northwest corner of Little Bahama Bank after losing its anchors in a sudden storm. However, the *San Antonio* was not supposed to be carrying treasure. According to all reports, the entire salvage had been placed aboard the lead salvage frigate, the *Madama do Brasil*.

Captain Herbert "Herbo" Humphreys, Jr. has been the primary salvager of treasure and artifacts from the *Maravillas* site since the Marx salvage effort in 1972.

There have been others who have obtained lease rights from the Commonwealth of the Bahamas. From 1973 to 1977 Jack Kelly of Tulsa, Oklahoma, and Grifon Corporation took over the Marx lease originally held by Seafinders, Inc. Norman Scott, with the 136-foot salvage boat *Privateer*, and Marty Meylach, with *Happy Hooker* worked the site in 1977 and 1978, under contract with Kelly. This writer made his first visit to the wreck site during this period through an invitation by Scott. In 1980 and 1981 Joe Barrow and Mike Daniels had the lease concession with Margaret Brandeis. In 1982 and 1983 Norman Scott's Expeditions Unlimited acquired lease rights and returned again to the Little Bahama Bank. In 1985 Art Hartman worked the wreck aboard the MV *Dare* in a joint venture with Senator Key of the Abacos. The next major salvor would be Herbert Humphreys in 1987. This is not to imply that others have not slipped over to the Little Bahama Bank to push some sand and pick through the scatter area. While many have found little or nothing, others have brought home handsome souvenirs of iron spikes, clay pipes, pottery shards, pieces-of-eight, candle holders, musket balls, silver spoons, pewter plates, and other assorted shipboard and household items.

Herbert Humphreys' salvage team, known as Marex International (Marine Archaeological Recovery, L.C.) has pumped the most capital into the effort, and has been the most consistently successful in modern times. His first major finds during 1988 and 1989 were highlighted with gold bars, pieces of fabulously detailed gold jewelry with emeralds and diamonds, lengths of golden rope chain, and numerous silver coins. In 1990 there would be yields of two-escudo gold coins, an ornate gold cross set with sixty-six emeralds, and an imposing gold brooch with eighty emeralds.

By 1991 Humphreys, now acutely affected with *Maravillas* fever, would uncover twenty-seven gold bars (approximately ninety pounds), twenty-five silver bars (approximately 506 pounds), forty gold coins, and a total of 6,085 silver coins (mostly of eight and four *reales*.)

During 1991 Marex purchased Bob Marx's research, notes and ship's logs. The hope was this additional data would provide directional clues to the long sought-after stern section of the *Maravillas*.

Another strong addition to the Marex team was John McSherry and his "gold sled." In 1992, aboard his vessel *Tail Hook*, he and his first mate, Betsy, successfully located another pile of wreckage on the scatter line of the *Maravillas*. Silver coins of the era of King Philip II (1556-1598) were recovered, as was a bronze cannon of English origin. These items, along with other artifacts, would predate the *Maravillas* by 100 years! What could they have possibly found?

Hank Hudson, former Vice President of Marex told it this way:

"The most bizarre item found on this site was a bronze saker cannon, ten feet in length and weighing 1,500 pounds. Its exterior, instead of the usual round shape, is twelve-faceted. It bears the inscriptions, 'JOHN AND ROBERT OWYN MADE THYS PESE ANNO DMN 1543, HENRICUS OCTAVUS.' The royal seal of Henry VIII, the Tudor Rose, surrounded by garter with crown is displayed as well. The Owyns (Owens) were chief bell and cannon founders for Henry VIII. This cannon is singular because of its origins, when and where it was found, and because very few examples of the Owyn brothers' work remain in existence. Two are in the Tower of London, and another is in the *Mary Rose* exhibit at Portsmouth, England.

"Alongside this beautiful bronze piece was found a large-bore, wrought iron swivel gun, known at the time as a 'murderer,' two cast iron cannon of Spanish origin, elephant tusks, over a dozen arquebus barrels (one with a partial wooden stock remaining), many cannon projectiles and musket shot, one gold bar, one intact storage, or 'olive' jar filled with magnetite (a black sand found on some Central and South American beaches), Venetian glass chevron trade beads, leg manacles, and a stone Indian celt (axe head). Also discovered are standing iron rigging from the ship itself, porcelain shards from the Ming dynasty export trade (Wan Li reign, 1573-1620), and over three hundred silver coins. The coins, though nearly destroyed by the long immersion in the sea, still show the crest of Philip II of Spain.

"Just a day or so later, and not far removed from this spot, three sections of Lombard cannon and a cache of coppery-looking bars of various sizes and shapes was found. Some of these bars weighed as much as forty pounds! Then, twenty-one gold bars marked from five kt to eight kt (20.8 percent to 33.3 percent content), twelve fine gold, small ingots and small pieces of bars. One silver ornament and a seated, smiling jaguar, about three inches high were also revealed. When the encrustation was removed from the 'copper' bars and disks, they were found to be well marked with tax stamps from Emperor Carlos I (1506-1556), so we knew they were not contraband and must have some value greater than copper. When we had samples assayed from these, they proved to contain copper, silver and gold, with a gold content of from ½ percent to 20 percent. It is now believed these bars are possibly melted down from Indian idols and jewelry, and were being transported back to Spain for further smelting. Such metal is known as 'tumbaga'."[141]

The word *tumbaga* was adopted by the Spanish from the Indians in the New World. It described gold, silver or copper alloys of low quality.[142] The Marex bars, weighing between five and twenty-five pounds, were roughly cast from crude clay or sand molds, after jewelry and other plundered Indian metals had been melted sufficiently to enable a fast pour into the mold.

Some 200 of the *tumbaga* bars, totaling about 2,000 pounds, were found containing a combined mixture of silver, copper and gold (although gold assayed at only about 5 to 6 percent in most of the ingots). There were, however, some twenty small bars which were primarily gold, and a handful of early gold money pieces consisting of small hand-chiseled chunks with carat markings.

Each bar was marked with an assay value, the initial of the person who did the assay, and the tax stamp or seal of King Carlos I. They were probably cast in Mexico during the mid 16th-century and, most significantly, they probably represent the earliest such bullion shipped from the New World back to Spain.

Today, the relatively small[143] ballast pile of the *Maravillas* lies in thirty-three to thirty-four feet of water. However, there have been times when it would be necessary to blow ten feet of sand off it.

The scattered trail of wreckage extends for several miles in a southerly and easterly direction, has a breadth of forty to fifty feet near the main wreck site, then tapers to about ten feet toward the end. (This is only after it stretches for an amazing distance of some three miles.)

Along this fascinating trail of treasure Humphreys and his team made discovery after exciting discovery. Most finds would boggle the minds of even the most conservative treasure hunters.

As an example, the emerald studded gold cross, and the two gold and emerald brooches were found in the "turtle grass" near the ballast mound. Also found were swords, muskets, emeralds, pieces-of-eight and ornate medals of the Order of Santiago. Gold bars, more silver coins and silver plates were dispersed one to two miles distant along the scattered path of treasure. Spikes, pins, musket balls, and silver coins and plates were discovered almost four miles from the primary ballast pile.

Was this trail the break-up route of the three-decked sterncastle? The first Spanish divers described the basic hull of the *Maravillas* as "completely intact." Indeed, so secure was the forward strong room that the 1657 expedition attempted to blast it open, but failed. Insofar as can be determined the total early salvage came solely from the site of the sunken hull. Later, after the wooden hull and deck timbers deteriorated, English salvors dredged around the wreck site in an effort to turn up treasure hidden in the soft sand bottom. This dredging could well have caused an even greater displacement of artifacts.

How far would a wooden chest loaded with silver coins have drifted? Probably not too far, unless storm tides and strong currents helped move it. Even if this occurred, could it have moved three miles? Spikes, musket balls and deck hardware were found along with valuable artifacts and treasure throughout the scatter area, indicating part of the ship's structure moved from the initial place of sinking. Evidence left in certain sections of the trail containing considerable debris and artifacts further indicate that something major happened there. Perhaps a large section of the poop deck settled in that spot, or a section of the stern containing several cabins where personal belongings were stored came to rest there.

Because of the extent of the scattered treasure trajectory, and

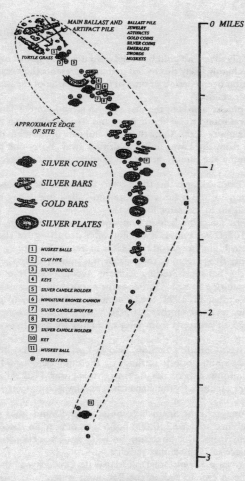

0 MILES

1

2

3

BALLAST PILE
JEWELRY
ARTIFACTS
GOLD COINS
SILVER COINS
EMERALDS
SWORDS
MUSKETS

MAIN BALLAST AND
ARTIFACT PILE

TURTLE GRASS

APPROXIMATE EDGE
OF SITE

SILVER COINS

SILVER BARS

GOLD BARS

SILVER PLATES

1 MUSKET BALLS
2 CLAY PIPE
3 SILVER HANDLE
4 KEYS
5 SILVER CANDLE HOLDER
6 MINIATURE BRONZE CANNON
7 SILVER CANDLE SNUFFER
8 SILVER CANDLE SNUFFER
9 SILVER CANDLE HOLDER
10 KEY
11 MUSKET BALL
✛ SPIKES / PINS

The Marex Scatter Trail

Along this fascinating trail of treasure Herbert Humphreys and his team made discovery after exciting discovery. Most finds would boggle the mind of even the most conservative artifact hunters. Was this trail the break-up route of the three-decked sterncastle, or is that huge target still waiting somewhere under the sand of Little Bahama Bank?

that not only silver and gold but shipboard items are spread over a distance, it is highly likely this mixed pattern represents the breakup and deterioration over a period of time of the sterncastle of the *Maravillas* and all it contained.

The precise words of the first Spanish salvors were: "The hull of the ship was found to be in one piece and structurally intact from the keel to the upper decks. Only the poop and part of the main deck had separated from the lower hull and drifted away. Forty-one guns are visible among the jumble of broken timbers and other wreckage, as are many silver bars."

This helps confirm this theory. We also know the Spanish divers worked only on the main wreck site and ballast pile. They returned time and again to this same location.

Christie's auction, held in London on October 3, 1990, brought a net of 107,169.40 pounds sterling, after deducting for their commissions, to Humphreys and the Marex investors.

Twenty-five percent of this balance was transferred to the Central Bank of the Bahamas Sterling Current Account on December 20, 1990, amounting to $51,736.03, as their contractual percentage.

On October 11, 1991, the Commonwealth of the Bahamas Public Treasury received another $15,970.81 as their 25 percent share in $63,883.25 of proceeds from sales by Marex for assorted coins and artifacts.

The next Christie's auction, held in London on May 28, 1992, brought 285,550 pounds sterling, or the equivalent of $411,655. The Commonwealth of the Bahamas' share was $102,914. These funds were credited to the Bahamas Treasury account on June 30, 1993.

The magnificent Spanish colonial emerald and gold pectoral cross combined sold for 210,000 pounds sterling to an absentee bidder[144] from Spain. This huge sum broke Christie's auction record for a single piece of 17th-century jewelry.

The royal *almiranta* of Don Matías de Orellana was the richest single galleon ever to sink in the Bahamian waters. Off and on, for twenty-seven years, the Spanish and other salvors worked the shipwreck. This proved one of the longest diving and salvage attempts on a single treasure site in ancient days.

Spanish salvors utilizing Indian divers recovered probably a third of the treasure cargo of the *Maravillas*. They left more on the bottom of Little Bahama Bank at *Los Mimbres*, and lost other bullion and coin to looters than they cared to admit. The salvage site is in open water. There are thousands of miles of Atlantic Ocean seas to the East and North. To the West, the Florida coast is only seventy miles away, but is separated by the swift flowing and extremely deep Gulf Stream. To the South, before reaching the settlement of West End on Grand Bahama Island, forty miles away, are only reefs and scattered rocks and islets. Walker's Cay, a small resort island frequented by sport fishermen, is the most northeasterly of the Abaco chain. It lies about forty miles from the *Maravillas* wreck site.

The unfortunate loss of life (605 people died) aboard this 900-ton galleon, together with its immense cargo of gold, silver and jewels, propelled the shipwreck into history. The Portobelo and Cartagena registers counted some 500 large bars of silver (weighing about 70 pounds each) and some 82,000 pieces-of-eight as officially recorded cargo aboard the *Maravillas*. There was no reference whatsoever to gold, emeralds or jewelry. However, Padre Diego stated in his memoirs: "There was five million in gold and silver on the king's galleon."

Jeronimo de Barrionuevo, chronicler of the King's Court in Madrid, reported: "The two ships, the *Maravillas* and the *Jesus, Maria y Josef* carried more than 12,000,000 between them."

Early salvors reported bringing up more than 1,000 bars of silver and twice as many pieces-of-eight (about 160,000) than were registered. Modern salvors have also recovered significant quantities of silver bar and coin, as well as fabulous finds of gold, emeralds and fine jewelry.

How much is left, and can it be recovered in any kind of economically feasible manner? This question will continue to be asked, and attempts will be made to find the answer, for at least another century.

GORDA CAY

Since the majority of the salvaged treasure from the Somovilla-Reyes second diving expedition was again lost at Gorda Cay, reports of what actually was recovered, taken to Havana, and later to Spain, are contradictory. We do know from these reports that large silver bars ranging in number from 144 to 160 were removed from the hull of the sunken *Maravillas* at *Los Mimbres*. We know also, either 130 or 132 were again salvaged from the Gorda Cay wreckage of the *Madama*, together with considerable worked silver, probably 150 silver bars, some silver cones, and a little specie—no more than 600 pieces-of-eight.

With this information, and despite not knowing the size and weight of the silver bars, we can place an estimated value of reported net salvage, after the Gorda Cay disaster, of about 170,000 pesos on what Somovilla and Reyes turned over to authorities in Havana and Spain.

There is no way to determine how much might remain today on the shallow reefs at Gorda Cay, before they drop off into deep water. The amount of silver looted by the English adventurers from Eleuthera was never completely reported for obvious reasons. The only data available was obtained from certain legal proceedings in Bermuda. These proceedings took place as a result of conflicts due to the dividing of the treasure from the two trips of the Eleutherans.[145]

It was rumored that native Bahamian fishermen worked the site between 1898 and 1903, but what they found was never officially reported. In August of 1950, Roscoe Thompson and Howard Lightbourn retrieved a seventy-two pound silver bar from Gorda Cay. It was later displayed by the Tourist Development Board in Nassau. The famed Florida Keys treasure salvor, Art McKee, is known to have recovered three more. They were unaware, at least at the time, where these silver bars came from. Today we can say with certainty, they represent the twice sunken *Maravillas* treasure lost on the *Madama do Brasil*.

SALVAGE IN THE BAHIA DE CÁDIZ

No known modern salvage has taken place on the ships sunk in 1656 in the Bahia de Cádiz. This is because Spain does not encourage salvage activity, particularly from outsiders. Nor does the country allow a potential salvor to retain anything he might discover. All items found within Spain's territorial waters, whether treasure or artifacts, are considered patrimony of that nation.

An extensive archives research and underwater search and mapping effort is currently being undertaken by archaeologists and historians of Spain's Department of Culture. Their purpose is to develop lists and charts of historically significant undersea sites that can be adequately excavated, and their finds properly conserved. This is a major project and likely will take decades. Cádiz has been a major seaport for centuries. There are hundreds of decaying and antediluvian vessels lost in the region, dateless and forgotten, since the dawn of history.

It is known the explosion of the *almiranta, San Francisco Javier,* blew out much of the bottom of the ship, taking ballast, bullion and heavy cargo directly to the ocean bottom. In all probability it is still today resting in a solitary pile on the sea floor about five miles off Cádiz. However, the upper decks, masts, sails and rigging drifted to shore in flames. The charred remains finally came to settle in about twenty-five feet of water, a mile offshore the time-worn gates of the old city. Within a month everything that could be reached was salvaged. Everything else sunk by the English fleet still lies on the bottom of the Bahia de Cádiz.

SANTA CRUZ DE TENERIFE, CANARY ISLANDS

After the English wipeout of the entire returning treasure fleet of 1657 at Santa Cruz, King Philip IV donated the armament retrieved from shipwrecks within the harbor to that important Spanish port. This was done in order to assuage, at least in part, the minds and hearts of the local citizens and those assigned to the military of the pummeled outpost.

Most of the treasure cargoes aboard the Spanish ships anchored at Santa Cruz were transferred to storage vaults within the thick walls of the fortress prior to the English attack. However, English reports reflect some pillage by crews sent aboard the merchantships to burn those Spanish vessels after they were abandoned by fleeing soldiers and sailors.

Spanish Captain General Egues y Beaumont later arranged for his preserved cargo of treasure to be transported to Spain aboard small trading vessels. These were less likely to be spotted by the English ships attempting to blockade the coast of Spain.

If there is any silver bullion or coins scattered among the harbor seafloor of this vintage Canary Island port, it is mixed with other discarded debris deposited over the centuries.

NOTES

Introduction

[1]C.H. Haring, *Trade and Navigation Between Spain and the Indies in the Time of the Hapsburgs*, p. 335.

Chapter 1

[2]Diverse spellings of the name appear in numerous documents. While the "b" and "v" were interchangeable at the time, this text uses Padre Diego's spelling as he signed it on official papers, Rivadeneira.

[3]The shallow waters in the Perico anchorage area forced the ships to enter and leave with the tide. However, it also provided a shallow and protected harbor for the galleons while they transferred the king's treasure and other cargoes to and from the warehouses on shore. Perico, the port of old Panama, was sacked and burned in 1671 by the pirate Henry Morgan and his buccaneers. In 1673, Panama City was built approximately eight kilometers west of the ruins of Perico.

[4]In 1659 Edward Barlow wrote about his first night aboard a frigate (*Barlow's Journal*, National Maritime Museum, Greenwich, England): "I was put into a cabin to sleep, a space much like some gentleman's dog kennel, for I was forced to crawl upon all fours, and when I was in . . . I could not hold my head upright, but being very weary I slept indifferently well."

[5]Punta Santa Elena owes its name to Francisco Pizarro, who discovered it on the day of the saint, August 18, 1525.

[6]Later named the Humboldt Current.

[7]Francis Drake is credited with naming Isla de Plata some seventy-five years earlier. Following a daring capture of the Spanish galleon *Nuestra Señora de la Concepción*, ladened with silver treasure, and enduring a return voyage of hardship, he was knighted by Queen Elizabeth. The unimposing island off the coast of the Presidency of Quito (today's Ecuador) became known as Isla de Plata, or Silver Island.

[8]The absence of the two avisos later provided the most damaging evidence against the captain general, especially as to why both *chinchorros* were sent ahead. Were they actually bringing advance news to Panama? Or were they headed to Paita or Guayaquil for some private trading, as was rumored?

[9]One Spanish *braza de mar* of the 17th century was the equivalent of 5.5 English feet.

[10]Indiferente, General 2574, folios 193, 194.

[11]The strong current provides further evidence as to why the *capitana* fell short of clearing Punta Santa Elena.

[12]*Patacon*, as used in Peru at the time, meant a hammered coin cut from a ribbon or sheet of silver to the approximate weight of an ounce. Struck by hand from a piece of silver shaped from the end of the bar it was referred to as a "cob." It later came to designate all kinds of pieces-of-eight, including the fine, round, mechanically milled ones of Potosí.

[13]From *Diaro de Lima*, by Josephe de Mugaburu, Captain of Infantry. Mugaburu kept a detailed dairy, as did his son after him, of the major events of life in Lima from 1640 to 1697. He was usually stationed at the palace of the viceroy and was well con-

nected to various political and social circles of Lima. The diary is considered a highly useful and generally reliable source of original information by all serious historians of Colonial Peru.

[14]Archivo General de Indias, Contratación 2425.

Chapter 2

[15]The cluster of rocks off Punta La Tintina, near Chanduy, is affectionately referred to as Los Negritos by Ecuadorans who commonly fish these waters. It is likely this is the ancient landmark General de Sosa mentioned.

[16]Don Jeronimo de Barrionuevo, *Avisos*, (1654-1658).

[17]Bernardo de Campos was later accused of being one of the biggest thieves of the ship's treasure.

[18]In addition to sea snakes, Vásquez de Velasco reported that "vile, maggot-like worms" were attaching themselves to the divers.

Chapter 3

[19]From *Armadas y Flotas de la Plata* (1620-1648), Fernando Serrano Mangas, Banco de España, 1990, p. 349.

[20]Archivo General de Indias, Indiferente 2693.

[21]After the loss of the *Maravillas* in 1656 and the subsequent delay of the *Jesus, Maria y Josef*, culminating with the destructive battle off Cádiz and the catastrophic loss of the entire treasure fleet at Tenerife in 1657, the *avería* would be temporarily fixed at ninety-nine percent in a desperate effort to help the king recover his losses.

[22]Archivo General de Indias, Indiferente 2693. Record of the Council of the Indies dated October 14, 1647.

[23]Archivo General de Indias, Indiferente 2501. Report from Don Gabriel de Ocaña y Alarcón to the President of the Council of the Indies, Madrid, January 17, 1645.

[24]*Imports of American Gold and Silver into Spain*, 1503-1660, Economic Quarterly, May, 1929, pp. 436-472.

[25]Archivo General de Indias, Contaduria 1726

[26]Alsedo y Herrera, *Compendio Histórico de la Provincia*, etc., p. 26.

[27]Juan y Ulloa, Noticias Secretas, p. 85.

[28]Archivo General de Indias, Lima 297, Recommendation to His Majesty from the Council of War.

[29]Lawrence A. Clayton, *Caulkers and Carpenters in a New World: The Shipyards of Colonial Guayaquil*, Ohio University, Center for International Studies, Latin America Series No. 8, Athens, Ohio, 1980.

[30]Ricardo Cappa, *Estudios Criticos*, p. 121.

[31]A *codo* was the equivalent of 23 inches.

[32]Lawrence A. Clayton, *Caulkers and Carpenters*, op. cit., p. 69.

Chapter 4

[33]Archivo General de Indias, Escribania de Camara, 1028c.

[34]From *Letters of the Lady—Travels into Spain*, London, 1692.

Chapter 5

[35]The official register of the *Maravillas* confirms Diego Portichuelo de Rivadeneira registered a total of 20,826 pesos alone, while in Cartagena.

[36]The Count of Bornos, Don Diego Ramirez de Haro, was the designated *Gobernador*. However, while in Vera Cruz he became ill and remained there.

[37]The compass rose was subdivided into points with each point equal to 111¼°. Example: North (N) = 0, North by East, (N x E) = 1 point or 11°15'. North, Northeast by North, (NNE x N) = 2 points or 22°30', North East by North, (NE x N) = 3 points or 33°45', North East, (NE) = 4 points or 45°00', etc. To change course by two points entails a directional shift by as much as 22.5°.

[38]Several survivors later testified not a soul was to be seen on the decks of the *capitana*, or anywhere thereabouts. This is in spite of the good lighting provided by the three bright lanterns on the stern.

[39]Psalm 18, Old Testament.

[40]Acts of Apostles, Chapter 27.

Chapter 6

[41]A square-rigged ship such as the *Jesus, Maria y Josef* was unable to sail more than approximately twenty degrees against the wind.

[42]The 680-ton galleon *Nuestra Señora de la Concepción* was lost in 1641 on *Los Abrojos*, (submerged rocks) east of Mouchoir Bank, about eighty miles north of Hispaniola (Dominican Republic). The vessel was ladened with a large cargo of silver bar and specie. These reefs later became known as Silver Bank because more than 50 tons of coin and ingots were lost there. As a result of the salvage of the sunken wreck in 1687, William Phips was later knighted by King James II, and rewarded with the Royal Governorship of Massachusetts in 1692.

[43]Known today as Aguadilla, Puerto Rico.

[44]One minute of latitude (1') is equivalent to one (1) nautical mile, equaling 1.15 statute miles. Consequently, there is a ten (10) nautical mile variance in these sun sights—a huge expanse of open water by any standards.

Chapter 7

[45]J.Veitia y Linage, *Norte de la Contratación de las Indias Occidentales*. Seville, 1672.

[46]Indiferente General 1870, memorandum dated January 17, 1630.

Chapter 8

[47]Access to the Bay of Cartagena was via the narrow channel of Bocachica, between Isla de Tierrabomba and the Baru peninsula. The castle of Bocachica was the fortress of San Luis de Bocachica. It served as a key bastion of defense for the city.

[48]The king's oath was a sanctioned prerequisite of loyalty and honesty for those entrusted with Spain's treasure.

[49]Today, the Straits of Florida.

[50]The Head of the Martyrs, today the lower Florida Keys near Key West.

[51]A method of utilizing small anchors (kedges) that can be rowed or placed in deeper water. By hauling in the lines (warping) the vessel is moved in that direction.

[52]State papers of John Thurloe, Secretary to the Council of State.

[53]The Count of Molina, Don Pedro de Messia y Tobas, was Mayor of Cádiz from 1650 to 1660. He was instrumental in convincing King Philip and his military engineers of the importance of improving the fortifications of the city. This work was finally begun in March 1657, after the disastrous battle with the English.

Chapter 9

[54]The message to the Governor of Lagos was delivered by two "responsible" men who were among the first prisoners released and taken ashore by the English.

[55]A *blanca* was the smallest existing silver coin in Spain at the time.

[56]F.C. Montague, *The Political History of England*, Vol. 7, p. 439.

[57]François Guizot, *Histoire de la Révolution d'Angleterre*, 11, pp. 260-261.

[58]Fernando Duro, *Armada Española*, V. 18-30.

[59]C.H. Firth, *The Last Years of the Protectorate*, Vol. 1, 1656-1657.

[60]Abbott's *Writings and Speeches of Oliver Cromwell*, Vol. 4, 1655-1658.

[61]Letter of General Mountagu to Secretary Thurloe.

[62]The number of eight hundred prisoners is stated in Stayner's report, but is probably an error. Five hundred is a more likely figure.

[63]Calendar of State Papers Domestic, Vol. 1656-1657, p. 194. Three hundred pounds sterling was approved for payment of the Baides brothers' new apparel and to provide "some money for their purses."

[64]The author has spent an exhaustive amount of time and money attempting in vain to locate the Baides brothers' paintings. They probably were burned in the great London fire of 1666.

[65]Indiferente General 1876, folio 770.

[66]Archivo General de Indias, Santa Fe 224.

[67]Archivo General de Indias, Indiferente General 770, references a complete list of treasure and cargo salvaged. A sampling of this extensive inventory compilation is as follows:

A chest, number 6, containing sixteen bars weighing from 62.5 *castilians* to 455 *castilians*. (A *castilian* was an ancient Spanish coin equal to ⅟₅₀ of a gold mark, and weighing 4.6 grams. A mark was equal to 230 grams, or 50 *castilians*, or 7.395 troy ounces. One troy ounce equals 31.103 grams. One troy pound equals 12 ounces, or 373.236 grams.) Because these weights are stated in *castilians*, it is likely these were gold bars ranging from about two-thirds a troy pound (.770) to 5.608 troy pounds. Another list described; "An unmarked green cargo trunk containing a quantity of wet letters and a small, delicate box containing images of Our Lady of Copacabana, with an attached note, 'To my lady Doña Francisca de Santillana, nun of the convent *Concepción Gerónima* of Madrid.'"

A definite confirmation of ownership was found in one chest, made in China and containing two golden pans, a golden goblet, four large, medium and small silver plates, a golden taller with 5-pieces, three chains of gold, two silver wash basins, a gold sword guard, and 12 solid, round, silver candlesticks, 11 with stems, all inscribed in ink, "Baides."

[68]It was recommended that these funds be held for the partial financing of next year's treasure fleet.

Chapter 10

[69]Known today as "Memory Rock," the lobstering is still very good.

[70]Futtock knee framing, linked with the ribs holding the deck.

[71]The stern section, torn horizontally from the rest of the ship.

[72]Hides were a typical cargo from Cuba, as were tobacco and cocoa.

[73]At 5.5 feet per *braza*, this defined a depth of forty-four feet. Most reports state the divers worked in six *brazas*, or thirty-three feet.

[74]Gulf Stream.

[75]Margarita Island, off the coast of Venezuela, was noted for its pearl divers. Some developed their free-diving capacity to remain submerged for over three minutes.

[76]One *castellano* equals ⅕₀ of one mark of gold, or 4.6 grams. It is not a coin, but a unit of accounting. Originally it was used as a coin, worth 490 *maravedises de plata*. The *castellano* did not exist as a coin in the 17th century.

[77]Court Records of Bermuda, (published by Lefroy, 1877-1879).

[78]Opportunistic Bermuda wreckers previously developed their own version of a diving-bell called the "Bermuda Tub."

[79]The *Madama do Brasil* was a strong vessel of 400 tons. It was built around 1650 for the Dutch West India Company. She was pierced for thirty guns, and carried twenty-six pieces of brass and iron. The vessel was manned by an eighty-member crew, and carried an additional ninety men, comprising two companies of armed soldiers and sailors.

[80]Near the border of what today is Venezuela and Colombia. Somovilla later reported the Negroes who were purchased by Juan de Ochoa were useless when diving in eight *brazas*. In fact, only a few of the Indians proved capable at the difficult and deep free diving.

[81]The total 1,500,000 pesos confirmed by Yriarte's report to His Majesty was an incredibly large amount of salvaged treasure. The unanswered question is this: If Yriarte reported recovering 1,500,000, how much was unreported? Later lawsuits brought against him indicate the probable total treasure he salvaged was much more than the amount he reported—much more! The other 120,000 pesos Yriarte reported delivering to Cartagena reached that port aboard a sister salvage ship.

[82]Yriarte did "not" return to Cartagena. He claimed to have been hit by such a fierce storm at latitude 44° that he was forced to head directly for Spain.

[83]Known today as Gorda Cay.

[84]This was learned in the later testimony of Pedro Gallegos, one of Somovilla's trusted sergeants who was on board the *Madama* for the second diving expedition and a subsequent one.

Chapter 11

[85]Archivo General de Indias, Santa Fe 198.

[86]These letters were brought personally to the Council of the Indies in Seville by the Marqués de Montealegre (who recently was named to the Council) as soon as he received them. This action initiated the beginning of a long series of law suits, ultimately leading everyone in Spain to believe much more salvaged treasure was recovered than was reported. And it had! *"El buceo se prestaba a grandes fraudes."* (The diving expedition lent itself to huge frauds.)

[87]The accusation was made that Juan de Somovilla Tejada recovered a chest, but did not list it among the salvaged inventory. The chest was said to have weighed seventy-one (71) pounds, and contained gold bars, gold doubloons, emeralds and other loose, precious stones and jewelry. Among the jewelry were seven *veneras* made of gold. These were badges or insignias of the Orders of Knighthood. Another piece of jewelry, a religious medallion, was described as a likeness of *Nuestra Señora de la*

Limpia Concepción, lavishly decorated with emeralds and diamonds. There was a reference to a gold rose, weighing four *castellanos* (about thirty-one grams.) Such detailed descriptions of the stolen plunder provided creditable evidence against the salvors.

[88]It is highly doubtful that, being Indians, they would have been permitted, or could have afforded to come the distance to Spain for their personal purposes. It is more likely they were brought to Spain forcibly, or otherwise by government officials in order to bring down the accused.

[89]A would-be salvor named Miguel Garcia de Villegas applied to the Council of the Indies for salvage rights to the 1641 wreck of the *Nuestra Señora de la Concepción*, prior to Gaspar de los Reyes seeking the concession. However, being consulted on May 28, 1666, the Council was of the opinion that Gaspar was the better candidate, "because of the experience he has in navigation of the Indies, and because he was the one who discovered the wreck of the lost *almiranta* on the sandbanks of *Los Mimbres.*"

[90]This virtuously indignant comment by Gaspar amusingly reflects the extraordinary irony of one embezzler condemning a fellow embezzler.

[91]There were eight divers from Florida who had been on the Yriarte *barquilla*, the small vessel sent to fetch firewood and water. This boat stayed at the *Mimbres'* site when Yriarte left.

[92]Archivo General de Indias, Indiferente General 2574.

[93]Contaduria 1435.

[94]Captain Rivera also stated that the previous year he was on deck on two occasions when 3,000 reales of eight were counted. This was twice the amount reported by Luzio in his final accounting to Havana.

[95]Contaduria 1155.

[96]Captain Melgar recommended that the salvors give hatchets, knives, beads, cloth, liquor, wine, etc., to the Florida Indian Chiefs, in exchange for the use of their divers. The divers were paid in silver pesos.

[97]A 45-foot vessel carrying 25 guns? Certainly, they could not have been large cannon, if there were, indeed any cannon at all on board.

[98]Today's hopeful salvagers should take note that here we have a specific reference from the men who made four successful salvage expeditions more than three centuries ago. Even after twenty-three years on the sea bottom, they could still locate the hull of the *Maravillas*, and it was on the sunken hull only that they worked.

[99]*Saulmone, Dictionnaire de l'Ancienne Langue Française et de tous ses Dialectes du IXe au XVe Siècle, Slatkine, Genève-Paris, 1982, Réimpression de l'édition de Paris 1891-1902, Tome VII, p. 327.*

[100]Present day Haiti.

[101]Governor of Saint Domingue from 1676 to 1683.

[102]Archivo General de Indias, Escribania 47a.

[103]Contaduria 3.

[104]The restamped pieces-of-eight were those pesos that had been counterstruck, as a result of the huge scandal uncovered in 1649 at Potosí, thus confirming their full value of eight *reales*, or their subsequent devaluation to seven or three *reales*, determined at the time by their weight.

[105]Contaduria 1435.

[106]Escribania 103B.

[107]Another Archivo General de Indias source (Escribania 1028B) related that treasure belonging to the 45 survivors included "thirty-five pieces of silver of different sizes and weights."

[108]This was the amount of treasure officially reported by Puerto Rican authorities. Others would testify later that the actual amount recovered exceeded 1,000,000 pesos, and that "the authorities profited handsomely to report a lesser amount." (Indiferente General 2574, folio 1382). Large silver bars were valued at 1,200 pesos each.

[109]Since most of the valuables recovered from Cayo de Rosario were silver items of a personal nature, placing any kind of value on them would be a guess.

[110]The amount of recovered treasure reported and delivered by Captain Ochoa was offloaded at Cartagena, as was the 120,000 pesos reported by Captain Yriarte, along with some of the cannon.

[111]The 1,500,000 pesos recovered by Yriarte was supposed to have been delivered to Governor Zapata in Cartagena, but according to our illustrious captain, "at 44° latitude he was hit by such a storm that he was forced to run with the wind which carried him all the way to his home port of Guetaria in Spain, where the silver and artillery were safely taken ashore."

[112]This total of 170,000 pesos is what was reported to auditors in Havana, after the shipwreck of the salvage vessel at Gorda Cay. We know it was not a complete tally of everything salvaged because a considerable amount of treasure had been buried at Gorda Cay, and other loot had been taken ashore at a small port in Cuba before the rescue vessel cleared with authorities in Havana.

[113]200,000 pesos was the amount reported taken by the French.

[114]It is not known whether there was another successful French attempt.

[115]The fleet of Captain General Enriquez de Guzmán returned to Spain with a registered amount of salvage totaling 33,767 pesos representing the king's half of the salvage award.

[116]The returning fleet of General Gaspar de Velasco brought back to Spain the registered amount of 41,300 pesos from salvage of the *almiranta*. This was represented to be the king's half share.

[117]This amount is a guess, based on the logs and comments of various English sea captains.

[118]This value in pesos does not include any value on the cannon which were salvaged. Also, some estimate must be added to reflect unreported or stolen amounts of treasure. This "plugged" figure should be considered at a minimum of 1,000,000 pesos.

Chapter 12

[119]mis *maravedis* in silver. Cesareo Fernandez Duro states the total value of the register was ten million pesos, another half million from Puerto Rico representing salvage from the *Maravillas*, brought earlier by Captains Tejada and Reyes.

[120]Stayner later stated Blake was disinclined to start a battle on Sunday.

[121]From *The Fighting Sailor Turned Peaceable Christian*, pp. 3-10.

[122]The only sails Stayner was able to hoist on the *Speaker* were the spritsail and sprittopsail.

[123]J. Campbell, *Lives of British Admirals*, 1893, Vol. II, pp. 291-293.

[124]Alonso de Davila was Governor of Santa Cruz de Tenerife. Don Diego later criticized the governor in front of the king for not doing more to help in the battle at Santa Cruz. "With sixty cannon mounted in the castle, although some were of small caliber, they were so poorly handled the enemy did not lose a single ship."

[125]Thomas Lurting reported the galleon he burned "had a great deal of silver on board, being a ship of about 800 tons. The other two were richly laden and about 700 to 800 tons."

[126]J. Campbell's, *Lives of British Admirals*, 1893, Vol. II, p. 121, "Memoirs of Admiral Blake."

[127]Bates, Elencus Motuum, Part ii, p. 323.

Chapter 13

[128]Reyes and Somavilla publicly reported the salvage of some 700,000 pesos as a result of three successive diving and salvage expeditions.

[129]There is considerable documentation in the A.G.I. Lima 253 in support of Father Diego's requests for a promotion. In these, his superiors, companions, shipwreck survivors and associates all write recommendations in his favor.

[130]The *Real Audiencia* took charge of governmental operations in Peru following the death of Viceroy Don Diego de Benavides while waiting for a new viceroy to be appointed. (Lima 67.)

[131]Because King Philip IV died in 1665, and his son Carlos II was only four years old, the Regency was assumed by the Queen mother.

[132]Contratación 5436, No. 29.

Chapter 14

[133]The *New York Times International*, Monday, April 14, 1997.

[134]Lima 60, The viceroy to the king, (1658. No. 66).

[135]According to Article No. 36 of the *Law of Internal Taxation*, any income for services rendered in Ecuador for foreigners would be taxed at a unique rate of "25 percent after expenses." However, according to Article No. 600 of the Ecuadoran *Civil Code*, the discovery of a treasure is similar to an invention or finding, activities not taxed as income.

[136]In 1998 we were able to accomplish a more realistic modification of this very unrealistic rule. Our division resulted in a 50%-50% split of everything recovered.

[137]Inca province which supplied the greatest number of Indian laborers to comply with the Spanish *mita*, a required period of servitude in the mines and smelters of Potosí.

[138]Even today the "trouble" is still there.

[139]On the old charts there are two references to the *Mimbres*. One near Bimini, and one north of Memory Rock (the *Tumbado*).

[140]One quarter of a league is 1,588 meters.

[141]The Marex Beacon, Vol. 11, Issue 9, Sept. 1992.

[142]Douglas R. Armstrong, *Tumbaga Silver for Emperor Charles V of the Holy Roman Empire*, 1993.

[143]It is likely the reason for the small amount of rock ballast is because the galleon was so heavily ballasted with silver bullion, chests of silver coins and other heavy cargo.

[144]It was rumored the absentee bidder was an entity of the government of Spain.

[145]J.H. Lefroy, *The History of the Bermudas*, 2 Vol., London, 1977-1979.

APPENDIX A
Composition of the Spanish Fleet and Comparison of Spanish/English Naval Ranks

The ship of the captain general, who was the commander-in-chief of the Spanish *flota* (fleet), was known as the *capitana*. English and Spanish terminology for naval ranks was not the same. An English commander-in-chief in the mid-17th century was referred to as general-at-sea, or admiral. His counterpart in Spain was known as captain general.

Second in command of the Spanish fleet was the *almirante*. His ship was referred to as the *almiranta*. English second-in-command might be referred to as admiral, vice admiral or commander, depending on the size of the fleet. The English ship carrying the flag of the second-in-command was called the vice-admiral. The rear admiral was generally third in command.

Third in command of a Spanish armada (the equivalent of the English rear admiral) was the *gobernador*, who was in charge of the infantry. He generally covered the rear squadron of the fleet. His vessel was referred to as the *gobierno*.

While some English blue bloods did postulate to high seafaring positions, most English high command positions were earned by years of experience at sea and at war. On the contrary, Spanish high command positions were often honorific and purchased by the occupant with the right connections. Most of these men expected to realize a fine return on their position through speculatory investments in New World commodities and products. This is not to imply that numerous lesser officials did not rise to high ranks in the Spanish Navy. In fact, many of them did.

Today, while the title of admiral, in English terms, outranks a captain, in the days of Old Spain the captain general was totally in charge. The admiral was second in command of the fleet. Captains, lieutenants and other career officers ranking under them were likely to have considerably more sea duty and experience, but not always. It depended on the man in charge, who he was and what he did to earn his stars.

APPENDIX B
Types of Treasure Shipped
Aboard *Carrera de Indias* Fleets

Barras

Large refined silver bars generally weighing between 65-75 pounds and valued at 1,000 pesos. The weight, fineness and serial number were stamped on each one.

Barretones

Smaller bars of refined silver of no standard weight or form. They generally weighed between 15-30 pounds.

Barretoncillos

Still smaller bars of refined silver, 5-15 pounds.

Tomillas

Bricks of silver.

Plata Plancha or *Plata Blanca*

Sheets of silver

Plata Piña

Poorly refined, unassayed porous silver, generally in the form of a cone. Sometimes in the form of a wedge (a part of a cheese-like wheel of silver).

Plata Labrada

Worked silverware consisting of plates, dishes, tureens, beakers, cups, candlesticks, forks, spoons, knives, frames, boxes, etc., made by Indian silversmiths to European designs, valued at the weight of the metal. (Since such items were considered for personal use, *plata labrada* was not subject to the *avería* tax. This contributed to a huge exploitation of this product category.)

Reales

Silver coins, the largest being the piece-of-eight *reales*, valued at a peso.

Gold

Large and small bars of assorted sizes and weights, as well as discs and coins.

APPENDIX C
Denominations and Conversions of Weights and Values

Maravedi de Plata Primarily a unit of calculation or measurement equal to ⅟₃₄ of one *real* of silver.

Maravedi de Vellon Equal to ½ a *maravedi* of silver.

Real de Plata A small silver coin worth 34 *maravedis*, or ⅛ of a peso.

Peso de a Ocho Piece-of-eight, equal to 8 *reales* of silver; equal to 272 *maravedis*; equal to 28.7 grams of silver, or one ounce. Most full-valued pieces-of-eight were rarely a full ounce, but 27.5 grams.

Marco de Plata Mark of silver was equal to 8 pieces-of-eight; equal to 230 +/- grams of silver; which was equal to ½ a Castilian *libra* (pound).

Marco de Oro Mark of gold was equal to 50 *castellanos*, or one *doblon* (*doubloon*).

Castellano Castilian, an early Spanish coin and later a measure of value, worth 490 *maravedis de plata*, being also equal to 14 *reales*, plus 14 *maravedis*.

Escudo A gold coin of 3.375 grams at 0.917 fineness, worth 550 *maravedis* during the mid-17th century, or about 14 *reales de plata*. *Escudos* of 1, 2, 4, and 8 were struck and the coin was later referred to as the legendary doubloon.

Ducado Ducat, gold coin, equal to 375 *maravedis*. The equivalent of 11 *reales*, plus 1 *maravedi* during the mid-17th century (up to 1680) or about 1½ pieces-of-eight.

Peso Ensayado   A measurement used in the New World for valuing bars of silver, especially worked silver, before the items were created, but including taxes and duties, i.e. the gross value. In the mid-17th century, 1 *peso ensayado* was the equivalent of about 1.62 pieces-of-eight.

Cajón de Plata   Chest of silver. As a registered shipment of money to Spain, a *cajón* contained 2,500 pieces of eight *reales*. In merchant trade a *cajón* contained 2,000 pieces-of-eight.

Talega   A strong, linen-cloth, sealed bag containing 1,000 pieces-of-eight. There were two *talegas* in a merchant's *cajón de pesos*. However, smugglers put more coin in some bags to evade taxes.

Libra   A Castilian pound, equal to 16 *onzas*, (ounces) or 460 grams.

Arroba   The equivalent of 25 pounds, or 11.5 kilograms.

Quintal   Equal to 4 *arrobas*, or 100 Castilian pounds.

APPENDIX D
Mid 17th Century

Distances and Measurements

Musket shot	200-300 meters (with accuracy approximately 150 meters)
Cannon shot	500 steps (from 2,200 to 2,500 yards)
Spanish *pie* (foot)	.283 meters, equal to 11.13 inches.
Spanish league	3.43 nautical miles ($\frac{1}{17.5}$ of a degree), or 6,352 meters
Spanish *palma* (palm)	.21 meter, or 8.27 inches
Braza (fathom)	One Spanish *braza de mar*, equivalent to 5.5 English feet
Cable length	608 feet

Latitude

Latitude is the angular distance measured north or south from the Equator. The early navigators learned that by recording the altitude of the sun just before, and just after, local apparent noon, their latitude could be determined from the highest point of altitude taken. Altitude is measured upward from the visible sea horizon, as an arc on the surface. One degree of latitude is equal to 60 nautical miles. One minute of latitude is equal to one nautical mile (a nautical mile is equal to about 1.15 statute miles). An astrolabe, predecessor to the sextant, was used to find the altitude of the sun (or a star). Depending upon the skills of the person using it, an astrolabe reading generally was accurate within 10 minutes of the actual position. Other than through the navigator's educated best guess, longitude (the distance measured east or west as an arc of the equator) was not accurately determined until a reliable time piece became available. This would be after 1707 when Englishman John Harrison created the clock (chronograph) and Greenwich Mean Time was established. GMT separates East from West, and today all countries utilize it as the time basis for determining longitude.

APPENDIX E

List of Persons Known to Have Been Aboard the 1654 Capitana, *Jesus Maria de La Limpia Concepción*

Capitán General (Captain General)	Don Francisco de Sosa
Capitán de Mar (Captain of Sea)	Bernardo de Campos
Maestre de Plata (Silvermaster)	Bernardo de Campos
Ayudante de Maestre de Plata y Artillero (Assistant Silvermaster and Chief of Artillery)	Juan Cortez
Piloto Mayor (Chief Pilot)	Captain Miguel Benitez de Alfara
Ayudante de Piloto (Assistant Pilot)	Captain Julio Caballero
Guarda Mayor (Chief Guardian)	Don Julio de Navarrete
Guarda (Guardian)	Francisco Gil
Contramaestre (Chief Boatswain)	Francisco Medero
Capitán de Compania de Infanteria (Captain of Infantry)	Don Francisco Tello de Guzmán y Medina (drowned later on the *Maravillas*)
Condestable (Master Gunner)	Julio Gomez Carvallo
Despensero (Steward)	Captain Domingo Fernández de Orozco
Escribano (Scribe)	Captain Bartolomé de Chavarria
Alferes (Midshipman)	Don Pedro Farfan
Alferes (Midshipman)	Don Jeronimo Lozano
Artilleros (Gunners)	Pedro de Inestrosa
	Francisco Davila
	Francisco de Fuentes
	Bernardo Ortiz de Menesez
	Francisco Rodriguez
Marineros (Seamen)	Juan Ramos (an Indian)
	Lopez Cavaillon
	Francisco Perez de Ircio
Soldados etc. (Soldiers and other military personnel)	Captain Don Julio de Melo
	Captain Julio Corrilla de Lagandara
	Captain Alonzo Perez Montejo
	Don Francisco Barragan
	Don Juan de Luna
	Jeronimo Locano

	Julio de Luna Giral
	Pedro Farfan de los Godos
Pasajeros (Passengers)	Geronymo de Cabrera
	Joseph Valdiviejo (resident of Callao)
	Francisco Brabo (merchant)
	Pedro de Inostrossa (cashier to the merchant, Brabo)

Many, many others were aboard the vessel. They remain unidentified. The majority of them were traveling to Panama, the Portobelo Fair and to Spain.

APPENDIX F
List of Persons Known to Have Been Aboard
the *Nuestra Señora de Las Maravillas*

* = Survived

In addition to Diego Portichuelo de Rivadeneira and the two pilots, Gaspar de los Reyes and Antonio Morales, there were forty-two other survivors as follows:

Seven soldiers
Nine passengers
Twenty-one sailors
Five cabin boys

Ships Officers:

Almirante (Admiral) Don Matías de Orellana

Capitán (Captain) Don Cristóbal de Salinas (also Captain of the Infantry on board, consisting of five officers and 148 men).

Maestre de Plata (Silvermaster) Don Diego de Yuste

* *Piloto Mayor* (Chief Pilot) Antonio Morales

* *Ayudante de Piloto* (Assistant Pilot) Gaspar de los Reyes

Guardián (Guardian) Ambrosio Altamirano

Contramaestre (Chief Boatswain) Juan Rodriguez

Maestre de Vela (Sail Master) name unknown

Maestre de Raciones (Master of Rations) Lucas de Quesada

Maestre de Jarcia (Chief Rigger) name unknown

Capellan Mayor (High Chaplain) Luis de Sierra

Cirugano (Surgeon) Josefe Cordé

Condestable (Chief Master Gunner) name unknown

Despensero (Supply Officer) Miguel Alonso

Alguacil (Bailiff) name unknown

* *Cabo de Escuadra de Guzmanes* (Chief of Midshipmen) name unknown

Buzos (Divers):

* *Buzo Mayor* (Chief Diver) Andre de Nicoleta

Buzo (Diver's Mate) name unknown

Trompeta (Trumpeter):
name unknown

Armero (Small Arms Keeper):
name unknown

Artilleros (Gunners):
* Fernando Camacho
* Alacaro García
* Juan de Messa
  Antonio de Vargas
  Antonio de Marante
  Pedro Simon
  Francisco de la Lama
  Andres Cassado
  Alonso Dias de Bergara
* Pedro Galán
  Francisco Dias
  Nicolas de Robles
  Francisco Navarro
  Francisco de Arenas
  Martin Moio
  Juan Muñoz
  Felipe Seguerra
  Andres del Mansibais
  Diego Sanchez
  Pedro Lopez
  Juan Perez de Solis
  Juan Alonzo Francisco
  Pedro Hittio
  Felipe García
  Cristóbal Martinez
  Bernardo Garcia
  Baltazar de Castro
  Pedro Montez Cabrera
  Bartolomé de Messa
  Juan Crespo

Marineros (Able Bodied Seamen):
There were fifty-three able seamen on board. However, we have only
a few of their names as most of the seamen drowned.
* Francisco de la Cumba
* Juan Ruíz
* Juan Salvador

Grumetes (Ordinary Seamen):

There were thirty-two ordinary seamen reported on board. We have no names.

Pajes (Ship's Boys):

There were forty *Pajes* listed as being on the ship.

* Simon Lopez de Miranda, age 18, was the only known survivor

Calafates (Caulkers):

* Juan de Sevilla
  Pedro de Ayllon

Carpinteros (Carpenters):

* Bartolomé de Castillo
  Mateo de Herrera

Toneleros (Coopers):

  Julio Jimenez
  Juan de Espinosa
* Francisco de Baraona

Arcabuceros (Harquebusiers):

There were reported to be at least forty on board.

Mosqueteros (Musketeers):

There were reported to be at least forty or more on board.

Pifanos (Fifers):

It is unknown how many were aboard the vessel, and how many lived or died.

Tambores (Drummers):

It is unknown how many were aboard the vessel, and how many lived or died.

Passengers:

* Dr. Don Diego Portichuelo de Rivadeneira
* Captain Don Domingo de Vega, Knight of the Order of Christ
  Miguel de Olocaran, Agent of His Majesty
  Many others, not identified nor counted.

APPENDIX G
The Naming of the *Maravillas* and
Biography of Admiral Orellana

Why was the *almiranta* named *Nuestra Señora de las Maravillas*? Maritime author, diver and researcher, Robert Sténuit reports:

The story begins in Madrid in 1624. A small community of Carmelites moved into a new convent on the Calle de las Palmas. The good nuns planted a garden in a walled-in land area to grow vegetables and flowers for the altar. Shortly before Christmas 1627, the nuns discovered a tiny, movingly beautiful statuette of the Child Jesus during an afternoon stroll in the garden. The painted wooden sculpture was found in a clump of white flowers called in Spanish, *Maravillas de Indias Mirabilis Imirabilis Jalapa*, or Marvels of Peru. (Also known as 'Four-O-Clock', since the plant's flowers, from the nyctaginaceae family, open in late afternoon.)

The nuns were so delighted, they knelt in admiration. They took the Child Jesus to the chapel, improvised a flowered altar and sang Christmas songs to honor Him. Every day for the following three years the nuns continued this simple, voluntary devotional to their beloved *Niño Jesus de las Maravillas*.

Moving back even further in history to the 13th century, a life-size wooden statue of the Virgin Mary was placed above the altar in a village church of *Rodas Viejas* in the province of Salamanca. She was venerated there for some 300 years. On one sad day in 1585, during a pastoral visit, the Bishop of Salamanca judged the beautiful carving of the Virgin to be so decrepit, the wood so rotten, that he ordered the statue be put away.

The bishop's action displeased the faithful villagers. A pious couple, the Gonzalez, obtained permission from the parson to move the statue to their own home so they could continue to honor her. In 1622, one of their sons inherited the Virgin. Some time later, the young Gonzalez, a muleteer and devout Christian, moved her to Madrid with his family.

Difficult times forced him to sell the Queen of Heaven to a tax collector. He immediately resold her for a profit to the constable, who stored her in the corner of an obscure, damp cellar while he searched for a buyer.

Strange phenomena, at the time believed to be the result of such an outrage to the Heavenly Mother, began occurring in the constable's house. Violent, repeated loud knocks shook the building at night. The worried constable ran back to the tax collector with the statue to return it. The tax collector, equally wary of supernatural powers of the sculpture, sold it to the first buyer he found. The new owner, Doña Ana Maria del Carpio, was the pious good wife of the well known sculptor, Francisco Albornoz.

The Holy Virgin became the focus of a devotional for not only the couple, but others on their block. Soon the entire neighborhood heard and quickly joined in the vigil. When Our Lady performed Her first registered miracle, resuscitating a child murdered by an angry hunter, the sculptor decided it was time to restore the statue. He replaced both hands and most of the head. Soon after, popular fervor became so widespread, on the advice of her confessor, Doña Ana Maria presented the statue to the church of the Convent of the Carmelites of Calle de las Palmas, so it could be viewed and shared with the public. As reported by various chroniclers, on February 1, 1627, the image of the Holy Virgin was solemnly transported to and installed in the church.

When the nuns and ladies of the parish dressed the old statue in the finest brocades, silks and laces, covered her in jewels, then raised her above the main altar, it appeared only natural that the recently discovered Little Jesus should be placed in the hands of His Holy Mother. He fit perfectly in Her arms.

From this time, and still today, the statue's arms are always decorated with fresh flowers of the Marvels of Peru. She remains passionately revered in Madrid as the *Santisima Virgen de Nuestra Señora de las Maravillas*, the most Holy Virgin of our Lady of the Marvels of Peru.

Her final consecration was soon to come.

In the same neighborhood, now *Barrio de las Maravillas*, stood the palace of the Dukes of Monteleon. In 1639, King Philip IV was warned that the Duke conspired against his policies and was organizing clandestine meetings in his home. One night the king, escorted by two of his courtiers, decided to see for himself who the conspirators were. From a vantage point near the convent he watched. He soon recognized the Duke's visitors. As Philip returned home late at night, his small group was attacked by six ruffians, brandishing swords. Within minutes one of them lay dead, the others put to flight. The king was seriously wounded and bleeding profusely.

Days later the remaining five ruffians were caught and hung on the *Plaza Mayor*, amid indescribable popular sentiment. His Majesty's injuries were severe. The wounds, despite a constant prayer vigil spread country-wide, were not healing.

The news quickly traveled to the Carmelites. They hastily sent the cloak of *Nuestra Señora de las Maravillas* to the palace. To the surprise and delight of all, as soon as the royal bed was covered with the cloak of the Virgin, His Majesty's wounds began to heal at an incredibly fast speed. Two days later the king was on his feet, deeply grateful.

He proclaimed himself patron of the convent, obliged himself to pay a generous annual rent and immediately ordered a new, larger church to be built at his expense. For the remainder of his life, until his death in 1665, he remained the most ardent devotee of *Nuestra Señora de las Maravillas*, even naming one of his new war galleons after her.

The original statue of *Nuestra Señora del Niño Jesus de las Maravillas* disappeared in the Spanish civil war in 1936. Despite the nuns' careful effort to hide the statue in the patio before fleeing the convent, it was destroyed by the militiamen. Following the war, two reproductions of the statue were made, both now in Madrid. Each holds a small statuette of the Child Jesus in Her hands. Both statues are claimed to be the original. They can be seen in the Church of the Carmelites Convent of *Nuestra Señora de las Maravillas y de los Santos Justo y Pastor* on Calle de las Palmas, Number 28. Other statues of the Virgin of the Marvels have been venerated. One in the Augustine monastery in Navarre in 1634, another is in the Church of *Nuestra Señora de las Maravillas in Sevilla*, and one is in Celiegin, Murcia.

One question will remain unanswered through history. As the richly laden Montealegre's *flota* was sailing back to Spain on the fateful night on January 4, 1656, on the edge of the dangerous Little Bahama Bank, why did Our Good Lady of the Marvels of Peru withdraw her protection from the galleon of Don Matías de Orellana?

The Orellana name was an old and proud one in all of Spain. Early members were associated with Pizzaro in Peru and Cortez in Mexico. This branch of the Orellanas, while financially comfortable, were not wealthy. Its first generation knights, the Orellana warriors were raised to be unceasingly loyal to family, king and Almighty Lord, and to serve each with dignity and honor.

Don Matías was the youngest of four brothers. He enjoyed a distinguished military career. Another brother, Don Pedro, previously served as general of the galleys in Naples. He also served as general of several *Tierra Firme* fleets. Both men were Knights of the Order of Santiago. Don Matías was ordained in 1639 after successfully proving his nobility to the High Council of the Order. The white cloak with red insignia of Saint James of the Sword was awarded him in the same house he was born, at Casas de Reinas. One year later, Matías de Orellana, now age thirty and already a *Capitán de Guerra*, found himself in Tarragona. Philip IV issued troops to Tarragona to restore order among the Catalans in the region, known to be attempting to form an alliance with France. The French army actually occupied the walled city, but departed soon after King Philip's show of strength.

As an ordained knight and army officer, the vow Don Matías accepted was to serve His Majesty for no less than six months at sea. In 1641 he served among the *Armada de Barlomento*, guarding the western Caribbean and the approaches to Cartagena. A year later he served on a galleon of the *Armada de la Carrera de las Indias*. An official document dated November 27, 1642 certified, "He has served diligently, with honor and competence."

In consideration of his past services the king graced him with the promise of two future posts as either admiral of the *Tierra Firme* fleet which sailed to the mainland of the South American continent, or admiral of the New Spain fleet, sailing to Mexico and Central America. Now on the officially designated waiting list, he would be appointed as soon as a vacancy appeared. His post as admiral placed him second in command of the entire fleet, behind only the captain general.

To his disappointment, however, in March 1643, he was ordered to serve another year on a warship bound for *Tierra Firme*. He attempted to resist by reminding Don Pedro Colomar of the Council of the Indies of his two promised posts.

His appeal was refused. Having faithfully promised to serve his king with honor and dignity, he presented himself in Cádiz on April 1, 1643. Reporting to the Marqués de Villafranca, Captain General of the Armada and Army of the Ocean Sea, he served for ten months, receiving 110 *escudos* a month. This extra duty enabled him to comply with his knightly obligation to serve His Majesty. In this capacity, though still not the designated *almirante*, he was a captain of sea and war, in charge of all the king's artillery and defense forces on board.

His ship was a Biscayan galleon of 580 tons (built in Biscay) the *Santiago de Galicia*, commanded by Antonio Sanz del Castillo.

Loaded with silver on its return voyage, the galleon developed a major leak in mid-ocean. Don Matías received much credit for getting the leaking vessel safely back to Spain.

Don Matías waited patiently all of 1645. His day finally arrived during 1646 when he was named admiral of the fleet scheduled to sail in 1647. He made several voyages to the Indies as fleet admiral when, on May 17, 1654, he was named second in command under Captain General Luis Francisco Nuñez de Guzmán, the Marqués of Montealegre. Their mission was to return to Spain with silver from the New World before an English fleet, known to be preparing to sail for the Indies, could stop them.

BIBLIOGRAPHY

A. ARCHIVE SOURCES

Chapter 1

A.G.I.(*Archivo General de Indias*)Seville

Contratación 2425, 5424, 5431, 5436

Indiferente General 2574

Lima 6, 7, 8, 56, 66, 67, 73, 253, 303, 304, 333

Other Primary Sources

Portichuelo de Rivadeneira, Diego. *Relacion del Viage*, Madrid, 1657

Mugaburu, Josephe de. *Diario de Lima*, 1717

Navarrete, Martin Fernandez de. *Biblioteca Maritima Española, Tomo I-II*, 1852

Alcedo, Antonio de. *Diccionario Histórico-Biografico de Peru*, Lima, 1931-37

Chapter 2

A.G.I.(*Archivo General de Indias*)Seville

Contaduria 1726, 1727, 1728B

Indiferente General 2574

Lima 297

Audiencia de Quito, selected legajos

Other Primary Sources

Actas del Cabildo Colonial de la Ciudad de Santiago de Guayaquil. Archivo Histórico de la Biblioteca Municipal de Guayaquil, published by Archivo Histórico de Guayas, Libro II, 1640-1649 and Libro III, 1650-1657

Archivo Nacional and Archivo Histórico del Ministerio de Hacienda y Comercio, Lima, Peru (Sección Colonial, 1548-1821)

Clayton, Lawrence A. *Los Astilleros de Guayaquil Colonial.* Publicaciones del Archivo Histórico de Guayas, Guayaquil, 1978

Chapter 3

A.G.I.(*Archivo General de Indias*)Seville

Contaduria 1726, 1727, 1728B

Indiferente General 2574

Lima 297

Audiencia de Quito, selected legajos

Other Sources

> *Actas del Cabildo Colonial de la Ciudad de Santiago de Guayaquil.* Archivo Histórico de la Biblioteca Municipal de Guayaquil, published by Archivo Histórico de Guayas, Libro II, 1640-1649 and Libro III, 1650-1657.

> Archivo Nacional and Archivo Histórico del Ministerio de Hacienda y Comercio, Lima, Peru (Sección Colonial, 1548-1821).

> Clayton, Lawrence A. *Los Astilleros de Guayaquil Colonial.* Publicaciones del Archivo Histórico de Guayas, Guayaquil, 1978.

Chapter 4

A.G.I.(*Archivo General de Indias*)Seville

> Contaduria 254, 570, 886, 1425

> Contratación 44A, 113B, 114A, 186, 1005, 2381, 2382, 3118, 3119, 3120, 3270B, 3297, 3874, 5178, 2900, 4484

> Escribania Camara 1028C, 1031B, 1928B

> Escribania General 1028A

> Indiferente General 115, 116, 770, 771, 1176, 1177, 1274, 2503, 2558, 2585, 2586, 2587, 2588, 2589, 2606, 2667

> Santo Domingo 102

> Santa Fe 4, 43, 75, 137, 138, 198

Other Primary Sources

> Barrionuevo, Jeronimo de. Avisos, Madrid, 1892

> Abbott's *Writings and Speeches of Oliver Cromwell,* Volume 4, 1655-1658, 1967

Chapter 5

A.G.I.(*Archivo General de Indias*)Seville

> Contaduria 3, 254, 570, 886, 1435

> Contratación 44A, 113, 186, 254, 607, 853, 970, 1005, 1658, 2381, 2382, 2900, 3118, 3119, 3120, 3270B, 3297, 3874, 4093, 4484, 4485, 5122

> Consulados *Lib.* 52, Leg. 475, 480

> Escribania Camara 47A, 103A, 103B, 103C, 592A, 1028, 1031, 1154B

> Indiferente General 115, 116, 770, 771, 1176, 1177, 1274, 1486, 1870, 1876, 2010, 2503, 2558, 2574, 2585, 2587, 2588, 2589, 2594, 2606, 2667, 2669

> Santo Domingo 102, 103B, 119, 120, 121, 122, 157, 225, 229, 233, 839.

> Santa Fe 4, 43, 75, 137, 138, 224

Other Primary Sources

   Barrionuevo, Jeronimo de. *Avisos*, Madrid, 1892

   Biblioteca Nacional, Madrid

   Duro, Cesar Fernandez. *Armada Española V*, Madrid, 1895

   Garraffa, Garcia. *Enciclopedia Heraldica*, Madrid, 1961

   Horner, Dave. *The Treasure Galleons*, New York, N.Y. : Dodd, Mead & Company, 1971

   Mendiburu, Manuel de. *Diccionario Histórico-Biografico del Peru*, Tomos V-VI, 1885

   Veitia y Linage, J. *Norte de la Contratación de las Indias Occidentales*, Sevilla, 1672

Chapter 6

A.G.I.(*Archivo General de Indias*)Seville

   Contratación 2381, 2382, 2900, 3118, 3119, 3120, 3121, 3122, 3297, 5122

   Escribania Camara 1028A, 1028B, 1028C, 1031B

   Lima 253

   Santo Domingo 102, 103C, 119, 120, 122

Other Primary Sources

   Portichuelo de Rivadeneira, Diego, *Relacion del Viage*, Madrid, 1657

Chapter 7

A.G.I.(*Archivo General de Indias*)Seville

   Contratación 2381, 2382, 3118, 3119, 3120, 3874

   Indiferente General 2596, 2685, 1870

Chapter 8

A.G.I.(*Archivo General de Indias*)Seville

   Contratación 3122, 5122, 5123, 4484, 4867, 5178

   Escribania General 1028A, 1028B, 2606

   Indiferente General 770, 970, 1176, 1177, 1876, 2503, 2504, 2606

Other Spanish Sources

   Duro, Cesar Fernandez. *Armada Española V*, 18-30, Madrid, 1895

   National Library of Madrid, B.N.-M.S., H86, F360

   Retegui y Bensuan, Mariano de. *Cádiz y el Comercio de Indias*, Sula

Gobierno Militar de Cultura, Cádiz, 1967

Barrionuevo, Jeronimo de. *Avisos*, Madrid, 1892

Portichuelo de Rivadeneira, Diego. *Relacion del Viage*, Madrid, 1657

English References

British Library

Firth, C.H. *The Last Years of the Protectorate, Vol. 1, 1656-1657*, 1907

Montague, F.C. *The Political History of England*, Vol. 7

Stace, M. (Ed.) *Bibliography of British History—Stuart Period, Cromwelliana*

A chronological detail of events in which Oliver Cromwell was engaged from 1642 to 1658. 1 vol., 1810

Extracts from *The Publick Intelligencer*, after 1649

Powell, J.R (Ed.) *Letters of Robert Blake*, Navy Records Society, Vol. 76, 1937

Calendar of Venetian and other State Papers

Calendar of State Papers Domestic. Letters to the Fleet Generals from Captain Richard Stayner aboard the *Speaker*

French Sources

Guizot, François. *Histoire de la Révolution d'Angleterre*, II, 260-261

Chapter 9

A.G.I.(*Archivo General de Indias*)Seville

Contratación 970, 2381, 2382, 2900, 3122, 3874, 4867, 5122

Escribania Camara 1028A, 1028B, 1028C

Indiferente General 770, 1876, 2504, 2606

Other Spanish Sources

Duro, Cesar Fernandez. *Armada Española V*, Madrid 1895

Calderón Quijano, & Altri. *Cartografia Militar y Maritima de Cádiz* (1513-1878), 2 Vol., Sevilla, 1978.

Fernandez Cano, Victor. *Las Defensas de Cádiz en la Edad Moderna*, C.S.I.C., Escuela de Estudios Hispano-Americanos de Sevilla, Sevilla, 1976.

English References

Firth, C.H. *The Last Years of the Protectorate*, Vol. 1, 1656-1657, 1907

Powell, J.R. (Ed.) *Letters of Robert Blake*, Navy Records Society, Vol. 76, 1937

Abbott's *Writings and Speeches of Oliver Cromwell*, Vol. 4, 1655-1658, 1967

The Thomason Tracts E1065. *A true narrative of the late success of the fleet of this Commonwealth upon the Spanish coast against the King of Spain's West India fleet in its return to Cádiz.*

Calendar of State Papers Domestic, Vol. 1656-1657

"The Life of Admiral Richard Stayner," *Dictionary of National Biography*

Campbell. J. *Lives of British Admirals*, Vol. 11

British Library, BM9300, 3411

French References

The *Gazette de Londres.* Numerous Issues of 1656, 1657

Dutch References

Hollandse Mercurius

Chapters 10 and 11

A.G.I.(*Archivo General de Indias*)Seville

Contratación 254, 1435, 1658, 3874

Escribania Camara 1031B

Indiferente General 770, 1177, 1486, 2010, 2574, 2574A, 2574B, 2596, 2606, 2606, 2699

Santo Domingo 103, 157, 225, 229, 233, 839

Consulados Lib. 52, Leg. 475, 480

Contaduria 1435

Indiferente General

Escribania General 1028B

Other Sources

Court Records of Bermuda

Lefroy, J.H. *The History of the Bermudas*, 2 volumes, London 1977-1979

The Marex Newsletter, Beacon

Chapter 12

A.G.I.(*Archivo General de Indias*)Seville

Indiferente General 770, 771, 2537, 2558

Contratación 2900 and 1943 (The Books of the Registers of the Entire Fleet)

Contratación 4925 (Summaries of gold, silver and goods shipped from the Indies under command of General Egues y Beaumont)

Contratación 3116 (*Papeles de Armada* 1652-1662), 5101

Other Spanish Sources

Museo Naval, Madrid. *Collección Vargas Ponce*, Serie II, Tomo 2, Doc. 28, f. 87-89

Biblioteca de la Real Academia de la Historia en Madrid. *Collección Salazar*, C-32/0-255, f. 214-257 (The Family Tree and the Descent of the Most Illustrious Family de Egues since the year 922)

Duro, Cesar Fernandez. *Armada Española*, Madrid, 1895

English References

Public Record Office, London

Calendar of State Papers Domestic 1656-1657

British Library, Maps Department

British Museum MS. No. 32093 and article in *The English Historical Review*, Vol. XX by Professor C.H. Firth, "The Battle of *Santa Cruz* Sir Richard Stayner's Narrative," also in Naval Miscellany, Vol. 40, 1910

"The Journal of John Weale 1654-1656," edited by Reverend J.R. Powell, published in Naval Miscellany, Vol. 92, 1952

Other English Sources

Campbell, J. *Lives of British Admirals*, Vol. FII, 1893

Clarendon, E. *The History of the Rebellion and Civil Wars in England, begun in the Year 1641*, Vol. III, Oxford, 1751 (** see notes)

Dutch Sources

Hollandtze Mercurius, March-April, 1657

Chapter 13

A.G.I.(*Archivo General de Indias*)Seville

Contratación 2900, 5122, 5424, 5431, 5436

Indiferente General 2606

Lima, 6, 8, 9, 57, 58, 59, 60, 61, 66, 67, 73, 253, 303, 304, 311, 333

Other Sources

Barrionuevo, Jeronimo de. *Avisos*

Mugaburu, Josephe de. *Diario de Lima*, 1717

Ballesteros, Jorge Bernales. *La Ciudad de Lima y sus Monumentos*, Escuela de Estudios Hispano-Americanos, Sevilla, 1979

Ballesteros, Jorge Bernales. *Edificación de la Iglesia Catedral de Lima (Notas Para su Historia)*, Sevilla, 1969

Vargas Ugarte, Ruben, S.J. *Historia del Seminario de Santo Toribio de Lima, 1591-1900*, Lima, 1969

Poma de Ayala, Felipe Guaman. *Nueva Cronica y Buen Govierno*

Portichuelo de Rivadeneira, Diego. *Relacion del Viage*, Madrid, 1657

B. INSTITUTIONS

SPAIN
SEVILLE
Archivo General de Indias
MADRID
Biblioteca Nacional (Departamentos de Impresos, de Manuscritos, de Bellas Artes, de Mapas y Planos, y de Bibliografia)
Biblioteca de la Real Academia de Historia
Biblioteca de Museo Naval
Archivo Histórico Nacional (Sección de Ordenes Militares Indice de Expedientillos y
   Datas de Habito de Cabelleros en Santiago, Calatrava, Alcantara y Montesa)
Biblioteca Salazar y Castro, Asociación de Hidalgos
VALLADOLID
Archivo de la Real Chancilleria
Archivo General de Simancas

ENGLAND
Public Records Office
British Library, Colonial State Papers
The National Maritime Museum, Greenwich
National Portrait Gallery
Courtauld Institute of Art
Oxford University
Historic Royal Palaces

FRANCE
Musée de la Marine
Bibliothèque Nationale

THE NETHERLANDS
Netherlands Royal Archives
Nederlandisch Historisch Scheepvart Museum

BELGIUM
Musée Royal

PERU
LIMA

Archivo Historico del Ministerio de Hacienda y Comercio (Sección Colonial, 1548-1821)

ECUADOR
GUAYAQUIL
Archivo Historico de la Biblioteca Municipal de Guayaquil (Actas del Cabildo Colonial de la Ciudad de Santiago de Guayaquil, Libro Segundo, January 17, 1640 - December 31, 1649; Libro Tercero, January 1, 1650 - July 23, 1657)

BERMUDA
Bermuda Library and Museum

NASSAU
Ministry of Public Safety and Transport

UNITED STATES
New York Public Library
Library of Congress

C. ORIGINAL DOCUMENTS OR PRIMARY WORKS

Seville, Spain
Archivo General de Indias
Portichuelo de Rivadeneira (Ribadeneyra) Dr. Diego. *Relacion del Viaje y Sucessos que tuvo desde que salio de la ciudad de Lima hasta que llego a estos Reinos de España*, Domingo Garcia y Morras, Madrid, 1657

Paz y Melia, A. *"Avisos"* of Don Jeronimo de Barionuevo, Madrid, 1892

Mugaburu, Josephe de, y Mugaburu, Francisco de (hijo). *Diario de Lima, 1640-1694*

Contaduria
     3, 114A, 225, 254, 1155, 1160, 1432, 1672, 2596, 2606, 2696, 2699

Consulados
     LIB 52, LEG 480 (1681)

Contratación
     113B, 114A, 574, 853, 970, 1005, 1365, 1943, 2381, 2382, 2896, 2900, 3116, 3118, 3119, 3120, 3121, 3122, 3270A, 3270B, 3297, 3298, 3752, 3874, 4093, 4094, 4095, 4097, 4484, 4848, 4867, 4897, 4925, 5101, 5122, 5123, 5178

Escribania de Camara
     47A, 48, 103B, 107B, 592A, 1027, 1028A, 1028B, 1028C, 1031B, 1087B, 1154B

Indiferente General
     117, 770, 1176, 1177, 1870, 1875, 1876, 2503, 2504, 2558, 2574A, 2574B, 2586, 2596, 2606, 2667, 2684, 2699

Lima
     57, 58, 59, 60

Mexico
   38

Santa Fe
   198

Santa Domingo
   71, 72, 75, 88, 102, 103, 106, 119, 120, 121, 122, 148, 157, 166, 225, 229, 233, 463, 535A, 535B, 848, 872, 945

D. GENERAL BIBLIOGRAPHY

Alcedo, Antonio de. *Diccionario Geográfico Histórico de las Indias Occidentales de America*, II, Madrid.

Alfaro Perez, J. *Diccionario Maritimo de Construcción Naval (Español-Ingles)*, Barcelona, S.D., Ediciones Garriga S.A., Paris 143 B. 11.

Alsedo y Herrera, Dionisio de. *Compendio Histórico de la Provincia Partidos, Ciudades, Astilleros, Ríos y Puerto de Guayaquil, en las Costas del Mar del Sur*, Madrid, 1741.

Armstrong, Douglas R. *Tumbaga Silver for Emperor Charles V of the Holy Roman Empire*, 1993.

Artinano y Galdacano, Gervasio. *Historia del Comercio con las Indias durante el Domino de las Austrias*, Barcelona, 1917.

Bakewell, Peter. *Miners of the Red Mountain, 1545-1650*, Albuquerque, NM: University of New Mexico Press, 1984.

Ballesteros, Bernales Jorge. *Edificación de la Iglesia Catedral de Lima*, Sevilla, 1969.

Bancora, Carmen. "Las remesas de metales preciosos desde el Callao a España en la primera mitad del siglo XVII," Revista de Indias, numero 75 (Enero-Marzo, 1959).

Barriga Villalba, Antonio María. *Historia de la Casa de Moneda*, Bógota: Banco de República, 3 volumes, 1969.

Baumber, Michael. *General at Sea Robert Blake and the Seventeenth-Century Revolution in Naval Warfare*, London: John Murray, 1989.

Bermudez, José Manuel. *Anales de la Catedral de Lima*, Lima, 1903.

Borah, W.W. *Early Colonial Trade and Navigation Between Mexico and Peru*, Ibero-Americana Magazine, Berkeley, CA: University of California Press, 1944.

Bradley, Peter T. *The Lure of Peru: Maritime Intrusion into the South Sea (1598-1701)*, 1989.

Bradley, Peter T. "Maritime defense of the Viceroyalty of Peru (1600-1700)," The Americas, 36, no. 2 (1979).

Burkholder, Mark A. and Chandler, D.S. *Biographical Dictionary of Audiencia Ministers in the Americas, 1687-1821.*

Burzio, Humberto F. *La Ceca de Lima (1565-1824)*, Fabrica Nacional de Moneda y Timbre, Numismática Publicación No. 5, Madrid, 1958.

Burzio, Humberto F. *La Ceca de la Villa Imperial de Potosí y la Moneda Colonial*, Facultad de Filosofía y Letras de la Universidad de Buenos Aires, Instituto de Investigaciones Históricas, Peuser, S.A., Buenos Aires, 1945.

Burzio, Humberto F. *Diccionario de la Moneda Hispanoamericana*, Santiago de Chile, 1956.

Calbeto, Gabriel. "Some Comments About This Sale of Potosí Mint Counterstamped Coins Struck in 1649-51 and Recovered From the Wreckage of the Spanish Treasure Ship the *Maravilla* (Lots 452-501)," from the Schulman Coin & Mint, Inc. catalog, New York, 1974.

Calcagno, Francisco. *Diccionario Biográfico Cubano*, 1878-1886.

Calderón, Quijano and Navarro Garcia. *Guia de Documentos, Mapas y Planos Españoles y Americanos*, Sevilla, 1962.

Calderón, Quijano, J.A. *Las Defensas del Golfo de Cádiz en la Edad Moderna*, Sevilla, 1976.

Campbell, J. *The Spanish Empire in America*, London, 1747.

Cappa, Ricardo. *Estudios Críticos acerca de la Dominación Española en America*, 20 volumes, Madrid, 1889-1897.

Castro, Javier de. *La Recuperación de Pecios en la Carrera de las Indias*, Universidad de Barcelona.

Castro y Bravo, Federico. *Las Naos Españolas en la Carrera de las Indias: Armadas y Flotas en la Segunda Mitad del Siglo XVI*, Madrid: Editorial Voluntad, 1927.

Cervera Pery, José. *Dos Facetes Navales del Reinado de Felipe IV*, Revista de Historia Naval I, 1982.

Cespedes del Castillo, Guillermo. "La Avería en el Comercio de Indias," Escuela de Estudios Hispano-Americanos de la Universidad de Sevilla, 1945.

Cespedes del Castillo, Guillermo. "La Defensa Militar del Istmo de Panama a fines del Siglo XVII y Comienzos del XVIII," Anuario de Estudios Americanos, IX, 1952.

Cespedes del Castillo, Guillermo. *Historia de España, VI, America Hispánica (1492-1898)*, Barcelona : Editorial Labor, S.A., 1983.

Chapman, Charles E. *Researches in Spain*, Berkeley, CA: University of California Press, 1918.

Chaunu, Pierre. *La Tonelada Espagnole au XVI et XVII Siècles*, Colloque International d'Histoire Maritime, 1 et 2, Paris, S.E.V.P.E.N., 1956, 1957.

Chaunu, Pierre. *Les Routes Espagnoles de l'Atlantique*, Colloque International d'Histoire Maritime, 9, Seville, 1967.

Chaunu, Pierre et Huguette. *Séville et l'Atlantique, 1504-1650*, 11 volumes, Paris, 1955-1959.

Chavez y Sanchez, Leopoldo Lopez. *Catalogo de la Onza Española*, Madrid: Editorial Iber-Amer, S.A.

Clarendon, E. *The History of the Rebellion and Civil Wars in England, Begun in the Year 1641*, Vol. III, Oxford, 1751.

Clayton, Lawrence A. *Cañones en Cañete*, 1615: "La Armada Real del Mar del Sur y la Defensa del Virreinato del Peru," Memorias del III Congreso Venezolano de Historia, Caracas, 1978.

Clayton, Lawrence A. "Caulkers and Carpenters in a New World: The Shipyards of Colonial Guayaquil," Ohio University, Center for International Studies, Latin America Series No. 8, Athens, Ohio, 1980.

Clayton, Lawrence A. "Ships and Empire; The Case of Spain," The Mariner's Mirror, 62:3, August, 1976.

Clayton, Lawrence A. "Trade and Navigation in the Seventeenth Century Viceroyalty of Peru," Journal of Latin American Studies, 7:2, May, 1975.

Codinach, Guadalupe Jimenez. *The Hispanic World 1492-1898*, Washington, DC: Library of Congress, 1994.

Dasi, Tomas. *Estudio de los Reales de a Ocho*, Valencia, 1950.

Davies, R. Trevor. *Spain in Decline 1621-1700*, New York and London: Macmillan & Company, Ltd., 1957.

Despertes, J. *Histoire des Naufrages*, Paris, 1828.

Dorta, Enrique Marco. *La Plaza Mayor de Lima en 1680*.

Duarte, Henrique Barbudo. *Diccionario Maritimo Ingles-Español*.

Duro, Cesar Fernandez. *Armada Española*, Madrid, 1895.

Duro, Cesar Fernandez. *Bosquejo Biográfico del Almirante Don Diego de Egues y Beaumont*, Sevilla, 1892.

Duro, Cesar Fernandez. *Disquisiciones Náuticas*, 6 volumes, Madrid, 1876-91.

Elliott, J.H. *Imperial Spain 1469-1716*, London, 1967.

Estrada Ycaza, Julio. *El Puerto de Guayaquil*, 3 volumes, Guayaquil, Ecuador, 1972-1974.

Fernandez Cano, Victor. *Las Defensas de Cádiz en la Edad Moderna*, C.S.I.C. - Escuela de Estudios Hispano-Americanos de Sevilla, Sevilla, 1976.

Firth, C.H. *The Last Years of the Protectorate*, Volume 1, 1656-1657, 1907.

Fischer, Jürgen. *Sammlung Religiöse Kunst*, Heilbronner Kunst-und-Auktionshaus, 1989.

Fuentes, Lutgardo García. *El Comercio Español con America (1650-1700)*, Sevilla, 1980.

Fuentes, Manuel A. *Lima or Sketches of the Capital of Peru*, London, 1966.

Gage, Thomas. *The English-American, His Travail by Sea and Land, or a New Survey of the West Indies*, London, 1648.

García Garraffa, A. & A. *Enciclopedia Heráldica*, Madrid, 1961.

Gil, Luis Suarez. *Diccionario Técnico Maritimo*, Madrid: Editorial Alhambra, S.A., 1981.

Gonzalez Suarez. Federico. *Historia General de la República del Ecuador*, 7 volumes, Quito, 1890-1893.

Guaman Poma de Ayala Felipe. *Nueva Crónica y Buen Gobierno*, a manuscript written in 1615.

Guizot, François. *Histoire de la Révolution d'Angleterre*.

Hamilton, Dr. Earl J. *American Treasure and the Price Revolution in Spain*, 1501-1650, Cambridge, MA : Harvard University Press, 1934.

Hamilton, Dr. Earl J. "Imports of American Gold and Silver into Spain, 1501-1660," Economic Quarterly, May, 1929.

Hamilton, Dr. Earl J. *Wages and Subsistence on Spanish Treasure Ships, 1503-1660*, Journal of Political Economy, 1929.

Hanke, Lewis. *Los Virreyes Españoles en America durante el Gobierno de la Casa de Austria*, Peru IV, Madrid, 1979.

Haring, C. H. *Trade and Navigation between Spain and the Indies in the Time of the Hapsburgs*, Cambridge, MA: Harvard University Press, 1918.

Harris, Robert. *Pillars and Portraits*, 2nd edition, 1969.

Hawkins, Richard. *Voyage into the South Sea*, London, 1622.

Herrera, Adolfo El Duro. *Estudio de los Reales de a ocho Españoles*, J. Lacoste, Madrid, 1914.

Herrera, Antonio Heredia. *Catalogo de las Consultas del Consejo de Indias.*

Herrera, Oria E. (Ed.) *Colección de Documentos Inéditos para la Historia de España y sus Indias*, Tomo II, Academia de Estudios Sociales de Valladolid, Madrid, 1930.

Hevia Bolaños, Juan de. *Curia Filipica, II, Mercancía y Contratación de Tierra y Mar*, Madrid, 1652.

Hidalguía. *Archivo General Militar de Segovia*, volumes 1-7, Madrid, 1961.

Hidalguía. *Orden de Santiago Siglo XVIII*, Madrid, 1977. -

Historia de la Ordenes Militares de Santiago, Calatrava, y Alcántara desde su fun-

dación hasta el Rey Don Felipe Segundo Administrador perpetuo dellas. Archivo General, Madrid.

Horner, Dave. *Shipwrecks, Skin Divers and Sunken Gold,* Dodd, Mead & Company, New York, NY, 1965.

Horner, Dave. *The Treasure Galleons,* Dodd, Mead & Company, New York, NY, 1971.

Hume, M.A.S. *The Court of Philip IV, Spain in Decadence,* London: E. Nash, 1907.

Jochomowitz, Albert. *Esplendor de la Antigua Lima,* Paris, 1958.

Kirsch, Peter. *The Galleon,* London: Conway Maritime Press, Ltd., 1990.

Lambert-Georges, Martine. *Les Ordres Militaires et les Indes,* Bordeaux, 1972.

Lastra y Terry, Juan de la. *Cádiz Trimilenario (Historia de Cádiz),* Barcelona: Ediciones de la Caja de Ahorros de Cádiz, 1980.

Letters of the Lady—Travels into Spain, London, 1692.

Lohmann Villena, Guillermo. *Los Americanos en los Ordenes Nobiliares,* Volumes 1 and 2.

Lohmann Villena, Guillermo. *Historia Maritima del Peru,* 10 volumes, Lima, 1972-1975.

Lorenzo, José de. *Diccionario Maritimo Español-Ingles,* Madrid, 1864.

Luis y Nava, Brusi. "La Falsificación de las Monedas ante las Leyes de Indias," Numisma no. 27, Julio-Agosto de 1957.

Lurting, Thomas. *The Fighting Sailor Turned Peaceable Christian,* London: William Phillips, 1813.

Lynch, John. *The Hispanic World in Crisis and Change 1598-1700.*

Lynch, John. *Spain under the Hapsburgs: Spain and America, 1598-1700,* New York, 1969.

Lyon, Eugene. *Search for the Mother Lode of the Atocha,* 1989.

Mangas, Fernando Serrano. *Armadas y Flotas de la Plata (1620-1648),* Banco de España, 1990.

Mangas, Fernando Serrano. *Función y Evolución del Galeon en la Carrera de Indias,* Madrid, 1992.

Manucy, Albert. *Artillery Through the Ages,* National Park Service Interpretive Series, History no. 3, Washington, DC: U.S. Government Printing Office, 1949.

Martinez Guitian, Luis. *Viajes de las Armadas de Galeones y Flotas a Tierra Firme y Nueva España, al Mando de D. Juan de Echeverri, Conde de Villa Alcazar de Sirga,* Gráficas Uquina, Madrid, 1949.

Marx, Robert and Jenifer. *The Search for Sunken Treasure*, Toronto, Ontario: Key Porter Books, Ltd., 1993.

Mateos, F. *Historia de la Compañia de Jesus en el Peru*, Madrid, 1912.

Mathewson III, R. Duncan. *Treasure of the Atocha*, Seafarers Heritage Library and Pisces Books, New York, 1987.

McIntyre, Loren. *The Incredible Incas and their Timeless Land*, Washington, DC : National Geographic Society, 1975.

McNickle, Andrew J.S. *The Lost Treasure of King Philip IV*, Bahamas Development Board, Nassau, 1952.

Means, Philip Ainsworth. *The Spanish Main: Focus of Envy, 1492-1700*, New York, NY: Charles Scribner's & Sons, 1935.

Mediavilla, Victor Herrero, and Lolita Rosa Aguayo Nayle. *Indice Biográfico de España, Portugal, e Iberoamerica*.

Medina, José Toribio. *Diccionario Biográfico Colonial de Chile*, 1906.

Mendiburu, Manuel de. *Diccionario Histórico-Biográfico del Peru*, Tomos V-VI, 1885.

Menzel, Dr. Sewall H. *The Potosí Mint Scandal and Great Transition of 1652*. West Palm Beach, FL: En Rada Publications.

Montague, F.C. *The Political History of England*.

Moreyra Paz-Soldan, Manuel. *La Moneda Colonial en el Peru*, Banco Central de Reserva del Peru, Lima, 1980.

Mur, Aurea L. Javierre and Maria Angeles Perez Castaneda. *Pruebas para Ingreso de Religiosos en la Orden de Santiago*, Spain.

Navarrete, Martin Fernandez de. *Biblioteca Maritima Española*, Tomo I-II, 1852.

Navarrete, Martin Fernandez de. *El Problema Maritima de España*, Sociedad Española de Artes Gráficas, Madrid.

Nesmith, Robert I. "Hoard of Lima and Potosí 'Cobs'," The American Numismatic Society Museum Notes, I, 1945.

Nesmith, Robert I. "The Coinage of the First Mint of the Americas at Mexico City 1536-1572," The American Numismatic Society, no. 131, New York, 1955.

Oliva, J. de Y. and L. Lopez-Chavez Sanchez. *Catalogo de los Reales de Ocho Españoles*, Madrid, 1965.

Ortiz, Antonio Dominguez. *Los Caudales de Indias y la Politica Exterior de Felipe IV*, Anuario de Estudios Americanos 13, 1956.

Ortiz, Antonio Dominguez. *Política y Hacienda de Felipe IV*, Madrid: Ediciones Pegaso, 1983.

O'Scanlon de Sacy, Timoteo. *Diccionario Maritimo Español-Ingles*, Madrid, 1831.

Pacheco Velez, Cesar. *Memoria de la Vieja Lima*, Lima, 1985.

Palacio, Diego García de. *Instrucción Naútica*, Editorial Naval, Museo Naval, Madrid, 1993.

Parry, J.H. *The Sale of Public Office in the Spanish Indies under the Hapsburgs*, Berkeley and Los Angeles, 1953.

Perez Balsera, José. *Los Cabelleros de Santiago*.

Perez Castaneda, Maria Angeles. *Pruebas para Contraer Matrimonio de las Ordenes de Calatrava*.

Perez de Sevilla, Vicente. *Cádiz en la Carrera de Indias*, Aula Militar de Cultura, Gobierno Militar, Cádiz, 1967.

Perez, J. Alfaro. *Diccionario Maritimo y de Construcción Naval*.

Peterson, Mendel. *The Funnel of Gold*, Boston: Little, Brown and Company, 1975.

Peterson, Mendel. *The Treasure of the Concepción* (essay) John G. Shedd Aquarium, Chicago, 1980.

Phillips, Carla Rahn. *Six Galleons for the King of Spain*, Baltimore, MD: The Johns Hopkins University Press, 1986.

Portal, Ismael. *Lima Religiosa*, 1535-1924, Lima, 1924.

Pradeau, A.F. *Numismatic History of Mexico*, 1933.

Puente y Gomez, Federico Fernandez de la. *Condecoraciónes Españolas, Ordenes, Cruces, y Medellas Civiles, Militares y Nobiliares*, Gráficas Osca, S.A., Madrid.

Pulido Rubio, José. *El Piloto Mayor, Pilotos Mayores, Catedráticos de Cosmografía y Cosmografos de la Casa de la Contratación de Sevilla*, Consejo Superior de Investigaciones Científicas, Seville, 1950.

Rades, Licenciado Frey Francisco de. *Crónica de las Tres Ordenes y Cavallerias de Sandiego, Calatrava y Alcántara*, Toledo, 1572.

Riva, Alfredo Basanta de la. *Sala de los Hijosdalgo*.

Rodriguez-Saigado, M.J. and the staff of the National Maritime Museum. *Armada 1588-1988*, London: Penguin Books in association with the National Maritime Museum, 1988.

Rodriguez Vicente, Maria Encarnación. *El Tribunal del Consulado de Lima en la Primera Mitad de Siglo XVII*, Madrid, 1960.

Romero, Emilio. *Historia económica del Perú*, 2 volumes, Buenos Aires, 1949.

Rubial García, Antonio. *El Convento Agustino y la Sociedad Novo Hispaña (1533-1630)*, Universidad Nacional Autonoma de Mexico.

Schafer, E. *El Consejo Real y Supremo de las Indias*, 2 volumes, Seville, 1935.

Schurtz, William Lytls. *The Manila Galleon*, New York, 1959.

Sedwick, F. *The Practical Book of Cobs*, 3rd edition, 1995.

Sténuit, Robert. *Treasures of the Armada*, New York, NY: E.P. Dutton & Co., Inc., 1973.

Suardo, Juan Antonio. *Diario de Lima*, Lima, 1935.

Tato, Julio Guillen. *Museo Naval Madrid Colección de Documentos y Manuscriptos Compilados por Fernandez de Navarrete*, Kraus-Thompson Organizations Ltd., Nendeln, Liechtenstein, 1971.

Terez y Rivas, Antonio. *Diccionario Maritimo Ingles-Español*, Madrid, 1896.

Thomazi, Auguste Antoine. *Les Flottes de l'Or: Histoire des Galions d'Espagne*, Revised edition, Paris: Payot, 1956.

Tippin, G. Lee and Herbert Humphreys, Jr. *In Search of the Golden Madonna*, Canton, OH: Daring Publishing Group, Inc., 1989.

Torres Ramirez, B. *La Armada de Barlovento*, Sevilla, 1981.

Ulloa, Juan Jorge and Antonio de Usher, Abbot Payson, *Spanish Ships and Shipping in the Sixteenth and Seventeenth Centuries*, Facts and Factors in Economic History. For Edwin Francis Gay, Cambridge, MA: Harvard University Press, 1932.

Ulloa Juan Jorge and Antonio de Usher. *Noticias Secretas de America*, vol. XXXI-XXXII, Biblioteca Ayachucho, ed. by Rufino Blanco-Fombona, 32 volumes, Madrid, 1918.

Vargas Ugarte, Ruben, editor. *Relaciones de viajes (siglos XVI, XVII, Y XVIII)*, Lima, 1947.

Vargas Ugarte, Ruben S.J. *Historio del Seminario de Santo Toribio de Lima*, 1591-1900, Lima, 1969.

Vasquez de Espinosa, Antonio. *Tratado Verdadero del Viaje y Navegación de Este Año de Seiscientos y Veinte y Dos que Hizo la Flota de Nueva España y Honduras*, Málaga, 1623.

Veitia Linaje, Josephe de. *Norte de la Contratación de las Indias Occidentales*, Sevilla, 1672.

Viera y Clavijo, José de. *Noticia de la Historia General de las Islas de Canaria*, Madrid, 1978.

Walsh, Michael. *Butler's Lives of the Saints*, San Francisco, CA: Harper Collins, 1991.

Zumalacarregui, Leopoldo. *Contribución al Estudio de la Avería en el Siglo XVI y Principios del XVII*, Anales de Economia 4, Madrid, 1944.

INDEX

ABOUT THE AUTHOR

DAVE HORNER is the author of several books, including *The Treasure Galleons, The Blockade Runners,* and *Shipwrecks, Skin Divers and Sunken Gold.* He pioneered sport diving and charter trips to sunken ships in the mid-Atlantic U.S., and is president of Maritime Explorations International. He lives in Maryland and Florida.